Prophecy Made Plain
For Times Like These

Prophecy Made Plain For Times Like These

by

Carl G. Johnson

❧ ❧ ❧
❧ ❧ ❧

MOODY PRESS
CHICAGO

Library of Congress Catalog Card Number: 72-77953

ISBN: 0-8024-6899-3

Printed in the United States of America

CONTENTS

5

FOREWORD

When I finished reading Dr. Carl Johnson's book, I was impressed. In these fifteen chapters the author has compiled more than 300 quotations from not less than 100 writers. He has read widely and has put together his findings in an orderly fashion.

My first reaction was, Do we need another book on Prophecy? But after examining *Prophecy Made Plain For Times Like These,* I concluded that it will serve a useful purpose. The Holy Scriptures never change. When a devout and earnest student of the Bible expounds the Word of God, he is teaching true prophecy and not prophesying. In preparing this book, Dr. Johnson did his homework. The student of prophecy will find in it a clear setting forth of the premillennial position and the pretribulation rapture of the church.

This is not a book with the stature of a religious classic nor the eloquence of a compelling drama. However it will inform and instruct and inspire the reader in the timely and timeless subject of prophecy. I intend to pass along this book to many persons. After you have read it, you will want to do the same.

Lehman Strauss

PREFACE

DR. WILBUR M. SMITH stated some time ago, "I believe that the study of the prophetic Scriptures is more important today, and that study more necessary for this day, than at any time, at least since the Reformation, if not since the days of the apostles."[1]

Dr. M. R. DeHaan wrote,

> Much of the confusion among believers is due to plain ignorance concerning prophecy. Thousands of believers, including ministers and preachers, avoid the study of prophecy because of the confusion which exists, but they have the horse behind the cart—the confusion is the result of *neglecting* the study of prophecy. Not one in a hundred of the members of our evangelical churches could give the order of events of the last days, and hence do not know what to look for. Ignorance of God's prophetic outline, failure to know God's program for the Church, the nations, and Israel, is the cause of the overwhelming amount of error and misunderstanding of the events of the future.[2]

This book has been written with the prayer that through it people will know "God's prophetic outline, . . . God's program for the Church, the nations, and Israel."

God told Habakkuk almost twenty-six hundred years ago, "Make it plain." He was speaking about the second coming of Jesus Christ. That this reference refers to the second coming of Christ is proved by its use in Hebrews 10:37: "For yet a little while, and he that shall come will come, and will not tarry" (compare Hab 2:2-4 with Heb 10:37-38). I pray that in these chapters, God will help me to "make it plain," so that the reader who reads may understand, and "that he may run that readeth it" (Hab 2:2)—he may run to others and share these truths with them.

9

I have found there is a real interest in prophecy, and in my evangelistic and conference work, I have noticed that when I speak on prophecy, Christians are stirred and sinners are saved.

This book took me eighteen months to write and was written while I was very busy in evangelistic and conference work in many states. I have tried to be simple and clear in writing, not using headlines to interpret the Bible, but using the Bible to interpret the headlines. I want this book to be helpful to those who desire to have a better understanding of "things to come" (Jn 16:13).

I have quoted many authors and I am very grateful to these men of God and the publishers who published their writings. Blaise Pascal, seventeenth century philosopher, remarked, "Certain authors, when they speak of their work, say, 'My book, my commentary, my history' . . . . They would do better to say 'our book, our commentary, our history,' since their writings generally contain more of other people's good things than of their own." This book contains many good things of other people, and I thank God that He has helped others to help us. I have studied and learned much in my study, and my own life has been enriched and stirred by these truths. Now they are being shared with others, with the earnest prayer that God will be pleased to use them to enrich and stir many, that together we may be ready for His coming (Mt 24:44): watching for Him (Mk 13:32-37); waiting for Him (1 Th 1:10); and working for Him (Jn 9:4).

The author graciously acknowledges the kindness of authors and publishers in giving permission to reproduce material in this volume.

1

WE SHOULD STUDY PROPHECY
Seven Reasons Why

BEFORE WE GIVE REASONS why we should study prophecy, it would be wise to define the word. The word *prophecy* comes from two words in the Greek language; *pro* means "for," "in front of," or "on behalf of," and the remainder of the word comes from *phanai,* "to speak." So a prophet is an individual who speaks on behalf of God. His message is twofold—to *forthtell* for the present and to *foretell* for the future.

There are many people today who never study prophecy. Some of them say that they can't understand the prophetic sections of the Bible, especially the book of Revelation, and so they neglect these portions of God's Word. There are others who have heard date setters make sensational predictions, exploiting prophecy instead of expounding it, who have brought the message of prophecy into disrepute. Then there are some who say that there is so much disagreement among Bible scholars in teaching prophecy that no one can be sure just what the correct interpretation is.

In spite of the excuses people make for not studying prophecy, God gives us a number of reasons why we should make a study of it.

BECAUSE GOD COMMANDS US TO

God commands in Isaiah 34:16: "Seek ye out of the book of the Lord, and read." Jesus commands in John 5:39: "Search the scriptures . . . they are they which testify of me."

Peter tells us: "We have also a more sure word of prophecy." Then he says, "Whereunto ye do well that ye take heed, as unto a light that

11

shineth in a dark place, until the day dawn, and the day star arise in your hearts" (2 Pe 1:19).

BECAUSE GOD CONSIDERS IT IMPORTANT

We speak of the seventeen books of the Old Testament, from Isaiah through Malachi, as books of prophecy, plus the book of Revelation in the New Testament. But there are other important prophecies in the Bible, in the Pentateuch, in the Psalms, in the gospels, in Acts, and in the pastoral and general epistles. Dr. James M. Gray, a former president of Moody Bible Institute, stated, "Taking it in bulk, more than one-half of the Bible is predictive, so that no further reason seems necessary why Christians should study prophecy."[1]

BECAUSE GOD WANTS US TO KNOW THINGS TO COME

God has promised, "The secret things belong unto the Lord our God: but those things which are revealed belong unto us and to our children for ever" (Deu 29:29). He also said, "Surely the Lord God will do nothing, but He revealeth His secret unto His servants the prophets" (Amos 3:7). God's prophets have had God's truths revealed unto them and they have spoken unto us. When we study the prophecies, we find what God is doing in the world and what He is yet going to do.

BECAUSE IT GIVES LIGHT IN DARK DAYS

Surely these days are dark days: dark morally and spiritually, dark nationally and internationally, dark politically and economically. The "more sure word of prophecy" is called "a light that shineth in a dark place" (2 Pe 1:19), and it gives us light on the path before us. The prophetic word is the only ray of light by which we can know the future. The outlook is dark, but the uplook is bright.

BECAUSE IT BRINGS COMFORT TO OUR HEARTS

If it were not for the truth that Jesus Christ is coming back again, there would be no hope and nothing to comfort our hearts. But we read in the Word of God: "For the Lord himself shall descend from heaven with a shout, with the voice of the archangel, and with the trump of God: and the dead in Christ shall rise first: Then we which are alive and remain shall be caught up together with them in the clouds, to meet the Lord in the air: and so shall we ever be with the Lord. Wherefore comfort one another with these words" (1 Th 4:16-18).

Dr. William Culbertson, in a prophecy conference, said, "Oh, the immeasurable comfort that comes to us as we contemplate the predictions which God has made concerning what will happen to those who love the Lord when He comes!"[2]

BECAUSE IT IS AN INCENTIVE TO HOLY LIVING AND SERVING

God's Word says in 1 John 3:2-3: "Beloved, now are we the sons of God, and it doth not yet appear what we shall be: but we know that, when he shall appear, we shall be like him; for we shall see him as he is. And every man that hath this hope [of Christ's second coming] in him purifieth himself, even as he is pure." Almost every time the second coming of Christ is mentioned in the New Testament, there is also a call to godliness and holy living.

Dr. Rufus W. Clark comments on this: "There is not a duty pertaining to the Christian life that is not quickened and rendered more imperative by the power of this blessed hope; not a virtue that it does not call into highest exercise; not a motive in the human heart that it does not purify and strengthen."[3]

Dr. R. A. Torrey told what the truth of the second coming of Christ did to him: "The latter truth [of the second coming of Christ] transformed my whole idea of life; it broke the power of the world and its ambition over me, and filled my life with the most radiant optimism even under the most discouraging circumstances."[4] Dr. Torrey was asked this question at a convention: "Is not the doctrine of Christ's personal and near coming one of practical power and helpfulness?" He replied, "It is transforming the lives of more men and women than almost any doctrine I know of."[5]

Dr. James M. Gray said: "There are at least five things which this hope effected in my life . . . it awakened a real love and enthusiasm for the study of every part of God's Word; it quickened my zeal in Christian service, especially in foreign missions; it delivered my mind from an over-weening ambition for worldly success and the praise of man; it developed patience and quietness in the face of unjust treatment; and it broke the bands of covetousness and set me free to give of my substance to the Lord."[6]

Speaking of "zeal in Christian service, especially in foreign missions," Dr. A. P. Stirrett, one of the most remarkable men in the history of the Sudan Interior Mission, gives his testimony:

> What finally brought me to my senses was a sermon on the return of our Lord and Saviour, Jesus, to this earth. The verse that especially struck me was, "Every man that hath this hope in him purifieth himself, even as he is pure."
>
> After the preaching, I went home, and gathering some things that were on my shelves that I would not like to be found with if Jesus came, I took them down into the cellar and threw them into the furnace.
>
> However, there came up before me more vividly my great sin of omission, my failure to go to tell those who knew not the gospel. The question was insistent—"Will Jesus be pleased, if He comes, to find you behind the counter?"
>
> For me there was only one answer, and so I gave up my work and sold my business, and started for the field.[7]

Because It Exalts Jesus Christ

We read in Acts 10:43: "To him [Jesus Christ] give all the prophets witness." Jesus said to the two disciples on the way to Emmaus, "O fools, and slow of heart to believe all that the prophets have spoken. . . . And beginning at Moses and all the prophets, he expounded unto them in all the scriptures the things concerning himself" (Lk 24:25, 27). Weymouth translates Revelation 19:10: "Testimony to Jesus is the spirit which underlies prophecy," and the Berkeley Version has a note on this verse which reads: "Christ is the center of prophecy just as He is the center of all Scripture." All prophecy from the book of Genesis through the book of Revelation relates to Him directly or indirectly.

Dr. James M. Gray said, "No one interested either in His past history or His ultimate triumph can afford to ignore its study."[8] He also has stated, "God never would have traced the exalted pathway of His Son through the long aisles of the future, had He not desired and expected us by our eye of faith to follow Him."[9]

I have given seven reasons why we should study prophecy—many more could be given. In times like these, we cannot afford to neglect this very important subject; and I pray that in these chapters God will enable me to write so clearly that the reader will see "prophecy made plain for times like these."

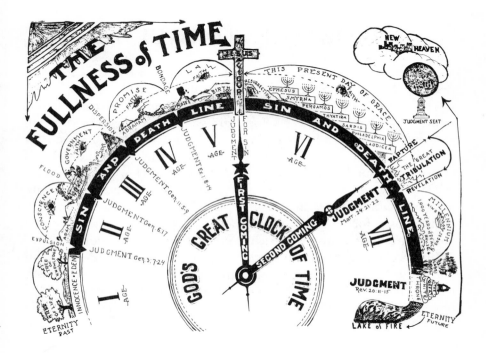

2

GOD'S GREAT CLOCK OF TIME

THE CHART, "God's Great Clock of Time" (shown on page 15), is a drawing by W. J. Dittmar and was published years ago by Union Gospel Press of Cleveland, Ohio. It is so simple and clear that I wrote to Union Gospel Press for permission to enlarge the drawing and put it on canvas for teaching. Permission was granted, and for years I have taught from this large canvas chart. I have taught this in my own church when I was a pastor, in other churches, in camps, in DVBS classes, and in conferences in this country and in the country of Trinidad. Sometimes I have taught the chart in one session, sometimes in four sessions, five sessions, eight sessions; and in my own church I taught it to my people every Sunday for six months.

In this chapter, I want to write briefly and give the reader a broad outline of God's working through the ages. I believe a person will have a much better understanding of God's Word if he sees that God has a plan and is working out His plan. This plan has been unfolding since the beginning of time and will continue until time has come to an end.

In God's plan there are various periods of times which we call dispensations or ages. It would be well to give some definitions of a dispensation at this point.

1. "A dispensation is a distinguishable economy in the outworking of God's purpose" (Dr. Charles C. Ryrie).[1]
2. "A dispensation is a period of time during which man is tested in respect of obedience to some *specific* revelation of the will of God. Seven such dispensations are distinguished in Scripture" (The Scofield Reference Bible).[2]

16

3. "A Dispensation is a period of time, or an age, conditioning human life on the present earth, during which God tests man, by means of some specific standard of conduct, in respect to man's obedience to the will of God. There are seven major dispensations recorded in God's Word, and under each one, man fails and God brings judgment" (Pilgrim Edition Bible).[3]

4. "A dispensation is a period of time during which God is testing man's ability to govern the earth. Inasmuch as man has a number of governmental ideas and theories, God gives man seven stewardships or dispensations. These constitute seven opportunities for man to make good, but history and prophecy unite to declare that all of man's theories of government are demonstrated by the seven dispensational tests to be fallacious and worthless. God uses the dispensations to reveal the deep seated reason for man's complete failure governmentally is because of his innate wickedness and depravity, which causes him to leave regeneration out of all of his governmental notions" (Clifton L. Fowler).[4]

5. "The word oikonomia bears one significance, and means 'an administration,' whether of a house, or property, of a state, or a nation, or as in the present study, the administration of the human race or any part of it, at any given time. Just as a parent would govern his household in different ways, according to varying necessity, yet ever for one good end, so God has at different times dealt with men in different ways, according to the necessity of the case, but throughout for one great, grand end" (W. Graham Scroggie).[5]

6. "An economy is an ordered condition of things. . . . There are various economies running through the Word of God. A dispensation, an economy, then, is that particular order or condition of things prevailing in one special age which does not necessarily prevail in another" (H. A. Ironside).[6]

7. "The word dispensation means literally a stewardship or administration or economy. Therefore, in its Biblical usage, a dispensation is a divinely established stewardship of a particular revelation of God's mind and will which brings added responsibility to the whole race of men or that portion of the race to whom the revelation is particularly given by God.

    "Associated with the revelation, on the one hand, are promises of reward or blessing for those responding to the obedience of faith, while on the other hand there are warnings of judgment upon those who do not respond in the obedience of faith to that particular revelation.

"However, though the time period (age) ends, certain principles of the revelation (dispensation or stewardship) are often carried over into succeeding ages, because God's truth does not cease to be truth, and these principles become part of the cumulative body of truth for which man is responsible in the progressive unfolding revelation of God's redemptive purpose" (Clarence E. Mason, Jr.).[7]

The Greek word *oikonomia* occurs eight times in the New Testament: Lk 16:2, 3, 4; 1 Co 9:17; Eph 1:10; Eph 3:2; Col 1:25; 1 Ti 1:4. The lexicons define this word as follows:

1. A dispensation, administration, management of family affairs, a stewardship (Parkhurst).
2. A stewardship, a dispensation (Westcott and Hort).
3. The management, oversight, administration of others' property (Thayer).
4. Management of a household or family, also public economy of states, administration, management, government (Liddell and Scott).
5. Management, administration (Schrevelius).
6. A stewardship, administration, an economy of things, a dispensation, a scheme (Robinson).
7. Management of family affairs, stewardship, administration, a spiritual dispensation, management, or economy (Groves).
8. Management and arrangement of a household (Donnegan).
9. The management of a house, a stewardship—N.T.—an apostolic stewardship, a ministerial commission in the publication and furtherance of the gospel, an arranged plan, a scheme, a due discharge of a commission (Bagster's Analytical).
10. Management of household affairs, a stewardship, a dispensation (Berry).
11. Economy, dispensation, stewardship (Strong).

No matter how intellectual, moral, or spiritual a Christian may be, unless he understands the dispensational structure of the Bible, he will never fully understand Bible doctrine.

Dr. Lewis Sperry Chafer, in his book, *Major Bible Themes,* says:

> As to time, the Bible may be apportioned into well-defined periods. These periods are clearly separated and the recognition of their divisions with their divine purposes constitutes one of the most important factors in true interpretation of the Scriptures. These divisions of time are termed dispensations. . . .
>
> It is probable that the recognition of the dispensations sheds more light on the whole message of the Scriptures than any other aspect of Bible study.
>
> Each dispensation, therefore, begins with man divinely placed in a new position of privilege and responsibility, and closes with the failure of man resulting in righteous judgments from God. While there are certain abiding facts such as the holy character of God which are of necessity the same in every age, there are varying instructions and responsibilities which are, as to their application, limited to a given period.[8]

Augustine said, "Distinguish the ages and the Scriptures harmonize."

THE SEVEN DISPENSATIONS

Many Bible scholars find seven distinct dispensations in the Biblical account of God's dealings with man, as begun in Genesis and ended in Revelation. These dispensations have been given the following titles: (1) innocence, (2) conscience, (3) government, (4) promise, (5) law, (6) grace, and (7) kingdom.

Within each dispensation can be seen four phases: (1) the testing of man, (2) the failure of man, (3) the judgment of God, and (4) the grace of God.

THE FIRST DISPENSATION—INNOCENCE

This dispensation or age began with the creation of man and ended with the expulsion of Adam and Eve from the Garden of Eden (Gen 1:26—3:23). Adam and Eve were created by God, put in a perfect environment in the Garden of Eden, and enjoyed fellowship with God in their innocency. Adam wasn't righteous, because he hadn't chosen good; and he wasn't sinful, because he hadn't chosen sin. We do not know how long they continued in their innocent state.

The testing of man. God gave them only one prohibition—they were not to eat of the tree of the knowledge of good and evil, and they were told of the punishment if they disobeyed: "Thou shalt surely die" (Gen 2:17). God made man a free moral agent and he can choose either righteousness or unrighteousness. God wants voluntary obedience. He does not make man a machine. In order for man to have an opportunity of choosing, Satan was allowed to tempt him. The devil came in the form of a serpent and deceived Eve (Gen 3:1). Adam was not deceived, but sinned willfully (1 Ti 2:14).

The failure of man. Eve yielded to the temptation, ate the forbidden fruit, and gave to her husband, Adam; and he ate (Gen 3:1-6). This is called the fall of man, and it proves that innocence is not sufficient to keep man from disobeying God.

The judgment of God. God brought judgment upon sin, and the penalty has affected the whole human race (Gen 3:7-19). Here are some of the effects of the fall:

Their eyes were opened (v. 7).

They knew they were naked (v. 7).

They were afraid (v. 10).

The serpent was cursed (v. 14).

Enmity was put between the godly and ungodly (v. 15).

Christ had to die for sin (v. 15).

The woman was cursed (v. 16): Sorrow in conception and subjection to husband.

The man was cursed (vv. 17-19): hard work and death.

The ground was cursed (vv. 17, 18):

They were expelled from the Garden (vv. 23, 24).

The whole human race is under the curse (Ro 5:12).

The grace of God. The grace of God is shown in His providing for them "coats of skin" (Gen 3:21) and clothing them. God Himself killed the animals, shedding their blood, which conveys the truth of Hebrews 9:22: "without shedding of blood is no remission." Dr. Louis T. Talbot has an interesting comment on this:

> The coats of skin could be had only on the basis of a death. To

take the skin from an animal is first to destroy the life. Here also is a prophetic picture—that on the basis of a death, the death of the Son of God, man would be clothed in a garment of righteousness that would fit him for the presence of a holy God. We have seen that when man fell, he made for himself aprons of fig leaves. Now God took those aprons away, and gave him a covering of His own making. Into the fig leaf apron God did not put one stitch; it was all the work of man. Into the coats of skins man did not put one stitch; it was all the work of God. Moreover, before Adam and Eve could be clothed with skins, the fig leaf aprons, the work of their own hands, had to be taken away. They had to be willing to exchange their aprons for the garments of God's provision. They had to be willing for the substitution to be made.

My brother, there are only two religions in the world today—that which gives to man a false hope, as represented by the fig leaf aprons; and that which makes man fit to stand in the presence of God, as represented by the coats of skin. The one is of works; the other is of grace. One presents man's futile effort to save himself; the other rests upon what Christ provides when He died on Calvary. Which of the two is yours today?[9]

The grace of God is also shown in the promise of a redeemer (Gen 3:15), who was to be the seed of the woman; this was the first intimation of the virgin birth of Christ. The seed of the woman, Christ, will bruise the head of the serpent's seed, prophesying the overthrow of Satan's government. The heel of the seed of the woman was to be bruised, speaking prophetically of the Saviour's death on Calvary for our sins.

It was also the grace of God that expelled them from the Garden, because if they had stayed there and partaken of the tree of life, they would have had to live forever in their sinful state. "So he drove out the man" (3:24). Dr. Arno C. Gaebelein said that if man had to live forever in his sinful condition, it would be like wandering in a dark, filthy swamp filled with reptiles and monsters.[10]

THE SECOND DISPENSATION—CONSCIENCE

The dispensation of conscience began with the fall of man (Gen 3:23), and ended with the flood (Gen 8:22). A period of 1656 years (cf. Gen 5:3–7:11—Adam lived 130 years and begat Seth; Seth lived 105 years and begat Enos; Enos lived 90 years and begat Cainan;

Cainan lived 70 years and begat Mahalaleel; Mahalaleel lived 65 years and begat Jared; Jared lived 162 years and begat Enoch; Enoch lived 65 years and begat Methuselah; Methuselah lived 187 years and begat Lamech; Lamech lived 182 years and begat Noah; Noah was 600 years old when the flood came. Thus, $130 + 105 + 90 + 70 + 65 + 162 + 65 + 187 + 182 + 600 = 1656$ years from Adam to the flood).

The testing of man. Under this dispensation, man was tested as to whether guided by his conscience, he would choose to do right or wrong. Without law or government, man became responsible before God to abstain from evil and do good.

The failure of man. During this dispensation, the people of the earth refused to do good, and we read, "And GOD saw that the wickedness of man was great in the earth, and that every imagination of the thoughts of his heart was only evil continually. . . . The earth also was corrupt before God, and the earth was filled with violence. And God looked upon the earth, and, behold, it was corrupt; for all flesh had corrupted his way upon the earth" (Gen 6:5, 11-12). God proved to man that if he were left to his own choice between right and wrong, he would always choose wrong. Some consciences are weak (1 Co 8:7); some are good (1 Ti 1:5); some are evil (Heb 10:22); some are seared (1 Ti 4:2); but none can be trusted to be a safe guide.

The judgment of God. We read in Genesis 6:6-7: "And it repented the LORD that he had made man on the earth, and it grieved him at his heart. And the LORD said, I will destroy man whom I have created from the face of the earth; both man, and beast, and the creeping thing, and the fowls of the air; for it repenteth me that I have made them." So after Noah had built the ark and he and his wife and three sons and their wives entered in, God sent a flood, "And all flesh died that moved upon the earth, both of fowl, and of cattle, and of beast, and of every creeping thing that creepeth upon the earth, and every man: All in whose nostrils was the breath of life, of all that was in the dry land, died" (Gen 7:21, 22).

The grace of God. Before God destroyed the earth by the flood, "Noah found grace in the eyes of the LORD" (Gen 6:8), and God saved Noah and his wife, his three sons and their wives, from death in the flood. "By faith Noah, being warned of God of things not seen as yet, moved with fear, prepared an ark to the saving of his house; by the which he condemned the world, and became heir of the righteousness which is by faith" (Heb 11:7).

Jesus said, "But as the days of Noe [Noah] were, so shall also the coming of the Son of man be" (Mt 24:37). As Noah was preserved in the ark and saved from judgment through faith, those who are in Christ through faith in Him will be preserved from judgment in the coming time of judgment. Grace was offered Noah and is offered to us today. If you are not in the ark of safety, the Lord Jesus Christ, enter in by faith today (2 Co 6:2; Ac 16:31).

THE THIRD DISPENSATION—HUMAN GOVERNMENT

This dispensation extended from the flood to the tower of Babel (Gen 9:1—11:9), a period of 427 years.

The testing of man. Man, in this dispensation, was given the responsibility of governing the earth righteously for God. Capital punishment was instituted (Gen 9:6). The government was to have complete authority to protect the lives of its citizens. This responsibility of governments to God, including the matter of capital punishment, has never been abrogated, and God still holds the rulers and the governments responsible.

The failure of man. Man failed God again in this dispensation and attempted to rule for himself instead of for God. God had told them, "Be fruitful, and multiply, and replenish the earth" (Gen 9:1). He wanted them to scatter and repeople the earth, but instead they said, "Let us make us a name, lest we be scattered abroad upon the face of the whole earth" (11:4). They built the tower of Babel in defiance of God. The sin of idolatry began here and spiritual degeneration followed.

The judgment of God. The people said "Let us make brick . . . let us build us a city and a tower . . . let us make us a name"; but the Lord said, "Let us go down, and there confound their language, that they may not understand one another's speech" (Gen 11:3, 4, 7). So He confounded their language, the building ceased, and they were scattered (vv. 8-9). This scattering was the beginning of nations and languages, and today there are about two thousand languages and dialects in the world.

The grace of God. God was merciful to them and chose one man,

Abraham, from among them to start a new nation which would belong to Him in a special way. From Abraham came the nation called Israel, later called Jews.

THE FOURTH DISPENSATION—PROMISE

This dispensation extended from the call of Abraham to the Exodus, a period of 430 years (Gen 12:1—Ex 19:2). God promised Abraham many important things: a great nation, a great name, a blessing, possession of the promised land, and the ultimate blessing of "all families of the earth" to be fulfilled in Abraham's seed, the Lord Jesus Christ (Gen 12:1-3; Gal 3:16).

The testing of man. The test was whether God's promises would be sufficient incentive to make Abraham and his descendants love the Lord and obey Him. Abraham's responsibility was to stay in the land which God gave him and not go down into Egypt. The descendants of Abraham were to abide in the land to inherit every blessing.

The failure of man. Abraham disobeyed God and went down into Egypt (Gen 12:10). He failed to trust God in the incident of Hagar and Ishmael (Gen 16), and lied again about his wife in Gerar (Gen 20). Isaac lied about his wife (Gen 26:1-11). Jacob deceived his father (Gen 27), and his twelve sons continually failed God and went to Egypt where they remained about 400 years.

The judgment of God. God brought upon them the judgment of slavery in Egypt, where they faced hard labor, sorrow, and threatened extinction.

The grace of God. God chose from among them a deliverer, a man called Moses, empowered him, and used him to lead the people out of bondage into the promised land.

THE FIFTH DISPENSATION—LAW

This period lasted from Mount Sinai to Mount Calvary, from the Exodus to the cross, about 1491 years (Ex 19:3—Mt 27:35). At Mount Sinai, the people of Israel accepted the Law when they told God, "All that the LORD hath spoken we will do" (Ex 19:8). God gave Israel the moral law, the ceremonial law, and the judicial law. In its entirety the Mosaic law contained 613 commandments—365 negative and 248 positive.

The testing of man. The test in this dispensation is whether man will faithfully live by the law, obey God's voice, and keep His covenant (Ex 19:5).

The failure of man. In order to be justified by the law, man must keep all of the law and must keep it all of the time (Ja 2:10; Gal 3:10). Even before Moses came down from Mount Sinai with the Ten Commandments, the people of Israel, at the foot of the mountain under Aaron's leadership, made a golden calf and began to worship it as an idol (Ex 32). Individually and collectively Israel broke God's law. Their unbelief caused them to wander in the wilderness forty years (Num 14:26-35). There was continued failure during the time of the judges (Judg 2:11-21:25). Judges 17:6 and 21:25 describe them well: "In those days there was no king in Israel, but every man did that which was right in his own eyes." During the era of the kingdom, they did no better (2 Ki 17:7-17, 19). After their captivity because of their sin, they returned to the land, but they continued to disobey God. The climax of their sin was when they rejected and crucified the Son of God (Ac 2:22, 23).

The judgment of God. Because of their failure to keep God's law, they were taken into captivity, first by Assyria and later by Babylon (2 Ki 17:1-18; 25:1-21). This dispensation ended in the judgment of sin on the cross in the death of the Lord Jesus Christ. "Christ hath redeemed us from the curse of the law, being made a curse for us: for it is written, Cursed is every one that hangeth on a tree" (Gal 3:13).

The grace of God. God's grace is manifested in many ways in this dispensation. He first spared the nation in answer to Moses' prayer (Ex 32:11-14). God sent deliverers in the time of the Judges (Judg 2:16). He forgave and restored them many times during the reign of the kings. After the captivity, He restored them to their land. God has continued to keep them, although they are scattered among the nations of the world. He withheld judgment on Jerusalem and the nation of Israel for about forty years after they had crucified Jesus Christ.

THE SIXTH DISPENSATION—GRACE OR CHURCH

This dispensation, called by some the age of grace, and by others the church age, began at Pentecost with the coming of the Holy

Spirit (Ac 2:1-4), and will end at the rapture of the church (1 Th 4:16, 17), extending from the descent of the Holy Spirit to the descent of the Lord Jesus Christ. This is the age of the Holy Spirit, and He is calling out from among the nations a people for His Name (Ac 15:14), the true church, made up of all those who truly receive Jesus Christ as their personal Saviour and Lord during this period. When the last soul is saved to complete the body of Christ, the church, then Christ will return to gather the church up to Himself.

The testing of man. The test in this age is whether man will receive the Lord Jesus Christ by faith as his personal Saviour. God offers man eternal life as a gift (Ro 6:23), and God says to man: "For by grace are ye saved through faith; and that not of yourselves: it is the gift of God: Not of works, lest any man should boast" (Eph 2:8, 9).

The failure of man. Unbelievable as it may seem, man has rejected God's offer of free grace during this age, and today, after almost two thousand years of God's grace and love offered to man, it is estimated that only about two percent of the world's population have received this wonderful gift and are saved. Dr. Frederick A. Tatford comments: "The majority of the world treat God's proffered grace with either apathetic indifference or bitter opposition, and relatively few respond to the offer of mercy and salvation in Christ."[11] The church has failed God and Scofield remarked: "The predicted end of the testing of man under grace is the apostasy of the professing Church."[12]

The judgment of God. This dispensation will end with the rapture of the church, when Christ returns for His own, and then comes the tribulation period, a time of judgment "such as was not since the beginning of the world to this time, no, nor ever shall be. And except those days should be shortened, there should no flesh be saved" (Mt 24:21, 22). More than one-half of the world's population will be killed in this time of judgment brought upon a Christ-rejecting world.

The grace of God. God's grace is shown throughout the whole age in offering salvation to the whole human race. His grace is shown in removing the church before the tribulation, and also in saving a great multitude out of the tribulation (Rev 3:10; 7:9-17).

THE SEVENTH DISPENSATION—THE KINGDOM

This is the last of the dispensations and the time period will be a thousand years; thus it is called the millennium (Rev 20). Six times in this chapter, God speaks of a thousand years (vv. 2, 3, 4, 5, 6, 7).

The testing of man. The test under this dispensation is whether man will live righteously upon the earth under the rule of Jesus Christ. Never will it be easier for one to live righteously, because during this period (1) the devil will be bound; (2) Christ will live and walk upon this earth and will rule righteously along with His church; (3) the curse will be removed from the earth, and the desert shall blossom as a rose; (4) war will be unknown; and (5) the knowledge of the Lord shall cover the earth as the waters cover the sea. Surely man should live righteously during this time.

The failure of man. Although people wonder how man could fail God under such favorable conditions, we find that even during this period some will rebel, and though Christ rules with a rod of iron, some will have to be accursed for their sin and rebellion (Is 65:20). Those born in this age are still of the Adamic, fallen stock and need to be saved on the basis of trust in the Lord Jesus Christ. Some render feigned obedience; and at the close of this period, when Satan is let loose, a great number follow him in revolt against God (Rev 20:7-9).

The judgment of God. When a person rebels openly during the millennium, he is cut off immediately in death, when he reaches the age of one hundred (Is 65:20). One rendering of Psalm 101:8, which some say refers to this time of judgment, is this: "Morning by morning I will destroy all the wicked of the land, that I may cut off all wicked doers from the city of the Lord."

At the close of the thousand years, when a great number revolt against God, His swift judgment follows, "and fire came down from God out of heaven, and devoured them" (Rev 20:9).

The grace of God. His grace is shown in that He protects the "beloved city," Jerusalem (Rev 20:9), and takes the redeemed into the eternal state with Himself.

Dr. William W. Orr comments: "Under every conceivable test man is shown to be a complete failure. This was not unknown to God. But now as a matter of record, it is proved to men. There is no possible hope for man except the grace of God."[13]

After the destruction of the followers of the devil, the devil himself shall be cast into the lake of fire and brimstone and shall be punished day and night forever and ever (20:10). The great white throne judgment follows, when all the wicked dead shall be resurrected and stand before God to be judged, and then cast into the lake of fire (20:11-15). "The heavens shall pass away with a great noise, and the elements shall melt with fervent heat, the earth also and the works that are therein shall be burned up" (2 Pe 3:10). "Nevertheless we, according to his promise, look for new heavens and a new earth, wherein dwelleth righteousness" (2 Pe 3:13).

In Revelation 21 and 22 God speaks of seven new things: 1.) a new heaven (v. 1), 2.) a new earth (v. 1), 3.) a new city (vv. 2, 10-27), 4.) a new people (vv. 3-5), 5.) a new temple (v. 22), 6.) a new light (v. 23), 7.) a new paradise (22:1-5).

He also speaks of ten "no more's" (21:1-27): no more sea, no more death, no more sorrow, no more crying, no more pain, no more temple (made by hands), no more sun, no more moon, no more night, and no more sin.

The promise to the one who is saved is: "He that overcometh shall inherit all things; and I will be his God, and he shall be my son" (21:7); but the promise to him who is lost is: "But the fearful, and unbelieving, and the abominable, and murderers, and whoremongers, and sorcerers, and idolaters, and all liars, shall have their part in the lake which burneth with fire and brimstone: which is the second death" (21:8).

Which will it be for you, my reader? If you are His son, you will be like Him for all eternity, enjoying all the blessings He has for His own; for He promises "that in the ages to come he might show the exceeding riches of his grace in his kindness toward us through Christ Jesus" (Eph 2:7). If you are not His son, you can become His son by receiving Christ as your personal Saviour and Lord, for He says in John 1:12: "But as many as received him [Christ], to them gave he power to become the sons of God, even to them that believe on his name."

God wants your love and fellowship throughout eternity. All of His future plans center about those who have been redeemed by the precious blood of Christ.

If you are not His son, for all eternity you will experience the second death, which is the lake of fire and brimstone, and forever you will be separated from God and His people. It's either become a son, or undergo the second death. As one unknown writer has said:

> The clock of life is wound but once, and no man has the power
> To tell just where the hands will stop—at late or early hour.
> To lose one's wealth is sad indeed, to lose one's health is more,
> To lose one's soul is such a loss as no man can restore.
> The present only is our own; live, love, toil with a will.
> Place no faith in tomorrow, for the clock may then be still.

3

UNDERSTANDING THE TIMES
And Knowing What to Do

IN 1 CHRONICLES 12:32 there is a short statement concerning the children of Issachar. It was said of them that they were "men that had understanding of the times, to know what Israel ought to do." There are some people today who have a knowledge of the times but not an understanding of the times. Only those who know the Lord and His Word understand the times and know what to do.

TIMES OF THE GENTILES

Jesus Christ said, "Jerusalem shall be trodden down of the Gentiles, until the *times of the Gentiles* be fulfilled" (Lk 21:24, ital. added). The times of the Gentiles began when Judah was carried into captivity by Babylon under King Nebuchadnezzar (2 Chr 36:1-21) and will end when Jesus Christ returns to earth in power and glory to destroy Gentile world power (Dan 2:34-35, 44; Rev. 19:11-21). Until that time, Jerusalem will be subject to political dominion of the Gentiles.

On June 7, 1967, during the Six-Day War between the Arabs and the Jews, the Israeli forces took the Old City of Jerusalem from Jordan, and many people thought the times of the Gentiles had been fulfilled, since Jerusalem was no longer "trodden down of the Gentiles." The people of Israel once again stood before the Wailing Wall in the Old City; and the Israeli commander who took the wall declared that none of those present had ever seen or done anything so great. Then—the story goes—he broke down and wept.

Although this might be called the shortest war in history, it also could be called one of the most important from a prophetic standpoint. For the first time in centuries, Jerusalem was again in the hands of the Jews. They say they will never give it up; but according to Revelation 11:1-2, during the last three and a half years of the great tribulation, Jerusalem will again be dominated by a Gentile power.

Though the times of the Gentiles are not yet ended, we can see that the end is drawing very close. The Jews are talking about rebuilding their temple, and they now have control of the land where it will be rebuilt. The stage is set for this as it never has been for nineteen hundred years, since the second temple was destroyed by Titus in A.D. 70. Surely the end of the age is near, and the coming of Christ for His own must be at the doors.

Dr. Charles C. Ryrie wrote recently, in his book *The Bible And Tomorrow's News*, "Of what significance is the present occupation of Jerusalem, then? It is important, because it has unified the city under a Jewish government. The land, too, has been enlarged so that one nation now occupies most of Palestine. All of this will make it easier for the man of sin to make a covenant with the Jews, as he will do at the beginning of the Tribulation. If that be so, the rapture of the Church is imminent. At any day, we may be caught up to be with our Lord."[1]

PERILOUS TIMES

Paul says in 2 Timothy 3:1: "This know also, that in the last days perilous times shall come." The Amplified New Testament renders this verse: "But understand this, that in the last days there will set in perilous times of great stress and trouble—hard to deal with and hard to bear." Notice that God wants us to understand this; He wants us to have an "understanding of the times."

The word *perilous* means "dangerous," "hazardous." As we read the newspapers and listen to the news today, it is not difficult to believe that we are living in perilous times of great stress and trouble.

Not only theologians and preachers are noticing the seriousness of the times, but scientists and statesmen are also speaking out. World leaders such as U Thant and Ralph Bunche, pointing to the arms race and the population explosion, are warning that organizations like the UN have only a short time left in which to do anything to forestall catastrophe.

The *Bulletin of the Atomic Scientists* has on its cover a clock which is called the doomsday clock. In 1968 "they advanced the hands to seven minutes to midnight—five minutes closer than its previous setting in 1963—and the first move forward (rather than backward) since 1953. . . . *Bulletin* editor Dr. Eugene Rabinowitch said the latest movement was necessitated by the 'dismal world record' of the past five years, during which nations have been 'drifting back to pre-atomic pursuits of their narrow national interests, with power politics again replacing attempts to build a stable, peaceful world.' "[2] As evidence of deteriorating conditions he noted the development of atomic weapons by France and Red China, the Arab-Israeli and Indo-Pakistani wars, escalation of the Vietnam war, and competition between America and Russia to produce an antiballistic missile—all timely issues when he was speaking.

H. G. Wells said shortly before his death, "Man and his world have come to a place where there is no way out." It is interesting to know that when Jesus was speaking of the last days, He said, "And there shall be signs in the sun, and in the moon, and in the stars; and upon the earth distress of nations, with perplexity" (Lk 21:25). The word *perplexity* in the Greek is *aporia*, which means "to have no way out."

Dr. Wilbur M. Smith, in his book *World Crises and the Prophetic Scriptures*, quotes Dr. Pitirim A. Sorokin, one of the most distinguished sociologists who has ever lived:

> We live amidst one of the greatest crises in human history. Not only war, famine, pestilence, and revolution, but a legion of other calamities are also rampant over the whole world. All values are unsettled. All norms are broken. Humanity has become a distorted image of its own noble self. The crisis is omnipresent and involves almost the whole of culture and society from top to bottom. It is manifest in the fine arts and science, in philosophy and religion, in ethics and law. It permeates the forms of social, economic, and political organizations and the entire way of living and thinking. There is every reason to expect that the disastrous effects of such calamities will fall upon us in a much more intensive and extensive scale during this catastrophic age of ours.[3]

Then Dr. Smith says, "The point I am making here is that we are, admittedly, in a great world crisis. Many believe it is so critical that they insist civilization is doomed and we are at the end of this age. Recently a brilliant young Christian scholar, a thorough conservative, having two doctorate degrees from well-known educational institutions, told me that a number of the professors of philosophy under whom he had been sitting the last four years, in his own hearing, threw out the question before their graduate students, 'May we not be at the end of everything?' "[4]

A. R. Pazhwak, past president of the U. N. General Assembly, recently stated: "If fools and folly rule the world, the end of man in our time may come as a rude shock, but it will no longer come as a complete surprise."[5]

Many scientists of our times are deeply concerned with the seriousness not only of the arms race and the population explosion, but also of the irreparable damage being done to our environment by our civilization. Dr. W. H. Pickering, director of Jet Propulsion Laboratory for California Institute of Technology, stated, "In half an hour the East and West could destroy civilization."[6] Yet other scientists feel that even without nuclear war, the problems of exhausted natural resources and overpopulation could still produce the same result before the end of the century.

Of course, the person who understands the Word of God knows that this world will be here for a long time before it will be destroyed. As promised, Jesus will come back at the end of this age and rule for one thousand years.

We have quoted from a few men other than theologians and preachers to alert you to what is being said about our times. Surely, these are "perilous times."

LATTER TIMES

Paul tells us in 1 Timothy 4:1: "Now the Spirit speaketh expressly, that in the *latter times* some shall depart from the faith, giving heed to seducing spirits, and doctrines of devils" (ital. added). A note in the Pilgrim Edition of the Bible at this verse says: "The latter days, or latter times, always refer to the last days of the age before Christ comes to reign."[7] Dr. Herman A. Hoyt, in his book *The End Times*, writes: " 'Latter' as a term used in connection with some events often refers to the end of the age. As for instance, 'In the latter times some shall depart from the faith' (1 Timothy 4:1)."[8] God wants us to have an understanding of this also, that we are at the end of this age and Jesus Christ may come at any moment. There are indications all about us that point to His soon return. In another chapter I want to give you some of them, but now let me give you a statement made by Dr. John F. Walvoord, president of Dallas Theological Seminary: "If there ever was a generation of Bible-Believing Christians who had a right to look forward to the coming of the Lord momentarily day by day, on the basis of what they see in the world, it is our present generation. Even unbelievers are telling us today that things cannot go on as they are much longer."[9]

After explaining a number of signs that indicate the coming of the Lord is very near, Dr. J. Dwight Pentecost, in his book *Prophecy For Today*, makes this statement: "When you see from all of these great movements how the stage is set so that these events could take place almost over night, I think there is only one conclusion that a person could make, and that is that the coming of the Lord *must* be drawing nigh. It is my absolute conviction that there is not one single line of prophecy that yet must be fulfilled in order for us to say, 'He can come now.' "[10]

What to do as Christians

Not only did the men of Issachar have an "understanding of the times," but they also knew "what Israel ought to do." I pray that you who have read this may now have a better "understanding of the times," and will be concerned as to what you "ought to do."

Time to awake

Paul said in Romans 13:11: "And that, *knowing the time*, that now it is high *time to awake* out of sleep: for now is our salvation nearer than when we believed" (ital. added). Surely, this is no time for God's people to be asleep, yet many of them are fast asleep.

Paul warns us, "Therefore let us not sleep, as do others; but let us watch and be sober" (1 Th 5:6). Jesus told us, "The harvest truly is great, but the laborers are few" (Lk 10:2), and commanded us: "Lift up your eyes and look on the fields; for they are white already to harvest" (Jn 4:35). What a tragedy that in this day when more than half of the world's population have never once heard the gospel, many of the reapers in the harvest are asleep. "He that gathereth in summer is a wise son; but he that sleepeth in harvest is a son that causeth shame" (Pr 10:5).

Ord L. Morrow, associate radio minister of the Back to the Bible Broadcast, wrote recently: "This is no day to be asleep! We see the signs of the Lord's coming, but let us not sit back and go to sleep. Of all the sad signs I think the sign of the sleeping saints is the saddest. Oh, that we might awake! Oh, that we might be ready and awake at His coming."[11]

"How long wilt thou sleep, O sluggard? when wilt thou arise out of thy sleep?" (Pr 6:9).

TIME TO SEEK THE LORD

God's Word tells us that "it is *time to seek the Lord,* till he come and rain righteousness upon you" (Ho 10:12, ital. added). It is time for Christians to "humble themselves, and pray, and seek [God's] face, and turn from their wicked ways." When this happens, God promises: "Then will I hear from heaven, and will forgive their sin, and will heal their land" (2 Chr 7:14). Let us, as Christians, obey the words of Jesus: "But seek ye first the kingdom of God, and his righteousness" (Mt 6:33). Let us say, with the psalmist: "Thy face, Lord, will I seek"; "O God, thou art my God; early will I seek thee" (Ps 27:8; 63:1). Thank God for His promises: "Those that seek me early shall find me"; "And ye shall seek me, and find me, when ye shall search for me with all your heart"; "he is a rewarder of them that diligently seek him" (Pr 8:17; Jer 29:13; Heb 11:6). Notice the word *seek* in all the above verses.

TIME TO JUDGE OURSELVES

"For the time is come that judgment must begin at the house of God" (1 Pe 4:17). The "house of God" refers to the true church, made up of all those who are born again in this age of grace. We should judge ourselves, examine ourselves, confess and forsake that which is wrong in our lives, and "cleanse ourselves from all filthiness of the flesh and spirit, perfecting holiness in the fear of God" (2 Co 7:1). In the light of the truth that "the night is far spent, the day is at hand," we should respond: "Let us therefore cast off the works of darkness, and let us put on the armor of light. Let us walk honestly, as in the day; not in rioting and drunkenness, not in chambering and wantonness, not in strife and envying. But put ye on the Lord Jesus Christ, and make not provision for the flesh, to fulfil the lusts thereof" (Ro 13:12-14).

What to Do As Unsaved

If you who are reading this are unsaved, may God help you to put your trust in Christ now and be saved before it is too late.

Time to be saved

God's Word warns: "Behold, now is the accepted time; behold now is the day of salvation." "Boast not thyself of tomorrow; for thou knowest not what a day may bring forth." "Today if ye will hear his voice, Harden not your hearts" (2 Co 6:2; Pr 27:1; Heb 3:7, 8). It's because of the longsuffering of God, because He is "not willing that any should perish, but that all should come to repentance" (2 Pe 3:9), that Christ has not returned; but one day (and it may be today) He will return, and if you are not saved when He comes, you will be left here on the earth to go into the awful time of judgment called the tribulation period and then into hell forever. "For God sent not his Son into the world to condemn the world; but that the world through him might be saved." "I am the door: by me if any man enter in, he shall be saved." "Believe on the Lord Jesus Christ, and thou shalt be saved." "That if thou shalt confess with thy mouth the Lord Jesus, and shalt believe in thine heart that God hath raised him from the dead, thou shalt be saved . . . For whosoever shall call upon the name of the Lord shall be saved." (Jn 3:17; 10:9; Ac 16:31; Ro 10:9, 13).

Let me close this chapter with some timely words from Dr. John F. Walvoord:

> The revelation of the prophetic Word was not designed simply to comfort and enlighten. The hope of the Lord's return should constitute an impelling challenge. The task is large and the days are few. It is time for searching of heart and purification of life. It is time for prayer and devotion, for sacrifice and effort. Now is the time to preach the good news of the Saviour Who died for the sins of the whole world that all who believe might live. It is time to press on

through closing missionary doors, through opposition, unbelief, and indifference. It is time to remind ourselves of that searching evaluation of our life and labors that awaits us at the Judgment Seat of Christ. The coming of the Lord is as near as our next breath, the next beat of our hearts, the next word of our lips. While we wait, may we be "steadfast, unmovable, always abounding in the work of the Lord" (1 Cor. 15:58).[12]

4

IS AMERICA HEADED FOR
DESTRUCTION?

I HAVE BEEN ASKED repeatedly, "Is America mentioned in the Bible?"
or, "How does the United States fit into prophecy?" As far as I have
been able to ascertain, there is no mention of this country in the
Bible. Dr. John F. Walvoord, in a chapter in his book *The Nations In
Prophecy*, says: "No specific mention of the United States or any
other country in North America or South America can be found in
the Bible. None of the rather obscure references to distant lands can
be taken specifically as a reference to the United States."[1] And a
comment from Dr. E. Schuyler English confirms this view:

> In the Bible there is no mention of the U.S.A. either by name or
> symbol. No lion, nor bear, nor leopard like those that symbolized
> Babylon, Persia, and Greece appears in the pages of Scripture to
> signify the United States. No ten-horned beast, 'dreadful and terri-
> ble, and strong exceedingly,' foreshadows the U.S. in the way that
> Rome's empire was characterized. Gog and Magog is a term that is
> applied to Russia in Holy Writ, but nothing of the sort signifies the
> United States. Predictive Scriptures are silent concerning the role
> that America will play in the last days.[2]

We know that today the United States of America is one of the two
most powerful countries in the world. God has richly blessed America and made her what she is. He has blessed us temporally, physi-
cally, and spiritually. The United States has only 6 per cent of the
world's population, yet she has:

        63 per cent of the world's manufactured goods
        58 per cent of the world's automobiles
        56 per cent of the world's telephones
        50 per cent of the world's wealth
        44 per cent of the world's trucks
        43 per cent of the world's radios,
        35 per cent of the world's electric output,
        29 per cent of the world's railroads,
        29 per cent of the world's petroleum,
        26 per cent of the world's steel,
        22 per cent of the world's coal.[3]

Not only have we been blessed with physical things, but God has also blessed us with spiritual things; and we have had strong churches and great institutions of learning. We have also been for many years the strongest base of operation for the missionary enterprise.

A French political philosopher, Alexis de Tocqueville, visited America when our nation was young. He came here to learn what magic quality enabled a handful of people to defeat the mighty British Empire twice in thirty-five years. He looked for America's greatness in her harbors and rivers, her fertile fields and boundless forests, her mines and other national resources. He studied America's schools, her Congress and her Constitution, without finding the secret of America's power. It was not until he went into the churches of America and heard pulpits "aflame with righteousness" that he found the secret of America's power and greatness. He returned to France and wrote this warning: "America is great because America is good, and if America ever ceases to be good, America will cease to be great."[4]

America has ceased to be good—she will cease to be great. John A. Stormer, in his book *The Death Of A Nation*, said, "Even if there were no communist threat, growing moral decay and spiritual bankruptcy will destroy America from within."[5]

Vance Havner said this about America: "If America continues to decline morally as it has over the past several years, we will have to change our national emblem from an eagle to a vulture."[6]

Dr. Harold Rawlings commented: "America is known as the land of the free and the home of the brave. But if the present rate of deterioration continues it will soon be known as the land of the 'spree' and the home of the 'rave.' "[7]

A number of people recently are saying that America is headed for destruction. A sampling of some of these statements appears in the following pages.

Arthur Kroch, a long-time Washington newsman of the New York *Times,* recently wrote a book entitled *Memoirs: Sixty Years on the Firing Line,* covering his sixty years as a newsman. He won the Pulitzer Prize three times. In this book he voiced the fear that the reign of the United States as a leading world power is nearing the end. In the closing paragraph of his book he says: "I have contracted a visceral fear. It is that the tenure of the United States as the first power in the world may be one of the briefest in history."[8]

Another prediction from Dr. Rawlings: "If our country continues to decline at its present rate, there will be no America as we presently know it by 1975. I am no prophet of doom. I am giving you the facts based upon the Word of God and based upon the trends we are seeing all around us."[9]

May Craig, longtime lady member of television's *Meet The Press* panel, wrote in a column for the *Sunday Telegram* of Portland, Maine: "Unless there is a change, deep-down in the American people, a genuine crusade against self indulgence and immorality, public and private, then we are witnesses to the decline and fall of the American Republic. Death on the highways . . . cheating from top to bottom in our society, get rich quick, break-up of the family, faltering foreign policy, reckless debt—these have destroyed nations before us. Why should we think we can take that path and change history?"[10]

Homer Duncan, editor of *Missionary Crusader,* wrote recently: "Not too many years ago, any person who spoke of impending danger was considered a fool and a fanatic. Times have changed. Events that are now taking place in our country are causing many to say, 'It is too late. There is nothing we can do.' Yes, the hour is late. Perhaps it is much later than any of us dare to believe. . . . We are like a jet that is in a power dive. We have not crashed yet, but we are rapidly speeding to our doom, and it may be that we have passed the point of no return."[11]

An editorial in *Christianity Today* asked this question "Has America passed her peak?" It answered: "The moral toboggan slide evident in our national life during the past decade leads many observers to speculate that America may have passed her peak and begun to decline as the moral and political leader of the world. . . . If Americans—Christians and non-Christians alike—do not soon repent of their sins of hatred, greed, violence, crime, divorce, and illicit sex—as well as other personal and social sins—turn to God, and live in accordance with His commandments, our decline will inevitably lead to the fall of the American nation."[12]

There appeared in the *Calgary Farm and Ranch Review* this article, unusually to the point for a secular magazine:

> One of man's most tragic weaknesses is his failure to benefit from the lessons of history. Yet those lessons have for centuries been recorded by scholars.
>
> Not the least of these was the famous historian Edward Gibbon, who dedicated many years of his life to future generations by his precise research into the causes and effects of social changes. In his classic, *The Decline and Fall of the Roman Empire,* he cited the five primary causes for the deterioration of that historic society:
>
> 1. The rapid increase of divorce and the undermining of the sanctity of the home.
> 2. The spiralling rise of taxes and extravagant spending.
> 3. The mounting craze for pleasure and the brutalization of sports.
> 4. The building of gigantic armaments and the failure to realize that the real enemy lay within the gates of the empire in the moral decay of its people.
> 5. The decay of religion and the fading of faith into a mere form, leaving the people without any guide. . . .
>
> In the light of today's conditions, the failings of ancient Rome make a rather sobering comparison with our own.[13]

Dr. John F. Walvoord gives a sober warning:

> History has many records of great nations which have risen to unusual power and influence only to decline because of internal corruption or international complications. It may well be that the United States of America is today at the zenith of its power much as Babylon was in the sixth century B.C. prior to its sudden downfall at the hands of the Medes and Persians (Daniel 5). Any realistic survey of moral conditions in the world today would justify a judg-

ment of God on any nation, including that of the United States. The longsuffering God has offered unusual benefits to the United States both in a material and religious way, but they have been used with such profligacy that ultimate divine judgment may be expected. The question is no longer whether America deserves judgment, but rather why divine judgment has been so long withheld from a nation which has enjoyed so much of God's bounty.[14]

The great Bible teacher Dr. Donald G. Barnhouse comes to the same conclusion about the biblical silence concerning America. And Dr. English, already quoted, echoes the suggestion that this country might be at its zenith as a world influence.

Recently I met a missionary from the Philippines, Rev. Frank Allen. He told me that while he was in a philosophy of education course at the University of Michigan in 1968, a member of Eldridge Cleaver's Peace and Freedom Movement spoke to this class these words: "We are determined to destroy the establishment; if we have to kill hundreds of thousands of people like you to do it, we will count it a privilege."

H. Rap Brown, in an article published in the French political weekly, *Nouvel Observateur*, said: "We are inferior in number. Therefore we have chosen guerrilla warfare as a solution which the situation imposes on us. We will concentrate on strategic points in the country—in the factories, the fields, and homes of whites. We can easily sabotage and destroy without ever firing a shot. We can, for example, destroy telephone lines, railways, airports, the electric and electronics installations. The life of every city in the U.S. depends on the electrical system. If it is paralyzed, so is the city. Thus, city by city, we will succeed in bringing America to its knees."[15]

The Communists are waging war to win the world. They are following detailed plans laid down over fifty years ago by Lenin, the man who brought Communism to Russia. In summary, this is Lenin's plan: "First, we will take eastern Europe, then the masses of Asia, then we will encircle the United States which will be the last bastian of capitalism. We will not have to attack. It will fall into our hands like an overripe fruit."[16] The specifics of Lenin's plans included fomenting racial and cultural hatreds, encouraging antagonisms between the generations, inspiring strikes and riots, setting wives against their husbands, and topping it all off with economic inflation.

Phillip Abbot Luce, who was a former Communist, in his book *Road To Revolution* describes how he actually sat in on meetings planning strategy for guerrilla warfare with the purpose of ultimately overthrowing the United States government.[17]

In his book *Masters of Deceit,* J. Edgar Hoover reveals the Communist plot to take over this country. He says the New Left has as its goal the destruction of the U. S. government. Mr. Hoover says the SDS is the primary spokesman for the New Left movement. He continues: "At the center of the movement is an almost passionate desire to destroy, to annihilate, to tear down. The Students for a Democratic Society has seized upon every opportunity to foment discord among the youth of this country."[18]

Not long ago, James Forman authored a twenty-five-hundred-word *Black Manifesto,* in which a small group of anti-American black revolutionaries vowed church seizures, disruptions, demonstrations, and demanded five-hundred million dollars in reparations from the American-Jewish community.[19] Rev. I. H. Jackson, president of the National Baptist Convention, representing over six million Negroes, said of the *Black Manifesto,* that it carries "as firm a message for the destruction of the United States of America as has ever been given."[20]

John A. Stormer, in his book, *The Death Of A Nation,* speaks of the Communists' plans: "Ultimately, the Communists . . . plan to bring America to a standstill. They can do it by coordinating riots in major cities with sabotage of electric power distribution, gas mains and water supplies. Communist plans for paralyzing U. S. cities have been exposed by Congressional Committees—although few Americans take the warnings seriously."[21]

Many Americans refuse to believe that America is in danger. They say, "It can't happen here." But America is headed for destruction. Whether this destruction will be from within or from without, I do not know. Whether we will be internally destroyed by Communist influence or destroyed by outright missile attack, I do not know. But I do know that God is going to bring judgment and destruction upon this country because of our sin.

In the Bible, God speaks of destroying people and nations. As I have searched the Scriptures to see why God destroyed them, I found these reasons.

SEVEN REASONS AMERICA IS HEADED FOR DESTRUCTION

"I know that God hath determined to destroy thee because . . ."
(2 Chr 25:16).

GOD DESTROYS PEOPLE BECAUSE THEY FORGET HIM

Psalm 9:17 says, "The wicked shall be turned into hell, and all the
nations that forget God." God warned His people in the Old Testament: "Beware that thou forget not the LORD thy God. . . . And it
shall be, if thou do at all forget the LORD thy God, and walk after
other gods, and serve them, and worship them, I testify against you
this day that ye shall surely perish. As the nations which the Lord
destroyeth before your face, so shall ye perish; because ye would not
be obedient unto the voice of the LORD your God" (Deu 8:11a, 19,
20). Israel forgot God and served other gods and was destroyed.
America too has forgotten God and is walking after other gods, serving and worshiping them, and is headed for destruction. God's Word
clearly says, "Now consider this, ye that forget God, lest I tear you
in pieces, and there be none to deliver" (Ps 50:22).

GOD DESTROYS PEOPLE BECAUSE THEY BECOME MATERIALISTIC

Israel was warned against materialism: "Lest when thou hast
eaten and are full, and hast built goodly houses, and dwelt therein;
and when thy herds and thy flocks multiply, and thy silver and thy
gold is multiplied, and all that thou hast is multiplied; then thine
heart be lifted up, and thou forget the LORD thy God. . . . And thou
say in thine heart, My power and the might of mine hand hath gotten me this wealth . . . I testify against you this day that ye shall
surely perish" (Deu 8:12-14, 17, 19). Our country has grown materialistic and this philosophy has crept into every facet of our lives.
Theodore Roosevelt said, at the very beginning of the twentieth century, "The things that could destroy America are prosperity at any
price, peace at any price, safety first instead of duty first, the love of
soft living, and the get-rich-quick theory of life." God's Word reminds us: "But they that will be rich fall into temptation and a snare,
and into many foolish and hurtful lusts, which drown men in destruction and perdition" (1 Ti 6:9).

GOD DESTROYS PEOPLE BECAUSE THEY DO NOT OBEY HIM

Moses speaks of what happens to those who do not obey God's Word: "Beware that thou forget not the LORD thy God, in not keeping his commandments, and his judgments, and his statutes, which I command thee this day" (Deu 8:11). America has flagrantly disobeyed God's Word and, according to the Bible, "Whoso despiseth the word shall be destroyed" (Pr 13:13).

GOD DESTROYS PEOPLE BECAUSE THEY ARE WICKED

In the days of Noah, "GOD saw that the wickedness of man was great in the earth, and that every imagination of the thoughts of his heart was only evil continually. And it repented the LORD that he had made man on the earth, and it grieved him at his heart. And the LORD said, I will destroy man whom I have created from the face of the earth" (Gen 6:5-7). Jesus mentioned the state of men's lives at the time of the Flood: "But as the days of Noe were, so shall also the coming of the Son of man be. For as in the days that were before the flood they were eating and drinking, marrying and giving in marriage, until the day that Noe entered into the ark, and knew not until the flood came, and took them all away; so shall also the coming of the Son of man be" (Mt 24:37-39).

Notice the pattern in the following verses, as indicated by italics. "The LORD preserveth all them that love him: but all *the wicked will he destroy.*" In Proverbs 11:3 is a similar statement: "The integrity of the upright shall guide them: but *the perverseness of transgressors shall destroy them.*" Speaking of the day of the Lord, Isaiah says that God will "lay the land desolate: and *he shall destroy the sinners thereof out of it*" (Is 13:9). Job asks the questions, "*Is not destruction to the wicked?* and a strange punishment to the workers of iniquity?" (Job 31:3), and again he asks: "Do ye not know . . . that *the wicked is reserved to the day of destruction?* they shall be brought forth to the day of wrath" (Job 21:29, 30). In Psalm 21:8-10, David speaks of what happens to the wicked who hate God: "Thine hand shall find out all thine enemies: thy right hand shall find out those that hate thee: Thou shalt make them as a fiery oven in the time of thine anger: the LORD shall swallow them up in his wrath, and *the fire shall devour them. Their fruit shall thou destroy from the earth,* and their seed from among the children of men."

Dr. Thorsten Sellen, foremost crime authority, said, "The United States has the worst criminal statistics of any country in the Western World."[22] J. Edgar Hoover, late director of the FBI, describes our country's moral conditions:

> Only one out of twelve persons in our country attends church. Seven out of eight children quit church and Sunday School attendance before they reach 15 years of age. Fifteen million sex magazines are printed monthly and read by one-third of the American people. There are more bar-maids in this country than college girls. One million American girls have venereal diseases; one hundred thousand girls disappear every year into white slavery. One million illegitimate babies are born annually and perhaps a million illegal abortions are performed annually. Our nation harbors three times as many criminals as college students. A major crime is committed every 22 seconds, an aggravated assault or rape every hour, a murder every forty minutes. There are 60 suicides in our nation daily. Three out of ten who start as light drinkers become drunkards.[23]

GOD DESTROYS PEOPLE BECAUSE THEY BECOME PROUD

God hates pride (Pr 6:16, 17), and in His Word we read repeatedly that He destroys people because of pride: "But when he was strong, his heart was lifted up to his destruction" (2 Chr 26:16); "The Lord will destroy the house of the proud," "Pride goeth before destruction, and an haughty spirit before a fall," "Before destruction the heart of man is haughty" (Pr 15:25, 16:18, 18:12).

One of the four sins which caused the destruction of Sodom was pride: "Behold, this was the iniquity of thy sister Sodom, pride, fulness of bread, and abundance of idleness was in her and in her daughters, neither did she strengthen the hand of the poor and needy" (Eze 16:49). Pride was the first sin mentioned. Hugh Ross Williamson, Anglican historian, writes of Sodom: "The correct understanding of Sodom is a proud, self-satisfied, materialistic society, acting with callous inhospitality to man and at the same time rejecting the true worship of God."[24]

The word *pride,* according to Webster, means an over-high opinion of oneself, exaggerated self-esteem, conceit, the showing of this in behavior, haughtiness, arrogance. Surely, America has become proud; she has "an overhigh opinion of herself; she has an "exaggerated self-esteem"; she is conceited; and she shows it by the behavior of her people in their haughtiness and arrogance. As Mr. Williamson said of Sodom, it also is true of us today—we are a "proud, self-satisfied, materialistic society, acting with callous inhospitality to man and at the same time rejecting the true worship of God."

Leonard Ravenhill, of Great Britain, points out: "Sodom had no Bibles. Sodom had no preachers. Sodom had no tracts. Sodom had no prayer meetings. Sodom had no churches, and Sodom perished. How will America and England be spared from the wrath of the Almighty? We have millions of Bibles, scores of thousands of churches, and endless preachers. And yet what sin!"[25]

GOD DESTROYS PEOPLE BECAUSE THEY BECOME SEXUALLY OBSESSED

God destroyed past civilizations because they had become sexually obsessed. Sodom and Gomorrah were completely destroyed for "giving themselves over to fornication, and going after strange flesh" and they "are set forth for an example, suffering the vengeance of eternal fire" (Jude 7). Peter says that God by "turning the cities of Sodom and Gomorrah into ashes condemned them with an overthrow, making them an ensample [example] unto those that after should live ungodly" (2 Pe 2:6).

Rome, Pompeii, Naples, and nation after nation, city after city, became preoccupied with sex and have been swept into oblivion. Today we are witnessing an unprecedented moral decline in America. It has been said, "The god of America is materialism and its goddess is sex." We have what is called the "new morality," which is nothing but the old immorality. We also have an approach to life problems called Situation Ethics, which teaches that every morally questionable act is judged on the basis of the situation surrounding its occurrence. The leading proponent of this view is Dr. Joseph Fletcher, professor of ethics at Cambridge Episcopal Theological School. According to him, the rightness or wrongness of an act is determined by the situation, not by an absolute moral code, such as the Ten Commandments. The situationist would say that *ordinarily* murder, adultery, and coveting are wrong—but not always.

According to the U. S. Public Health Service, approximately 250,000 girls annually leave high school to become mothers; 70 per cent of the brides in the United States have lost their virginity before marriage; there are more than 150,000 cases of rapes and assaults in the U. S. yearly; there has been a 36 per cent increase in illegitimate births in six years.

Dr. Graham Blaine, Jr., of the Maternity Center Association in Manhattan, said, "Illegitimate births in the United States have tripled in the past 25 years."[26]

It is tragic, but true, that the same day, June 25, 1962, that the U. S. Supreme Court banned prayers and Bible reading from America's public schools, it also opened the U. S. mails to a magazine published for homosexuals.[27] U. S. Post Office officials estimate that 500 million dollars worth of mail order pornography—dirty books, postcards, and filthy magazines and movies—are mailed to millions of young people every year. Mr. Hoover, in an FBI *Law Enforcement Bulletin,* said: "The publication and sale of obscene material is big business in America today. . . . It is impossible to estimate the amount of harm to impressionable teenagers and to assess the volume of sex crimes attributable to pornography, but its influence is extensive. Sexual violence is increasing at an alarming pace. Many parents are deeply concerned about conditions which involve young boys and girls in sex parties and illicit relations. . . . Pornography in all its forms, is one major cause of sex crimes, sexual aberrations and perversions."[28]

Dr. Goodrich Schauffler observes: "Our youth, in particular, have been engulfed in the flood of Hollywood's insane emphasis on sex."[29]

Professor Hermann Sasse of Australia says that in America, as well as Western Europe, our standards of morality have sunk far below the level of Russia or Red China to that of the Greek and Roman civilizations in their stages of complete disintegration. "This is not the subjective impression of a few malcontent churchmen, reactionary politicians, and romantic laudatores temporis acti; it is the substantial verdict of well-informed sociologists, historians, jurists, economists, and medical scholars, men with a worldwide outlook and experience in all countries of the Western World."[30]

Dr. Mary Steichen Calderone, executive director of the Sex Information and Education Council of the United States, Inc. (SIECUS), was asked by a senior high student, "What is your opinion of premarital sex relations among teenagers?"

She replied, "Nobody from up on high determines this. You determine it. I don't believe the old 'Thou shalt nots' apply anymore."[31]

Vance Packard, in his book *The Sexual Wilderness,* gave a breakdown of the percentage of premarital experience among American women, stating that 57 percent in the East, 48 percent in the West, 32 percent in the South, and 25 percent in the Midwest had no moral scruples.[32]

At the University of California at Berkeley, an estimated thousand couples are living together, unmarried. At the University of Pennsylvania, which has as its motto "Learning without morality is vain," the dean of women has announced the university has dropped the rule which prohibits female students from spending the night in the apartments of single males. This is fast becoming the rule in other colleges and universities throughout the country.[33]

The Courier Mail, a publication from Brisbane, Australia, carried this statement: "We are not living in ordinary times. . . . The morals with which we have grown up are being cast aside. . . . God has been dethroned; sex has been deified."[34]

Pageant magazine noted, "Adultery seems to be as widely practiced as it must have been in the orgiastic days before the Flood."[35]

The U. S. Public Health Service officials announced that by 1964, venereal diseases in the fifteen- to nineteen-year-old group had increased 232 percent since 1957. By 1966, doctors in St. Louis reported that syphilis cases among teenagers in metropolitan St. Louis had increased 600 percent in the same period.[36]

In an article in *Redbook* magazine in November 1967, entitled "Sex Before Marriage: A Young Wife's Story," the author says, "I feel premarital sexual experience in a stable relationship is healthy. . . . I feel that young adult couples—and I stress young adult—who have a healthy attitude toward sex can benefit greatly from a premarital relationship. . . . I hope to bring my daughters up to share my ideas."[37]

The first of the "Rules For Bringing About Revolution," published by the Communists in 1919, says: "Corrupt the young; get them away from religion. Get them interested in sex. Make them superficial. Destroy their ruggedness."[38] It is plain to see that the Communists are succeeding in carrying out this rule as we see so many young people in this country who are corrupt, who are not interested in religious things, who are interested in sex, who are superficial, and who lack ruggedness.

Newsweek magazine ran an article, widely quoted, entitled, "Our 'Anything Goes' Society—Where Is It Going?" in which are found these paragraphs:

> The old taboos are dead or dying. A new, more permissive society is taking shape. Its outlines are etched most prominently in the arts —in the increasing nudity and frankness of today's films, in the blunt, often obscene language seemingly endemic in American novels and plays, in the candid lyrics of pop songs and the undress of the avant-garde ballet, in erotic art and television talk shows, in freer fashions and franker advertising. And, behind this expanding permissiveness in the arts stands a society in transition, a society that has lost its consensus on such crucial issues as premarital sex and clerical celibacy, marriage, birth control and sex education; a society that cannot agree on standards of conduct, language and manners, on what can be seen and heard. . . .
>
> These new postures alarm many citizens, psychologists and social thinkers who see in this rapid destruction of taboos a dangerous swing toward irresponsible hedonism and, ultimately, social decay. "It is the inevitable mark of decadence in our society," says British social commentator Malcolm Muggeridge. "As our vitality ebbs, people reach out for vicarious excitement, like the current sex mania in pop songs and the popular press. At the decline and fall of the Roman Empire, the works of Sappho, Catullus and Ovid were celebrated. There is an analogy in that for us."[39]

Not only do we see the magazines, movies, plays, songs, books, pictures, TV programs, and advertising media advocating sex, but many of our religious leaders are following them in their teaching.

Rev. Harry Williams, dean of England's Trinity College, was quoted as saying: "Premarital or extramarital intercourse might be not only permissible but also a healing action in which Christ is present."[40]

Rev. Howard Moody, of the United Church of Christ, one of nine clergymen interviewed by *Playboy* magazine, said, "Are we able to say with dogmatic assurance that ALL extramarital sex is bad and destructive to the marriage relationship? As Reverend Adams indicates, most men engaged in counselling know that there are situations in which extramarital affairs have saved marriages, rather than destroyed them."[41]

In New Zealand, Rev. Allan Pyatt, noted dean of Christchurch, issued a statement saying: "Liquor, sex, gambling and dancing, if used properly, can lead to a fuller life."[42]

Gordon Clanton, a Presbyterian minister, said recently in the magazine, *Christian Century*: "For some time now theologians of the 'liberal bent' have been hinting at the emergence of a 'new morality.' They have been brave enough to say that nonmarital sex is not necessarily wrong. Now we must go further and proclaim that, properly understood and lovingly practiced, sex outside of marriage is a positive good—nonsinful, recreational sex is a possibility—the church should be seeking to weaken rather than strengthen the hold of morality on society."[43]

Rev. Ernest Harrison, in his book, *A Church Without God*, says: "If love is satisfied, then adultery is not wrong. In the case of premarital intercourse the problem is even easier."[44]

Mr. Truman Douglas, vice president of the National Council of Churches, stated: "We must have church support for the sexual revolution many of our youth today are committing."[45]

Professor Pitirim Sorokin, Harvard sociologist, has warned:

> We are victims of a sex mania as malignant as cancer and as socially menacing as Communism. Our sex obsession is reflected in the ever-mounting divorce rate, the upsurge in sex crimes, the emphasis of sex in radio and TV programs, stage plays and movies, popular songs, pictures, reading matter and advertising. Our civilization has become so preoccupied with sex that it now oozes from all the pores of American life. Unless America conquers her sex obsession, she will go the way of ancient Greece and Rome.[46]

God's Word clearly teaches that the wrong use of sex is sinful, and He will judge those who indulge in illicit sexual relations. Here are some of His warnings: "Thou shalt not commit adultery" (Ex 20:14, Mt 5:27); "Flee fornication" (1 Co 6:18); "abstain from fornication" (1 Th 4:3); "Flee also youthful lusts" (2 Ti 2:22); "Marriage is honorable in all, and the bed undefiled: but whoremongers and adulterers God will judge" (Heb 13:4).

God destroys people and nations who continue "giving themselves over to fornication, and going after strange flesh," like Sodom and

Gomorrah who "are set forth for an example, suffering the vengeance of eternal fire" (Jude 7). Paul warns that those who practice adultery and fornication will not inherit the kingdom of God (*see* 1 Co 6:9, 10).

If America will not conquer her sex obsession, she may go the way of ancient Greece and Rome. Bruce Dunn, in an article entitled "Watching A Nation Die," gave this warning: "No civilization, no empire, no nation has survived obsession with sex and impurity."[47]

GOD DESTROYS PEOPLE BECAUSE THEY BECOME APOSTATE

Peter wrote a warning that even as there were false prophets among the Israelites, there will also be false teachers in the church. These men will bring in serious heresies, going so far as to deny the very Lord who paid the price for their salvation. Their deadly example will be followed by many, and because of them the true way of salvation will get a bad reputation. Peter also warned that these men, possessing a desire for material things, will use their speaking ability to take advantage of the Christians. But, he concludes, their judgment has been building up. Their condemnation is on the way. (*see* 2 Pe 2:1-3)

Paul too asserted that when Jesus returns He will bring vengeance to those who do not know God and rejected the gospel. Their punishment will be eternal and destructive; they will be forever banished from the presence and glory of God. (*see* 2 Th 1:7-9)

Paul said, "For many walk, of whom I have told you often, and now tell you even weeping, that they are the enemies of the cross of Christ: *Whose end is destruction,* whose god is their belly, and whose glory is in their shame, who mind earthly things" (Phil 3:18, 19, ital. added).

Ladies of the Methodist Church used the book *Basic Christian Beliefs* as the guide for their 1961 Lenten Bible study program. The author, Frederick C. Grant, was one of the translators of the Revised Standard Version of the Bible. He denies that Jesus Christ had to die for man's sins. He says: "To describe the death of Christ as a 'propitiation' clearly implies an angry God who must be placated by the death of a sinless person: but this is not the meaning of the New Testament. . . . Nowhere does Jesus suggest or even imply that divine forgiveness is conditioned upon his own death."[48]

The literature of the World Council of Churches (WCC) also denies man's need to be born again and saved. *Study Encounter* is published four times a year by the WCC and distributed in three languages on college campuses and to Christian youth groups around the world. Volume 1, Number 2, was issued in the spring of 1965 and included an article on "Conversion and Church Practices." Based on a message delivered at a WCC Youth Conference, the article said:

> Certainly in the Gospels one simply does not find a Jesus who is the first Evangelical Churchman! As a matter of fact, if it is the function of the preacher to "pluck brands from burning," one can only say that Jesus is rather irresponsible! When he confronts the crowds, he does not speak of their eternal destiny . . . He tells them how damn lucky they are to be alive and that there is no need to overdo it with their prayers![49]

In recent years, the United Presbyterian Church replaced the 300-year-old Westminister Confession of Faith with a new, "modern" confession which pays lip service to the Bible as the Word of God and then describes the Scriptures as ". . . the words of men, conditioned by the language, thought forms, and literary fashions of the places and times at which they were written."[50]

In a recent issue of *Christianity Today* were these words:

> The extent of liberalism in the churches can be seen from the Glock and Stark survey, parts of which were highlighted in *The Gathering Storm of the Churches* by Jeffrey K. Haddon. Haddon says that of the respondents, 87 per cent of the Methodists, 95 per cent of the Episcopalians, 88 per cent of the Presbyterians, 67 per cent of the American Baptists, and 77 per cent of the American Lutherans did not believe that the "Scriptures are the inspired and inerrant Word of God not only in matters of faith but also in historical, geographical, and other secular matters." In answering the question whether "Adam and Eve were individual historical persons," 82 per cent of the Methodists, 97 per cent of the Episcopalian, 84 per cent of the Presbyterians, 55 per cent of the American Baptists, and 51 per cent of the American Lutherans said no. Sixty per cent of the Methodists, 44 per cent of the Episcopalians, 49 per cent of the Presbyterians, 34 per cent of the American Baptists, and 19 per cent of the American Lutherans did not "believe that the virgin birth of Jesus was a biological miracle." Fifty-eight per cent of the Meth-

odists, 60 per cent of the Episcopalians, 54 per cent of the Presby-
terians, 35 per cent of the American Baptists, and 22 per cent of the
American Lutherans agreed that "Hell does not refer to a special
location after death, but to the experience of self-estrangement,
guilt, and meaninglessness in this life." The churches have been
overtaken by liberalism and by repudiation of the Bible as the Word
of God.[51]

From the comments and quotes in this chapter, the consensus of
many informed and concerned persons can be summarized by the
following statements:

> America has forgotten God.
> America has become materialistic.
> America has disobeyed God.
> America has become wicked.
> America has become proud.
> America has become sexually obsessed.
> America has become apostate.
> America is headed for destruction.

General William K. Harrison was asked the question: "Do you
have any worries or fears concerning our nation, for instance?" He
answered: "Well, yes. I say this. First of all as a Christian, I am one
who does study the Bible. I am convinced that this age is coming to
its end in what Christ referred to as the tribulation so great that if
God doesn't shorten it nobody would survive. And I think the United
States, particularly, deserves the judgment of God. No other country
that I know of has had the blessings from God that we have in a
material way, spiritual way and a political way, and yet I know of
no country which has apostasized from God to the extent that this
one has."[52]

William H. Walker, former dean of a Bible college, wrote in his
book *Will Russia Conquer the World?*:

> As a loyal and patriotic American citizen the author loves his
> country and would like to predict a glorious and prosperous future
> for our nation. It is with a heavy heart that he contemplates the
> inevitable decline and destruction of America. Would to God she
> would repent!
> National repentance, however desirable and necessary, is never-

theless very remote. Although still possible, a national turning to God is very unlikely. America has traveled too long, too far, and too fast down the road that leads to moral and spiritual ruin. She has passed the point of "no return."

There comes a time when it is too late to save the ship. It is then imperative to expend all efforts to rescue as many passengers aboard as possible. That time has come in America. Those who work conscientiously to patch up and keep the ship afloat are to be commended. Every true American should do all in his power to preserve our way of life as long as possible. But God's promise of salvation is not for America as a nation, but for individuals in the nation who dare to believe His Word.[53]

When Peter preached on the day of Pentecost, he testified and exhorted the people, saying, "Save yourselves from this untoward generation" (Ac 2:40). The Amplified New Testament gives the verse like this: "Be saved from this crooked (perverse, wicked, unjust) generation." This is a crooked, perverse, wicked, unjust generation, and it is headed for destruction. But God will save individuals from it "who dare to believe His Word." "Believe on the Lord Jesus Christ, and thou shalt be saved" (Ac 16:31). "That if thou shalt confess with thy mouth the Lord Jesus, and shalt believe in thine heart that God hath raised him from the dead, thou shalt be saved. For with the heart man believeth unto righteousness; and with the mouth confession is made unto salvation. For whosoever shall call upon the name of the Lord shall be saved" (Ro 10:9, 10, 13).

If you are not saved, you can put your trust in the Lord Jesus Christ, and then, instead of being headed for destruction, you will be headed for heaven.

STRIKE FROM SPACE

Six years ago, a pastor friend of mine gave me a copy of the book *Strike From Space,* published in 1965, in which the authors, Phyllis Schlafly and Chester Ward, tell of the secret plan for a surprise nuclear attack against the United States. Brig. Gen. William H. Wilbur, USA (Ret.), recipient of the Congressional Medal of Honor, author of *Guideposts to the Future* and *Freedom Must Not Perish,* said of this book: "This is a powerful book. The authors have skillfully assembled pertinent facts which have an urgent bearing on our security and our survival. They have made a convincing case against Communism and against those misguided Americans who refuse to recognize the seriousness of the threat that confronts us. It should be read by every American."[54] Every military and nuclear authority who has communicated with the authors of *Strike From Space* since its publication has confirmed or corroborated its basic themes.

Since I first read this book, I have followed closely in the newspapers and news magazines the articles concerning Russia's plan to "bury" us. Krushchev boasted when he was in power: "History is on our side. We will bury you."[55] ". . . we want—not only want but have dug—quite a deep hole, and shall exert efforts to dig this hole deeper and bury the capitalist system forever."[56]

In this chapter, I want to share with you some of the things I have learned about a possible strike from space.

In a long speech on January 6, 1961, Krushchev interpreted the Moscow Manifesto, which was adopted by the Communist parties of the world in late 1960. The AP Moscow Bureau called it the most important Soviet pronouncement since the end of World War II. Krushchev revealed the broad plan by which the Soviet Union intends "to destroy the United States by nuclear weapons," without itself being subjected to fatal, or even seriously crippling, damage from U.S. retaliation. The speech was immediately recognized by the press and the politicians as a Communist blueprint for world conquest. The American Security Council *Washington Report* analyzed it as containing "plans to eliminate the United States as 'the enemy of the people of the world,' by preventive war." The most comprehensive evaluation was made by Dr. Stefan T. Possony, Director of the Hoover Institute at Stanford University, and published by the Government Printing Office. Extensively documented, brilliantly developed, and logically irrefutable, his 100-page analysis is the most authentic exposé of the secret Soviet war plan, a plan which "utilizes massive deception to bring about, through (a) the unilateral weakening of the free world, (b) the moral paralysis of free world governments, and (c) the demoralization of public opinion, the capitulation of the United States. Failing in this strategy, the Soviet intends to destroy the United States by nuclear weapons."[57]

A blueprint for "burying" the United States was published in the Soviet Union in 1962. Not unlike *Mein Kampf* in spirit, the book *Soviet Military Strategy* suggested a massive, all-out, surprise attack as soon as military superiority could be achieved. The goal, of course, is to destroy the United States without receiving major damage in turn. This 450-page book cannot be lightly waved away; it was edited by Marshall V. D. Sokolovskii and thirteen other senior officers of the Red Army, including nine generals.[58]

In the fall of 1967, two authoritative studies appeared. One was *The Soviet Military Technological Challenge* by a distinguished panel at the highly respected Center for Strategic Studies of Georgetown University. The other was *Peace and the Strategy Conflict*, an impressive book by William R. Kintner, a former member of the Planning Staff of the National Security Council. These two studies, reported in a *Reader's Digest* article, confirmed that unless present trends are quickly reversed, the United States seems certain in the 1970s to find itself in a markedly inferior strategic position with the Soviet Union. The possible military and political results could be disastrous.[59]

Kintner pointed out in his book that missile accuracies are constantly improving, for the Soviets as well as for us, and it is likely that by 1970 the Soviets will be able to drop ICBM (Inter-Continental Ballistic Missile) warheads within 1500 feet of bull's eye.[60]

These studies make it ominously clear that the true goal of the Soviet Union is not "mutual deterrence" but actual military supremacy. "Leading Soviet strategists time and again publicly have insisted that victory in nuclear war will go to the side that is best prepared to wage nuclear war, and that the Soviet Union is so preparing itself; and Kintner finds that the Soviets lay great stress on the value of a preemptive surprise attack—with no formal declaration of war. Moreover, says Kintner, America will be their main adversary."[61]

Dr. George S. Benson, in his syndicated column, reported recently on Russian military activity in Cuba. From interviews with over 2,000 Cubans came reports of vast, subterranean missile complexes in Cuba, commanded by Russian technicians and soldiers. The direc-

tor of the Citizens Committee for a Free Cuba conducted these interviews and reported fifty "completely credible stories" of eyewit-
ness observations.

> Among the hundreds of Russian missiles, manned by Spanish-
> speaking Russian launching crews and kept in Russian-built and
> Russian-commanded arsenals deep beneath the mountains of south
> western Cuba (scarcely more than 100 miles from Miami) are three
> species which are labeled in Spanish: "Washington Derecha," "Wash-
> ington Centro," "Washington Izquierda." Translated, the labels
> read: "Washington Right," "Washington Center," "Washington
> Left."
> The labels indicate the various regions of sprawling metropolitan
> Washington D.C. toward which the Cuban-based Soviet H-bombs
> are to be fired.
> The missiles, approximately 70 feet long and 7 feet in diameter,
> are capable of hurling their H-bombs 1200 to 1500 miles. They are
> Russian IRBM, and they (together with some larger ones) are today
> pouring into Cuba in ship bottoms camouflaged to fool American
> U-2 "spy" planes and "spy" satellites. . . .
> Some of our most knowledgeable anti-Communists in Congress
> accept these reports. If so, a Soviet-controlled Cuba poses a clear
> and present danger to the United States, a "missile crisis" that must
> be faced.[62]

The book *Strike From Space* states as its thesis that the Soviet
Union is planning a surprise nuclear attack against the United States.
The authors point to various factors as confirmation of this thesis:
certain developments in Soviet weapons programs, increases in
Soviet military budget, and statements of Soviet leaders. But their
most convincing and dramatic confirmation is the diary of Colonel
Oleg Penkovskiy, a Soviet missile expert, chairman of a scientific
committee, and intelligence officer. He was executed for passing
information to the British and Americans. As quoted in *Strike From
Space*, Penkovskiy says:

> The Soviets have adopted the new military doctrine of the sudden
> strike employing atomic and hydrogen bombs for their strict guid-
> ance. . . . To be the first one to deliver a nuclear strike is important
> . . . because it concerns the entire course and the outcome of the
> war. . . . This plan has been worked out in every detail and is on

file in the General Staff. Staff exercises have been conducted in accordance with this plan. That is the Soviet position. . . . I know the extent of their preparations . . . the plan to strike first, at any cost. I know their missiles and their warheads. . . . Imagine the horror of a 50-megaton bomb with an explosive force almost twice what one expects. . . . I must defeat these men. . . . God will help us in this great and important work.[63]

Another question answered by the authors of *Strike From Space* concerns the moral possibility of a nuclear attack on the American people. A surprise nuclear bombing of an entire nation is not too horrible for the Communist mentality, considering past massacres which have been conducted in Communist satellite nations. Seven million starved Russians and twenty million liquidated Chinese testify to the Communist willingness to take human life. "Every Communist government, from Russia, to Cuba, to North Vietnam, has ruthlessly murdered and persecuted thousands of its own innocent people simply for the purpose of enforcing discipline on the nation. Why should the Communists suddenly develop any qualms about liquidating 149 million Americans—especially when they hate us anyway for standing in the way of world 'peace' under Communism?"[64]

There is no question in my mind about Russia's plan to strike from space and destroy us. She has ICBMs of 100-megaton size, which can reach our country in just thirty minutes and, according to Schafly and Ward: "If the Kremlin launched its ICBMs at us today, all our Defense Department could do would be to give us a 15-minute warning of the disaster. They could not shoot down a single enemy missile."[65]

A one-megaton bomb is equal to one million tons of TNT. The two bombs which fell on the two Japanese cities were equal to only 20 thousand tons of TNT, yet the one dropped on Hiroshima on August 6, 1945, killed 70 thousand people. At least 80 thousand were burned or injured; the entire center of the city was demolished; a 47-square-mile area was ravaged; and 60 thousand buildings—two in every three—were destroyed or badly damaged. The one dropped three days later on August 9, 1945, on Nagasaki, killed 39 thousand people; many more than this were injured; and nearly all buildings within one and one-half miles of this blast were wiped out, and most structures within the next mile were damaged.[66]

The deaths and damage done by a bomb equal to 20 thousand tons of TNT were horrible. But the destruction which would be caused by a 100-megaton missile, five thousand times more powerful, is almost beyond the realm of the imagination.

Representative Craig Hosmer of California, a member of the Joint Committee on Atomic Energy, and chairman of the House of Republican Conference Committee on Nuclear Affairs, wrote a scenario of the U.S. being hit by just eighteen bombs of 100-megaton size each:

> At precisely 2 o'clock in the afternoon of a clear fall day, almost the entire States of Massachusetts, Rhode Island and New Jersey burst into flames. So did New York City, Hartford, Philadelphia, Baltimore and Washington, D.C. Essentially the entire East Coast from Portland, Me., to Norfolk, Va., up to 150 miles inland, became one raging, all-consuming fire storm.
>
> At the same moment a 170-mile-wide, 22,500-square-mile circle of flame erupted across southern portions of Louisiana, Mississippi and Alabama, from New Orleans and Baton Rouge through Biloxi to Mobile, destroying all within it. Detroit, Toledo, Cleveland and half of Ohio met a similar single fate, as did portions of Wisconsin, Illinois and Indiana, from Milwaukee through Chicago, on to Gary and South Bend.
>
> On the Pacific Coast, flames consumed Portland and Seattle and everything between them. A fiery torch descended on California's northern population and industrial centers of San Francisco, Oakland, San Jose, Stockton, Sacramento and Vallejo.
>
> Simultaneously, 9 million southern Californians, including another major fraction of the nation's scientific and industrial talent, were incinerated in a band of fire from Oxnard, north of Los Angeles, to San Diego and the Mexican border.
>
> Three 100-megaton bombs, optimized for thermal-heat-radiation, had exploded at altitudes below 50,000 feet to create the East Coast conflagration, and over each of the other six areas described, one more had detonated. At the same instant, eight 100-megaton monsters had burst in a spread over U.S. ICBM complexes in the triangle from Arkansas to Montana to Arizona, incidentally igniting Phoenix, Tucson, Little Rock, Wichita, Cheyenne, Kansas City, Great Falls and many more cities.
>
> The eighteenth hostile warhead exploded 4,000 feet below the

waters of the Pacific on slopes of the Aleutian Deep. It created a tidal wave 28 to 70 feet high, which speeded at over 200 mph to destroy Alaskan, Hawaiian and otherwise undamaged Pacific Coast areas.

Fire storms—a hundred times more intense than World War II's which consumed Hamburg and other German cities—raged in part or all of 34 of the 50 States. . . .

Considerable loss of life outside the fire storms occurred from suffocation. Major casualties also resulted from winds of more than hurricane proportions feeding oxygen to the blazes. In all, a fair portion of the continent's oxygen was used up by combustion. Not enough was left in many places to support life. . . .

Three of every five Americans were dead and the nation's military-industrial back was broken.

What I have said so far is that Russia plans a strike from space. I have not said that she *will* strike us. I do not know whether God will permit this to happen. Some Bible scholars think that because of our awful wickedness and departure from God, God will permit us to be destroyed. God's Word promises: "The wicked shall be turned into hell and all the nations that forget God" (Ps 9:17).

God warned His people in the Old Testament: "Beware that thou forget not the LORD thy God in not keeping his commandments, and his judgments, and his statutes, which I command thee this day . . . And it shall be, if thou do at all forget the LORD thy God, and walk after other gods, and serve them, and worship them, I testify against you this day that ye shall surely perish. As the nations which the Lord destroyeth before your face, so shall ye perish; because ye would not be obedient unto the voice of the LORD your God" (Deu 8:11, 19, 20). Israel would not obey God; and God permitted a wicked nation, Assyria, to come and take them out of their land into captivity and repeople their land with other people. Judah would not obey God; and God allowed a wicked nation, Babylon, to destroy them and take most of them into captivity.

There are some prophetic scholars who say that before God destroys Russia (about the middle of the tribulation period), He will first permit Russia to destroy us because of our decline in political, social, moral, and spiritual integrity.

God clearly says in His Word, "And at what instant I shall speak concerning a nation, and concerning a kingdom, to build and to plant it; if it do evil in my sight, that it obey not my voice, then I will repent of the good, wherewith I said I would benefit them" (Jer 18:9, 10). He also promises, "If that nation, against whom I have pronounced, turn from their evil, I will repent of the evil that I thought to do unto them" (Jer 18:8). Dr. Gerrit Verkuyl, editor-in-chief of *The New Berkeley Bible*, comments on these four verses: "The Lord's action is not arbitrary but always in accordance with our behavior toward Him."[67]

I pray that America will repent of her sins and return to God, for God has promised: "If my people, which are called by my name, shall humble themselves, and pray, and seek my face, and turn from their wicked ways; then will I hear from heaven, and will forgive their sin, and will heal their land" (2 Chr 7:14). Surely our land needs healing, and it is either revival or ruin for us. May it be revival.

CHRIST WILL STRIKE FROM SPACE

Very soon Christ will leave heaven and come suddenly for His church. He will strike quickly when He "shall descend from heaven with a shout, with the voice of the archangel, and with the trump of God: and the dead in Christ shall rise first: then we which are alive and remain shall be caught up [in a moment, in the twinkling of an eye (1 Co 15:52)] together with them in the clouds, to meet the Lord in the air: and so shall we ever be with the Lord" (1 Th 4:16, 17). Three times in Revelation 22 Jesus says, "Behold, I come quickly . . . And, behold, I come quickly . . . Surely I come quickly" (vv. 7, 12, 20).

I am not sure whether Russia will strike from space; but I am very sure that Christ will strike from space, and His own will go up to meet Him in the air. Every unsaved person will be left on the earth when Christ strikes from space. One second after He comes will be too late to be saved for those who have heard the truth and rejected it (2 Th 2:10-12). If you are not ready for Christ's strike from space, receive Him as your personal Saviour and Lord at this moment, and He will save you (Jn 1:12; 6:37; Ro 10:9, 10, 13).

GOD WILL STRIKE FROM SPACE

After Christ strikes from space, God then will strike from space, but in judgment. During the seven-year period which follows Christ's coming for His church, over one-half of the world's population will be killed as God brings judgment upon a Christ-rejecting world.

When Russia and her armies start to invade Israel sometime during the first part of this seven-year tribulation period, God will strike from space in judgment upon Russia and her armies (*see* Eze 38:18-22). When God strikes Russia and her armies in judgment, He will turn their weapons on each other; they will suffer plagues, great injuries, flooding rain, hailstones, fire, and brimstone. He will completely destroy their armies and send fire on the land of Russia. It will take seven months for the Israelis to bury the dead that fell in their land (Eze 38:21, 22; 39:2, 6, 12).

God will strike from space in judgment, and one-fourth of the world's population will be killed through famine, violence, and wild animal attack (Rev 6:8).

God will strike from space in judgment, and the sun will turn black; the moon will become red as blood. The stars, or possibly meteorites, will fall to the earth; the sky, or atmosphere, will disappear, like a scroll being rolled up; mountains and islands will move out of their places. Rulers, men of wealth and high position, leaders, men of accomplishment—both servants and masters—all will hide themselves in the caves and rocks of the mountains, looking for escape from the judgment of God (Rev 6:12-17).

God will strike from space in judgment and a third of all trees and green grass will be burned up; a third of the creatures in the sea will die; a third of the ships on the sea will be destroyed; many people will die because of bitter poison in the waters. One-third of the sun, moon, and stars will be affected. Locusts will torment men so severely for a five-month's period that they will beg for death, but God will not permit them to die. Finally, a third of the remainder of the population of the earth will be killed (Rev 8:9).

God will strike from space in judgment and sores will come upon men; the sea will have a quality like the blood of a dead person, and every living thing in the sea will die; the rivers and springs will also be turned into a substance like blood. The sun will scorch men with a great heat, and men will chew their tongues because of pain. A great earthquake will take place, and Jerusalem will be divided into three parts. The cities of the nations will collapse; every island will vanish and mountains will disappear; and hailstones weighing over one hundred pounds will fall upon people (Rev 16).

God will strike from space in judgment, and millions will be killed at the Battle of Armageddon; the beast (or Antichrist) and false prophet will be cast alive into the lake of fire; and the rest of the armies gathered against Jerusalem will be killed (Rev 14:14-20; 19:11-21; Is 24:6; Zec 14:12). (Later chapters will more fully discuss these "strikes from space": the rapture, the tribulation, the invasion of Israel by Russia, and the battle of Armageddon.)

In the light of the fact that there may be a strike from space by Russia at any time, or that Christ could strike from space at any time to take His own to Himself, and in the light of the fact that God will strike from space in awful judgments soon, may every reader of this book who is not saved "prepare to meet thy God" (Amos 4:12) and heed the words of Jesus: "Therefore be ye also ready: for in such an hour as ye think not the Son of man cometh" (Mt 24:44). In order to be prepared and ready, there must be "repentance toward God, and faith toward our Lord Jesus Christ" (Ac 20:21). May you repent (Lk 13:3), and believe on the Lord Jesus Christ right now (Ac 16:31; 2 Co 6:2), because every day of delay leaves a day more to repent of, and a day less to repent in.

5

SEVEN SIGNS OF THE SECOND COMING

Which No Other Generation Has Seen

THERE ARE MANY SIGNS given in the Word of God to reveal to us the second coming of Christ to earth. These signs point to the end of the age and events which will follow the rapture. The rapture of the church is a signless event—God has not revealed when it will take place. It is presented in Scripture as always imminent, possible at any moment. The present world situation provides a number of indications that the rapture may be very near.

Dr. J. Dwight Pentecost writes: "While the translation, or the rapture of the Church is without any signs to warn us of its proximity, yet there are foreshadowings of events that will come to their consummation after the Church is gone that are already appearing on the world scene. And because of these things, we believe the Rapture which has to precede these specific prophetic events could and must be very near."[1]

This chapter shows and discusses seven signs of the second coming of Christ which no other generation has seen—signs which are before us today and which have tremendous significance: 1) the return of the Jew to Palestine, 2) the rise of Russia, 3) the departure from the faith, 4) the ecumenical movement, 5) the forming of the four world-power blocs, 6) increase in travel and knowledge, and 7) the beginning of birth pangs of a new age.

THE RETURN OF THE JEWS TO THE LAND OF PALESTINE

Perhaps the most significant sign is the return of the Jews to the land of Palestine. God promised the land of Palestine to the Jews back in the days of Abraham (Gen 12:1-3, 7; 13:15-17; 15:5-7; 17:1-8). They were told that if they obeyed God, He would bless them (Deu 28:1-14), and if they disobeyed God, He would chasten them (Deu 28:15-68). They disobeyed God and were taken into captivity by the Assyrians and Babylonians hundreds of years before Christ. They returned from their captivity to the land of Palestine, but again in A.D. 70 they were expelled from their land. For almost twenty-six hundred years, Palestine has been under the control of Gentile people, since the days of Nebuchadnezzar (about 586 B.C.).

The Jews have been scattered over the entire earth for almost nineteen hundred years, but God promised many times in His Word that He would return them to their land (Deu 30:1-5; Is 11:11, 12; Jer 16:14, 15; 23:7, 8; 32:37-42; Eze 34:11-31; 36:24-38; 37:21-28; Amos 9:14, 15). God promised that the Jews would continue as long as the sun, moon, and stars endure (Jer 31:35, 36); and He has preserved them as a distinct people. At the beginning of the twentieth century, there was not a single Jewish village in all their land, and only about twenty-five thousand Jews could be found scattered throughout Palestine.

During World War I, Palestine was made ready for the Jew. At that time, Jerusalem was occupied by the Turks. Its capture by the British was accomplished in a meaningful way. Out of Egypt a long line of British soldiers marched, led by General Edmund Henry Allenby, a Christian. When Allenby was a child, he had been taught to close his prayer with a special plea for Israel: "Forget not Thine ancient people. Hasten the day when they shall be restored to Thy favor and to their land." As he and his troops approached the city of Jerusalem, he was much concerned about not destroying the city and holy places. On the night before the British were to attack Jerusalem, he spent the night in prayer and Bible study. Sometime during the night, God gave him a verse of Scripture, Isaiah 31:5, which he used at the break of day as his strategy against the city. On December 11, 1917, he sent wave after wave of his planes flying low over Jerusalem, and, as a result, the Turks fled from the city. No bombs were dropped, not a shot was fired, not a drop of blood was shed. He assembled his troops before the city and read Isaiah 31:5 to them: "As birds flying, so will the LORD of hosts defend Jerusalem; defending also he will deliver it; and passing over he will preserve it." Then he announced, "Men, this day has this scripture been fulfilled before your very eyes."

General Allenby's name was appropriate for the occasion, too. In the Turkish language it would be pronounced "Allah-bay," which would mean to a Mohammedan, "prophet of God," or "sent of God." It had been a tradition of the Moslem priesthood for centuries that when a leader by that name comes, Jerusalem must go back to the Jews.

In commemoration of the bloodless, miraculous occupancy of Jerusalem, the Allenby Bridge, spanning the Jordan River, was built. At a reception honoring Allenby in London, he said, "I never knew that God would give me the privilege of helping to answer my own childhood prayer."

During World War I, England found it impossible to obtain an adequate supply of wood alcohol for the production of acetone, which was sorely needed for the manufacture of explosives. Dr. Chaim Weizmann, a Jewish professor active in the cause of the Jewish people, had engaged in research into the production of synthetic acetone from starch and, at the request of the British government, undertook the task of developing the process and building factories for large-scale production. His services to England in this respect were of such outstanding value that the government intended to bestow an honor upon him. But Mr. Weizmann declined the offer and asked instead for a home for the Jew in Palestine.

On November 2, 1917, Lord Balfour, who was then foreign secretary, wrote the following letter to a prominent and wealthy Englishman who, as a member of a distinguished Jewish family, represented the Jews of England.

> Dear Lord Rothschild: I have much pleasure in conveying to you, on behalf of His Majesty's Government, the following declaration of sympathy with Jewish Zionist aspirations, which has been submitted to, and approved by the Cabinet.
>
> His Majesty's Government view with favour the establishment in Palestine of a national home for the Jewish people, and will use their

best endeavours to facilitate the achievement of this object, it being
clearly understood that nothing shall be done which may prejudice
the civil and religious rights of existing non-Jewish communities in
Palestine, or the rights and political status enjoyed by Jews in any
other country.

I should be grateful if you would bring this declaration to the
knowledge of the Zionist Federation.[2]

This letter is known as the Balfour Declaration, and "was hailed by
Jews all over the world as an act of national liberation comparable to
the decree of Cyrus of Persia which led to the re-establishment of the
Jewish Commonwealth in Judea after the Babylonian Captivity,"
according to Paul Goodman.[3] When a Jewish State was proclaimed
on May 14, 1948, Dr. Chaim Weizmann become the first president of
Israel.

World War I prepared the land of Palestine for the Jew. World
War II prepared the Jew for the land of Palestine. Under Hitler's
atrocities, six million Jews were slaughtered, and as a result, a conviction came to the Jewish people: "No matter how well we have at
first been received in the nations where we have gone, we have
sooner or later become the victims of persecution and if we are going
to die anyway—we will die in our own land." In 1920 there were
only 58 thousand Jews in Palestine. By 1935 the population had
grown to 375 thousand. But in 1946 it doubled to 675 thousand,
and in 1952 it reached the 1½ million mark. By 1967 the population
was 2 million, 635 thousand.[4] The immigrants have come from 107
countries of the world. Almost fifty thousand new immigrants came
to Israel in 1970.

On May 14, 1948, the British terminated their mandate over Palestine, and the new state of Israel was proclaimed that same day. As
soon as Israel was officially recognized a nation by the UN, war
broke out between the Jews and Arabs. When it became clear that
Israel could not be crushed, the Arab nations agreed to sign armistices
with Israel; however, there were continual border skirmishes. Finally,
in reaction to obvious Egyptian preparation for attack, Israel invaded
the Sinai peninsula in 1956. A UN cease-fire was arranged, but it
could only be maintained by UN police patrol. In May, 1956, these
UN forces were withdrawn; and war between Israel and the Arab
nations broke out on June 5, 1967. On Wednesday morning, June 7,

just two days after the fighting began, Israeli soldiers broke through the gates of the Old City and began to run ecstatically through Arab sniper fire to the Western Wall. A shout went up as the wall was sighted; and hundreds rushed forward to the great, time-worn stones, laughing, weeping, and praying. Hours later, General Moshe Dayan came to the wall and said, "We have returned to the holiest of our holy places. I give you my word, we shall never be parted from it again."[5] Israel's chief of staff, General Yitzhak Rabin, described the effect of these events on his forces: "The strain of battle, the anxiety which preceded it, the sense of salvation and direct confrontation with Jewish history itself, cracked the shell of hardness and shyness and released well-springs of emotion and stirrings of the spirit . . . in its symbolism an act so rare as to be almost unparalleled in human history."[6]

Sanche de Gramont, in an article in the *Saturday Evening Post* entitled "Battle For Jerusalem," wrote: "They had realized the two thousand-year-old prophecy of recovering Jerusalem." A Jewish friend inquired, "Whose prophecy was that?" The reply was, "The answer is in Luke 21:24."[7]

Omer, the Labor Federation's paper, had an editorial on June 7, 1967: "The greatest day of all has come: Jerusalem, Israel's eternal capital, is not divided any more . . . The Lord has brought about this day."[8]

Up until the capture of the older part of Jerusalem on June 7, 1967, there were two Jerusalems—the Old City on the east, which belonged to Jordan, and the New City on the west, which had become the capital of Israel. These two parts of the city had been separated by no-man's-land for nineteen years, and they were united by the Israeli victory on June 7. Earlier that week, a woman of Bnei Brak, an orthodox suburb of Tel Aviv, began hoarding flour as the Old City's fall drew near. She insisted on having flour to make cakes for the Messiah's coming. If not for Messiah, then for the great prophet who will herald Him.

One thing is still missing—the rebuilding of the temple in Jerusalem. According to Scripture, a temple will be rebuilt in Jerusalem, and the man of sin, the Antichrist, will confirm a covenant with the Jews for a period of seven years. In the middle of this seven-year period, the Antichrist will break his covenant and will sit in the temple demanding worship as God (Dan 9:27; Mt 24:15; 2 Th 2:3, 4; Rev 11:1, 2).

As soon as the Six-Day War ended in June, 1967, speculation arose about possible rebuilding of the temple. There is only one place where it can be built, according to the Scriptures, and that is Jerusalem (2 Chr 6:6). Mount Moriah was where the two previous temples were built—the first built by Solomon, about 1000 B.C., and the second built by the Jews when they returned from the Babylonian captivity, about 516 B.C. It is logical to expect the third one to be erected there also. However, there are some obstacles to rebuilding the temple. On Mount Moriah now stands the Dome of the Rock, the second holiest place of the Moslem faith, recently completely rebuilt at the expense of many millions of dollars. Israeli historian Israel Eldad was quoted as saying: "We are at the stage where David was when he liberated Jerusalem. From that time until the construction of the temple by Solomon, only one generation passed. So it will be with us."[9] When he was asked what would become of the Moslem shrine, the Dome of the Rock, Eldad answered, "It is, of course, an open question. Who knows? Perhaps there will be an earthquake."[10]

These two quarter-page advertisements were carried in the *Washington Post*, the first on May 21, 1967, just two weeks before the war, and the second on June 10, 1967:

TO PERSONS OF THE JEWISH FAITH ALL OVER THE WORLD

A project to rebuild the "TEMPLE OF GOD" in Israel is now being started. With Divine Guidance and Help the Temple will be completed. It will signal a new era in Judaism. Jews will be inspired to conduct themselves in such a moral way that our Maker will see fit to pay us a visit here on earth. Imagine the warm feeling that will be ours when this happy event takes place. "THIS IS MY GOD" by Herman Wouk is the book that was the inspiration for this undertaking. GOD will place in the minds of many persons in all walks of Jewish life the desire to participate in this work. Executive talent, Administrators, and Workers on all levels are needed. All efforts will be anonymous. GOD will know those desiring to participate.

Please write to Box M-917, The Washington Post. Under no circumstances send contributions. LABEL LETININ

"GOD'S WILL WILL PREVAIL"
TO PERSONS OF THE JEWISH FAITH ALL OVER THE
WORLD
THE MILITARY VICTORY WON BY THE HEROIC MEN,
WOMEN AND CHILDREN OF ISRAEL UNDER MIRACULOUS
CIRCUMSTANCES IS A GIFT OF GOD. THIS VICTORY WAS
A SIGN BY OUR MAKER THAT NOW IS THE TIME TO
REBUILD "THE TEMPLE OF GOD."
"GOD'S WILL WILL PREVAIL"

LABEL LETININ

The Scriptures speak of a final regathering of Israel to the land of Palestine, which will be in three stages. First, a number will go back to the land and form a political state, making it possible for them to enter into a covenant relationship with their Gentile neighbors, spoken of in Daniel 9:27. Then, as a result of the covenant, there will be a further regathering of the Jews and a great increase of wealth, which will be one of the reasons why Russia will invade Israel, as predicted in Ezekiel 38-39. Following the second coming of Jesus Christ to establish His kingdom on the earth, the regathering will finally be completed; and the entire nation of Israel, after she is judged, and the rebels are purged out, will be ushered into the land that God promised Abraham (Eze 20:33-44; 39:25-29; Zec 13:8, 9; Ro 11:25-27).

The present state of Israel is the first phase of this final regathering of the Jews, and soon the covenant will be signed between Israel and her Gentile neighbors. This covenant apparently will not be signed until after the rapture of the church, since the Antichrist, or man of sin, will not be revealed until after the church is gone (2 Th 2:1-10); so the present state of Israel is precisely what we can expect at the time of the rapture of the Church. Dr. Walvoord comments: "If the rapture occurs before the signing of this covenant, as many premillennial scholars believe, it follows that the establishment of Israel in the land as a preparation for the covenant is a striking evidence that the rapture itself may be very near."[11]

In a television program, the Joe Pyne show, a Jewish rabbi was asked about Israel's real reason for being back in "the Land," as they call it. Without hesitation, the rabbi replied, "To await the coming of the Messiah."

Dr. Jacob Gartenhaus, a Hebrew Christian, wrote recently:

> The eyes of the world are focused upon Israel—the land and the
> people—as never before in history. Not a day passes that the secular
> press, television, radio, etc., do not call attention to what is trans-
> piring. Many friends have written in asking, "Is This the Time?"
> The Lord Jesus said, "Jerusalem shall be trodden down of the Gen-
> tiles until the times of the Gentiles be fulfilled" (Luke 21:24). Now
> Jerusalem is again a Jewish city and the Jews have vowed never to
> let it go. The Lord must have had these days in mind when He said,
> "And when these things begin to come to pass, then, look up, and
> lift up your heads; for your redemption draweth nigh" (Luke 21:28).
>
> I have been a student of prophecy for about fifty years. I have
> spoken and written on the subject; I have tried not to be dogmatic
> concerning the order of events; I have always granted anyone the
> right to differ with me. My mind has not been closed to helpful
> suggestions. But of this one thing I am certain: events which we are
> witnessing today are like those of Biblical times. A land is being
> reborn and a spiritual revival is on the way. During my recent visit
> to Israel I saw prophecies of centuries being rapidly and literally
> fulfilled. Only the willfully blind fail to see God's hand in it all.
>
> The tragedy of it is that in most of the seminaries and churches
> little mention is made of the miracle of Israel's regathering. But
> thank God for the faithful remnant who do realize that our redemp-
> tion draweth nigh, that time is short and therefore we need to re-
> double our efforts for reaching our Lord's own brethren who are yet
> to play a great part in the evangelization of this world. In the light
> of this, our task becomes more urgent.[12]

Hal Lindsey, in his book *The Late Great Planet Earth,* stated,
"With the Jewish nation reborn in the land of Palestine, ancient Jerusalem once again under total Jewish control for the first time in 2600
years, and talk of rebuilding the great Temple, the most important
prophetic sign of Jesus Christ's soon coming is before us."[13]

Dr. Walvoord also concurs, "Of the many signs indicating the end
of the age, few are more dramatic and have a larger Scriptural foundation than the revival of Israel as a token of the end of the age."[14]

Dr. F. A. Tatford summarizes:

> There are indications in current events that the days so long fore-
> told cannot be far distant. The countries of the west are beginning
> to come together; a further attack from Egypt is expected before

long; an intervention then from Russia seems inevitable; the threat from the Far East is slowly materializing; nearly 2½ million Jews are already in the land and Israel is a State once again. The stage is set and the shadows of the actors are seen in the wings: soon the play will commence. But before then, the church of believing Christians will have been translated from this scene at the Coming of Christ (I Thessalonians 4:15-17). If the fulfillment of prophecy seems imminent, the rapture of the church may be about to take place. Until that happens, the Divine plan for Israel is held in abeyance, but all the indications suggest that its implementation cannot long be postponed.[15]

THE RISE OF RUSSIA

Dr. M. R. DeHaan says of this sign, "If we were to choose the three most outstanding signs of the coming of Christ, we would have no difficulty in placing the rise of Russia among those first three signs."[16] In 1917, there was a revolution in Russia; at the end of World War II she was a broken nation with her major cities destroyed and much of her manpower lost in war; but today she is one of the two most powerful countries in the world. Up until very recently, the United States was the most powerful country in the world; but some are saying that Russia is now number one in power. The American Security Council, in a brochure sent out in late 1970, reported, "The United States is now Number Two in Strategic Power."[17]

According to the prophecy in Ezekiel 38-39, Russia will invade Palestine "in the latter years," "in the latter days," when Israel "is gathered out of many people," when "they shall dwell safely all of them," when they "are at rest" (38:8, 11, 16). (*See* Chapter 9, "When Russia Invades the Middle East".) Though Israel is not now dwelling safely and at rest, she is back in her land, and Russia desires her territory. Today, for the first time in world history, Russia could invade Palestine to fulfill this prophecy of Ezekiel 38-39, because Israel wasn't in the land as a nation until May 14, 1948.

Dr. Walvoord writes concerning this prophecy:

> An invasion of Israel in the twentieth century by Russia seems a likely development in the end of the age. The fact that Russia has risen to such power in our day sets up a situation which, coupled

with Israel's return to the land, establishes the basic conditions set forth by Ezekiel for the fulfillment of its prophecy.

Though all the factors are not yet fulfilled and it can hardly be said that Israel is dwelling safely in their land at the present time, the rise of Russia coupled with the return of Israel to the land puts two major component parts together in a prophecy which would have been impossible of fulfillment prior to the twentieth century. The situation of Israel dwelling in unwalled villages is a modern situation, not true in the ancient past. Never during a period when Israel was in the land was Israel threatened by an army from the far North. . . . The rise of Russia therefore is another factor in the contemporary situation in which the stage is being set for the final drama of the end of the age.[18]

Dr. Lehman Strauss, in the book *The End of This Present Age,* writes:

The rise of Russia is one of the significant signs of the times which points to the return of Christ to take His own out of this world. It is not until after the Church is raptured that the man of sin, the antichrist, will show himself. It is not until then that the king of the north will strike. There is only one hope for the child of God. It is that blessed hope of Christ's return for His Church (Titus 2:13). It seems that man is reaching his last extremity. How comforting for the true believer in the Lord Jesus Christ to know that soon, possibly in the lifetime of this generation, he will be with his Lord and Redeemer![19]

THE DEPARTURE FROM THE FAITH

In I Timothy 4:1, Paul says, "Now the Spirit speaketh expressly, that in the latter times some shall depart from the faith, giving heed to seducing spirits, and doctrines of devils." In 2 Timothy 3:1, God gives nineteen characteristics of the kind of life which departure from the faith, or apostasy, promotes:

"This know also, that in the last days perilous times shall come. For men shall be lovers of their own selves, covetous, boasters, proud, blasphemers, disobedient to parents, unthankful, unholy, without natural affection, trucebreakers, false accusers, incontinent, fierce, despisers of those that are good, traitors, heady, highminded, lovers of pleasures more than lovers of God; having a form of godliness, but denying the power thereof: from such turn away." You will notice that these verses are a description of those "having a form of godliness, but denying the power thereof." Men in every generation have denied the reality of God, but the denial of the power has come from those outside the Christian church. Now, for the first time in history, the denial of the power comes from inside the Christian church, from those who have "a form of godliness," men who say that God is dead, so-called "Christian atheists." They deny the power—God; they keep the form. They are wolves in sheep's clothing.

Peter speaks of the time when "there shall be false teachers among you, who privily shall bring in damnable heresies, even denying the Lord that bought them" (2 Pe 2:1). Today, many of the religious leaders deny the deity of Christ and His substitutionary atonement. Most of the seminaries of today deny the doctrine of the verbal inspiration of the Scriptures, the virgin birth of Christ, His substitutionary death, His physical resurrection from the dead, and His coming again. Modernism now permeates every major denomination, and the control of every major denomination is in the hands of modernists.

Walvoord writes of the departure from the faith: "It is not necescessary to wait for some future day to have these prophecies of the departure from the faith fulfilled. The world-wide sweep of neo-orthodoxy, presenting a new and confusing form of unbelief in the central doctrines of faith, has been influential. Even worse is the demythologizing approach of Bultmann and the anti-God movement which is emerging in liberalism. Though departure of the faith is characteristic of all periods of church history, there never has been an hour in which it has been more evident than today."[20]

The Ecumenical Movement

This sign is closely related to the preceding one, but is distinct from it. The word *ecumenical* comes from a Greek word *oikoumene,* meaning "the inhabited world," or "worldwide." It is applied to one large religious body with its influence embracing the entire inhabited earth.

The dream of a united church was in the minds of church leaders back in 1910, at the World Conference on Missionary Cooperation in Edinburgh. It was a topic for discussion in 1925 at the Universal Christian Council on Life and Work at Stockholm. Again, in 1927 at Lausanne, it was discussed at the World Conference on Faith and Order; and those in attendance stated that, in order to find a common ground of belief, it was time to rethink those church doctrines and traditions where differences existed.

The World Council of Churches was formed in Amsterdam on August 23, 1948. The primary object of the World Council of Churches is the reunion of Christendom, and Dr. Douglas Horton, the chairman of the American Committee for the World Council, said at Amsterdam in 1948, "An effective welding of the Christian Churches of the world into a single unit characterized by Catholic continuity and Protestant freedom in Christ is the burden of our hopes."[21]

At the Second Assembly of the World Council of Churches at Evanston in 1954 and at the Third Assembly at New Delhi in 1961, the ecumenical movement continued to create interest and gain influence.

COCU, which means Consultation On Church Union, plans to bring together about 25 million church members in America from nine different denominations. When they are united, they will call themselves the Church of Christ Uniting and will include the African Methodist Episcopal Church; the African Methodist Episcopal Zion Church; the Christian Church (Disciples of Christ); the Christian Methodist Episcopal Church; the Episcopal Church; the Presbyterian Church in the United States; the United Church of Christ; the United Methodist Church; and the United Presbyterian Church in the United States of America. It is the announced purpose of COCU to bring into this union, sooner or later, all the churches of Christendom.

The Protestant groups will unite with the Catholic and Greek Orthodox religions. We can see already these three groups coming together for meetings, discussions, and mergers. The framework of a world church already erected will come into play more noticeably after the rapture of the true church. All true Christians will be taken at the rapture, leaving millions of unsaved church members who will make up the apostate world church. It is estimated by men of God of the past and present that between 85 and 90 percent of the church members in America are lost.

According to the Word of God, at the end of this age there will be a world church which will be associated with the world government of that time. This world church is pictured in Revelation 17 as a whore or harlot (vv. 1, 5, 15, 16). A harlot is an unfaithful woman professing faithfulness to a certain man. This world church professes faithfulness to Christ, but in reality is unfaithful to Him.

This world church will exercise great political power. She is pictured as sitting upon "a scarlet coloured beast" (v. 3), and upon "many waters" (v. 1), which means that this church will for a while during the tribulation control the political powers of that day, which control the masses of world population in a religious way (v. 15). A note in the Pilgrim Bible at Revelation 17:3 says: "The false church, the religious power, is pictured here as seated upon the Beast, the political power. That means that the false religious power shall control, for a time, the secular or political power."[22]

The superchurch will be destroyed by the Antichrist and the western federation of nations at the midpoint of the tribulation period (Rev 17:16, 17). They will make her "desolate," withdrawing all political and military support. They will make her "naked," taking away all outward glamour and attractiveness. They will "eat her flesh," seizing all her wealth and leaving her standing like a skeleton. They will also "burn her with fire," which indicates that her buildings, shrines, altars, images, and finery will be destroyed or confiscated.

God's Word warns, "Come out of her, my people, that ye be not partakers of her sins, and that ye receive not of her plagues" (Rev 18:4). Though this command of separation is especially to those who will be in the tribulation period, it is applicable at all times. Every true Christian should separate himself from this unscriptural and apostate system.

After writing more than four pages on the ecumenical trend, Dr. Charles C. Ryrie concludes:

> What is the relation to prophecy of the present ecumenical trend? The answer is not difficult. The present trend seems to be preparing the way for the final apostate religious system. The widespread character of the present apostasy in the visible church, the union of various groups into larger denominations without regard to doctrinal consideration, the increasing openness of Catholic and Protestant groups toward each other, the constant intrusion of church bodies into political affairs, and the replacing of the authority of the Bible with the presumed authority of man all seem to say very loudly that the coming of a climax is not far off.

How should a true believer react toward such truths? He should have a deep Spirit-generated compassion for those who are being deceived today into trusting a theology or an organization that cannot save. He should be increasingly burdened, while there is yet time, to take the true message of life and forgiveness to those who otherwise have no hope. And, above all, he should deepen his loyalty and fidelity to the Lord who loved him enough to die for him.[23]

The Forming of Four World Power Blocs

The Bible predicts that at the end of this age there will be four great world powers surrounding Israel. There will be a great power to the north of Israel. This refers definitely to Russia. We read in Ezekiel 38 and 39 about this northern army coming against Israel in the last days. To the south of Israel there has arisen recently the United Arab Republic, led by Egypt, which has openly avowed to push Israel into the Mediterranean Sea. To the east of Israel a backward nation has come on the scene and become one of the greatest threats to the whole world, namely, Red China. Along with other nations of the east, Red China will march to Armageddon (Rev 16:12-16). Walvoord comments, "Never before has an invasion from the Orient upon the Holy Land been more likely than in our generation."[24] Finally, to the west of Israel, we are seeing for the first time the beginnings of a revived Roman Empire. The nations of Europe are drawing more and more together for economic survival as well as by fear of Russia. This western power will eventually become ten nations, which are spoken of in Daniel 2:37-45; 7:7, 19-27; Revelation 13:1 and 17:12, 13.

The Common Market is possibly a forerunner of the ten nations which will eventually merge to form the United States of Europe. Former Secretary of State Dean Acheson recently stated: "The success of the movement toward unity in the west of Europe is no longer in doubt. Only the rate of progress is undecided. The Coal and Steel Community, Euratom, the Common Market, have been accepted. A common currency and political community are on the way."[25] In 1958, six European countries—Belgium, France, Holland, Italy, Luxemburg, and West Germany—established the European Economic Community, or the Common Market.

On Saturday, January 22, 1972, Britain, Ireland, Norway, and

Denmark entered the European Common Market. The Beckley *Post-Herald* stated:

> Their entry created a giant new 10-nation economic force in the world that could rival Russia and the United States in trade. The prime ministers of the four Western nations signed the entire treaty, which takes effect Jan. 1, 1973. . . . When the treaty goes into effect next January, it will forge Western Europe into a single trading bloc with a combined population of 255 million and a combined gross national product of $565 billion. Officials said it could become a formidable trading rival for both the United States and the Soviet Union.

In an exclusive interview with France's Jean Monnet in the October, 1970, issue of *Reader's Digest*, Mr. Monnet was asked: "Mr. Monnet, how do you view present prospects for European unity?" He answered:

> I am optimistic. Europe is once again on the move. The Common Market is going to be enlarged. I have no doubt that the recent applications of Britain, Denmark, Norway and Ireland to join the Market will achieve success. When that occurs, the European Economic Community will be enlarged from a market of 186 million people to one of 250 million—a market bigger than that of the United States—bringing with it the prospect of ever-increasing trade, production and prosperity.
>
> Moreover, the community is not going to be enlarged; it will gradually evolve into a true economic and monetary union, much like what you have in America. Indeed, we will ultimately create a United States of Europe. [He closed his interview by saying:] Does that sound utopian? Look at the distance we have already come. Here we have a group of proud and ancient nations, which have clashed frequently in commerce and in war, and which have somehow, out of a shared sense of necessity, agreed to fuse a large measure of sovereignty in common European institutions. Nothing like it has ever been done before. The process of united European action may stumble at times, but it is forging ahead. The nations of Europe are on their way to forming one large community: the United States of Europe.[26]

The French Foreign Minister, De Murville, said, "The weight which the Common Market will carry, with its networks of interest and involvement across the world, will be such that it will eventually become a *world system.* Its very size will force it to deal on a world scale and to accept what will be its role as a global trading system. If then the Common Market is still in Europe, it will be an entirely new Europe. This Europe of *nine or ten nations* will be necessarily new politically speaking."[27]

From a future brief alliance of ten nations will come a powerful ruler (Dan 7:8), to whom the ten nations, very powerful at that time, shall surrender their sovereignty (Rev 17:8-13). A note in the *Pilgrim Bible* at Daniel 7:8 states: "This represents someone very important in prophecy. He appears under different names in prophetic passages (see Daniel 9:26, 27; 11:36-45; 12:11; Matthew 24:15; II Thessalonians 2:4-8; Revelation 13:1, 4-10, 14, 15). After the Church has been caught up to Heaven (I Thessalonians 4:16, 17), a powerful ruler will arise among the ten kings of the Roman Empire, who will subdue three of the ten kings. He will be especially characterized by his blasphemy against God and his persecution of the Jews (see vss. 23-26)."[28] Western Europe is now in desperation, looking for a great leader who can solve its problems. Belgium's premier said recently: "The truth is that the method of international committees has failed. What we need is a person, someone of the highest order of great experience, of great authority, of great energy. Let him come and let him come quickly. Either a civilian or a military man, no matter what his nationality, who will cut all red tape, shove out of the way all committees, wake up all the people and galvanize all governments into action. Let him come and let him come quickly."[29] This man will be the beast, or Antichrist, spoken of in the Word of God (Rev 13:17; 1 Jn 2:18).

Dr. F. A. Tatford, in his booklet "The Common Market," concludes:

> It would be foolish to maintain dogmatically, as some have done, that the Common Market, or the European Community, is to be identified with a revived Roman Empire or with the federation of ten kingdoms of which prophecy speaks. On the other hand, it is certainly clear that an extraordinary resemblance exists between the prophetic picture and that which is at present being painted before our eyes. The similarity is, in fact, so marked that we may well be seeing today the initial stages in the formation of the great Western

power which is to appear after the translation of the church from this scene. If the fulfilment of prophecy seems to be looming up, then the return of our Lord for His church cannot be far distant.[30]

The Increase in Travel and Knowledge

In Daniel 12:4, Daniel was told by the messenger from God: "But thou, O Daniel, shut up the words, and seal the book, even to the time of the end: many shall run to and fro, and knowledge shall be increased." For centuries, the book of Daniel was a sealed book, but in the last few years there has been an increase in the interest of people in prophecy; and Daniel and Revelation are being studied and understood by Bible students as never before. Dr. William W. Orr says of this verse: "Evidently the time of the end means the end of Gentile dominion, or what we might call, the end of the age of grace."[31]

Daniel then gives two of the signs of the end: "many shall run to and fro"—increased travel; and "knowledge shall be increased"—increased knowledge.

The increase in travel

Only a few years ago travel was quite limited. Those who traveled went on foot, on horseback, by horse and buggy, oxcart, or some other slow process. For six thousand years of man's history, his speed was confined to that of the horse. More than two hundred years ago, Sir Isaac Newton said, "The time is coming when men will travel 50 miles an hour." Voltaire, the skeptic, ridiculed Newton's prediction with, "Now look at that mighty mind of Newton who studied gravitation. When he became an old man and got into his second childhood, he began to study the book that is called the Bible. And it seems in order to credit its fabulous nonsense we must believe that the knowledge of mankind will be so increased that we will be able to travel at the rate of 50 miles an hour. The poor dullard! No man can travel at the rate of 30 miles an hour and get his breath!"[32]

There were no paved roads, no automobiles, no airplanes, and consequently people did not travel too far from their own homes. But then came the automobile, paved roads, trains, airplanes, and other means of transportation by which people can travel almost anywhere they wish. Automobiles and trains travel over one hundred miles per hour, and planes now travel hundreds of miles per hour. Russia's new supersonic airliner, the TV 144 with Aeroflot, travels fifteen hundred miles per hour—twice the speed of sound. People think nothing now of traveling thousands of miles on their vacations. Someone has well said, "The world today is literally a human race on wheels." Cars, trains, steamships, and planes are being used to transport people all over the world to fulfill the scripture "many shall run to and fro."

THE INCREASE IN KNOWLEDGE

This sign is concurrent with the one above, within the last few years. Dr. John Wesley White says the words "knowledge shall be increased" are much stronger in the Hebrew and give this idea: "A sudden knowledge explosion will occur at the time of the end."[33] It has been reported that 90 percent of all scientists who ever lived are living now. There are fifteen thousand different scientific journals being published regularly, many with a world-wide circulation. Another report says that 90 percent of all drugs being prescribed by physicians today were not even known ten years ago. Three-fourths of all the people who will work in industry will be producing products that have not yet been invented or discovered. In a single day, modern man now undertakes enough research to fill seven complete sets of Encyclopedia Britannica. According to Robert Oppenheimer, half of the knowledge we have today was acquired over a period of ten thousand years. The other half was acquired in the last fifteen years, and this acquisition may be doubled in the next five years. Nearly twenty million of the young people of the world are in universities or colleges today. In this country, 46 percent of Americans between the ages of eighteen and twenty-one are in institutions of higher learning, according to Arthur Schlesinger, Jr. A computer has recently been built which can perform fifty-five billion transactions in one second, according to Dr. John Wesley White.[34]

Recently, our country has succeeded in putting men on the moon and bringing them back to earth safely. Gavin Hamilton wrote concerning men in space:

> I cannot but believe that this adventure into space on the part of the nations, particularly the United States and Russia, claims priority

in the realm of signs. It seems to pin-point the truth embedded in the words 'knowledge shall be increased' (Daniel 12:4). While this Scripture can be applied to practically every realm of human knowledge, I feel that science has outstripped everyone. The splitting of the atom has released indescribable, almost unimaginable power, which thrusts the capsules into space with men aboard.[35]

Dr. M. R. DeHaan commented: "Truly this is the age of travel and education. One stands in reverence and awe before the Word of God which described twenty-five hundred years ago, the very conditions which would prevail in these days in which we are living. To the enlightened Bible student, this increase in travel and education spells just one thing—*the coming of the Lord is at hand.*"[36]

THE BEGINNING OF BIRTH PANGS OF A NEW AGE

When the disciples of Jesus came to Him as He sat upon the Mount of Olives shortly before His death, they asked these questions: "When shall these things be? [the destruction of the temple in Jerusalem spoken of in verses 1 and 2], and what shall be the sign of thy coming, and of the end of the world [age]?" (Mt 24:3). Jesus answered with these words, "Take heed that no man deceive you" (24:4). Then He warned them about false Christs who would come (24:5), wars and rumors of war (24:6), and then said, "All these things must come to pass, but the end is not yet." False Christs and wars and rumors of war were not the sign of His coming. There have been false Christs through the centuries, and many wars and rumors of wars throughout the history of the world.

But when we read Matthew 24:7, 8, the scene is changed, and Jesus gives us a fourfold sign of His coming:

"For nation shall rise against nation, and kingdom against kingdom: and there shall be famines, and pestilences, and earthquakes, in divers places." Then Jesus said, "All these are the beginning of sorrows." Dr. A. T. Robertson renders this "the beginning of travail" and then comments, "The word means birth-pangs. . . ."[37] W. E. Vine, in his *Expository Dictionary of New Testament Words*, renders the word *sorrows* in the Greek as *odin* and then makes this statement: "a birth pang, travail, pain, 'sorrows,' Matthew 24:8."[38] Dr. Arthur I. Brown writes of "the beginning of travail": "A new world is about to be born and a new millennial age introduced. As human birth is always accompanied by pains, so this world-birth. The first great pain is the world war, then you see famines, pestilences and earthquakes on an increasing scale. Watch for this sign and its accompanying disasters and you will know the end is near."[39]

Not everyone agrees on the interpretation of Matthew 24. A number of commentators give a variety of interpretations to this chapter. Some say it pertains only to the Jews; others say it speaks of both the Jews and the church. Some say its events are all in the future; others say that some verses refer to events which have already occurred and some to future events. As I have studied this chapter, I am convinced that we have in the first eight verses a picture of this present age. From verse 9 through verse 28, Jesus is speaking of the tribulation period, and verses 29-31 speak of the revelation of Jesus Christ.

WORLD WAR

When Jesus said in verse 7 that "nation shall rise against nation, and kingdom against kingdom," He used an Old Testament idiom, found in two passages of Scripture (2 Ch 15:6 and Is 19:2), which describes a war which begins with one nation coming against another nation, and growing to include all the nations before the eyes of the prophet. The whole world is before the eyes of Jesus in Matthew 24, and He sees a war which will include all of the major nations of the world. In 1914-1918, World War I involved all the nations of the world with the exception of seven minor nations: the three Scandinavian countries, Spain, Portugal, Holland, and Switzerland. All of the other nations were enveloped in World War I—93 percent of them. According to the *Encyclopedia Americana* and the book *Why Wars Must Cease,* in World War I the combined armies totalled 65,000,000 men, and there were 37,500,000 total casualties. One out of every four soldiers died. One English statistician, Crammond, sets the direct cost of that war at $210,000,000,000, and the direct and indirect cost at $370,000,000,000.[40]

FAMINES

Famine always follows war. Following World War I came the great Chinese famine in 1920, about which the *London Times* gave a summary on December 15, 1920: "The population now totally destitute in Chihli is 6,000,000; in Shantung, 2,500,000; in

Honan, 3,500,000; in Shensi, 1,000,000; in Shansi, 500,000—a total of 13,500,000." Then, only eighteen months later, the Volga Valley in Russia was swept by famine. Louis S. Bauman quotes statements by contemporary observers:

> The Archbishop of Canterbury said at the time: "Never in the history of the world has a condition of things existed comparable to the ghastly death by famine of whole millions of men, women, and children." The famous Doctor Nansen, having accurate knowledge, said, "The famine is beyond all doubt the most appalling that has ever happened in the recorded history of man." . . . "Thirty thousand Russians are dying of starvation every day," D. M. Panton of London wrote. In 1929 the Chicago *Tribune* wrote of another great famine in China: "Latest reports on the famine indicate 30 million persons are afflicted instead of the 20 million first reported. . . . Competent authorities expressed fear that 15,000,000 persons might perish." . . . In North China alone, the China Famine Relief, U.S.A., with headquarters in N.Y., printed in its appeal: "The tragedy of over 8,000,000 human beings having starved to death is one of the most terrible in history."[41]

The Bible predicts for the future a great famine during the tribulation, seen in Revelation 6:5-8, when one-fourth of the world's population will die by the "sword, and with hunger." Right now, every day, ten to twelve thousand people die from hunger and starvation, and another eighty to one hundred thousand die each day due to diseases caused by malnutrition. *Science News* reports, "Some experts say the Great World Famine is already upon us."[42] One South Dakota senator observed: "Half a billion people go hungry every day of their lives. Another billion are undernourished because of a shortage of protein in their diet, and at least 3 million children die of malnutrition each year!"[43]

Dr. Raymond Ewell, vice-president of the State University of New York, former adviser to the government of India, declares: "It is hard for us sitting in rich, comfortable, overfed America and of course, the Western World to realize that the GREATEST DISASTER in the history of the world is just around the corner."[44] He gave the warning that the world is running out of food, and declared, "This is the biggest, most fundamental, and most nearly insoluble problem that has ever faced the human race."

Not only do Bible teachers and preachers warn the world of famine coming, but many of the serious thinkers of the world are giving us warning. Surely, this age must be coming to an end very soon.

PESTILENCES

Terrible pestilences followed World War I. The *London Times* reported that six million people died in twelve weeks' time from what was called the "Spanish influenza," and they reported, "This plague is five times more deadly than war. Never since the Black Death has such a plague swept over the face of the world."[45]

In India five million died because of it; in the Arctic whole Eskimo villages were wiped out by it; in the Fiji Islands 85 percent of the people were stricken; in the United States of America, 500,000 people died; and the total figure given for those who died because of this pestilence is 20 million. No country on earth escaped its ravages. Major Norman White, sanitary commissioner for India, declared, "It is an epidemic in many respects without parallel in the history of disease."[46]

Dr. Dale M. Yocum of a Kansas City Bible college reports: "There is a graph in one of my college text books showing the various causes of death in the past 100 years. It is interesting to note that just about the year 1920 there was a curve of death-producing agencies which rises higher than any other time before it or after it and that curve was caused by influenza immediately after the First World War."[47]

EARTHQUAKES

Jesus said there would be "earthquakes, in divers [many or different] places." The greatest earthquakes that have ever shaken this world have all come since the close of World War I. Several of them shook the whole earth. An official report of the earthquake in China in December, 1920, gave the loss of life around the Ching Ting Choo district as three hundred thousand, and a C.I.M. missionary said that "working on this proportion, it would mean that between 500,000 to 1,000,000 lost their lives." *The World Encyclopedia* said this earthquake was three times as deadly as any earthquake ever recorded before World War I, and that others since that time have been far more destructive than any recorded earthquake before that time.

An article appeared not long ago in *Changing Times,* the Kiplinger magazine:

30 Seconds From Now, Another Earthquake

It's a fact. Every 30 seconds the ground shakes somewhere on the globe. And people near enough to feel the stronger tremors can only wonder: Is a catastrophic earthquake being born? Or will the earth just shudder for a moment and spare us?

Luckily, most rumbles come and go quickly, after rattling the windows like a phantom subway train. Of a million or more quakes a year, fewer than one-tenth of 1% pack the power to kill and destroy, and of these only 20 or so occur near enough to populated areas to make much difference.

By comparison the Alaskan quake of 1964, one of the worst disasters to strike an American state, destroyed $450,000,000 worth of property and killed 131 persons, including those drowned under giant waves generated by the furious shaking.

Odds are that a calamity of this scale will again occur somewhere along a dangerous earthquake zone rimming the Pacific Ocean. But don't rule out any place. Destructive earthquakes have hit Missouri, Hawaii, Massachusetts, Montana, Nevada and South Carolina. Lesser tremors have shaken coastal areas from Maine to Florida. Not long ago people in Denver began feeling surprise tremors.

Outside the United States quakes are most likely to strike in the South American, Asian and New Zealand quarters of the Pacific bowl, or in a vast earthquake belt stretching from the Indian Ocean through the Himalayan Mountains, the Caucasian Mountains and the Alps of Europe.

In this century earthquakes have killed more than 900,000 people, about 1,250 of them in this country. Property damage reaches into billions of dollars.[48]

A major earthquake rocked southern California on Feb. 9, 1971, causing widespread damage estimated in the billions of dollars; sixty or more persons were killed, and hundreds were injured. President Nixon declared it a major disaster. Richard L. Worsnop, writing about this earthquake in the Raleigh *Register,* May 21, 1971, stated, "In a sense, the city is still shaking as it totals up the damage from what a U.S. Government study calls 'the most important earthquake in history.' (But not the most destructive. The Peruvian earthquake of May 31, 1970, killed more than 65,000 people; it was the greatest seismic disaster in Western Hemisphere history.)"

R. W. Neighbor, writing in the *Gospel Herald* about earthquakes and similar disturbances, says, "There is no doubt that we are beginning to reach the age the Bible has described as the *great tribulation* period. Great cataclysms may be expected on the earth in the near future."[49]

Mr. Robert J. Little, one of the members of a panel of three Bible teachers of Moody Bible Institute, as they discussed "Bible Prophecy and the Mid-East Crises," said:

> In practically every generation there have been wars and rumors of wars. There have also been earthquakes, famines and pestilences in every generation and people have pointed to these events as evidences of the end time. Now I don't think they were mistaken in feeling that way, even though it was not the time of the end. For it has been God's intention that every generation should live in the expectancy of the Lord's return. Now I do believe the present signs are intensified beyond perhaps anything that has been seen before, which leads me to think we *are* in the time of the end. . . .[50]

After Jesus gave the fourfold sign in Matthew 24:7 and said, "All these are the beginning of sorrows" (v. 8), He spoke of the tribulation period which is yet future (vv. 9-28). In verses 29-31, He discussed the revelation of Jesus Christ, when He comes back to the earth. Then in verses 32-34, by the law of recurrence, He comes back to the subject He left in verses 7 and 8 and says: "Now learn a parable of the fig tree; when his branch is yet tender, and putteth forth leaves, ye know that summer is nigh: So likewise ye, when ye shall see these things, know that it [margin, He] is near, even at the doors. Verily I say unto you, This generation shall not pass, till all these things be fulfilled" (vv. 32-34). The Greek term for "all these things," found in verse 33, is *panta tauta*, which is the same term found in verse 8, "all these." So when we see "all these things," we can know that the coming of Christ "is near, even at the doors." Then Jesus made a very important statement which has been misunderstood by some Bible scholars through the years: "Verily I say unto you, this generation shall not pass, till all these things be fulfilled" (v. 34).

There are at least three different interpretations of "this generation." Some have said that it referred to the generation to which

Christ spoke. This could not be the correct interpretation, because many generations of people have come and gone since then; and some of the things mentioned in this chapter have not yet been fulfilled.

Another interpretation is that "generation" here means the race or nation of Israel. A note in the Scofield Bible at Matthew 24:34 says: "Gr. *genea,* the primary definition of which is 'race, kind, family, stock, breed.' (So all lexicons.) . . . The promise is, therefore, that the generation-nation, or family of Israel—will be preserved unto 'these things'; a promise wonderfully fulfilled to this day."[51] Thousands of Bible students have accepted this for years. In his book *The World's Crisis and the Coming Christ,* Dr. T. J. McCrossan, foremost Greek scholar and formerly instructor in Greek at Manitoba University, wrote:

> Literally, this reads: "Verily I say unto you, the generation, this generation (he genea haute) will in no wise have passed away, until all these things have come to pass." This means the generation living —our own generation. How may we be absolutely sure of this? Because of the demonstrative pronoun haute that ALWAYS refers to the one person or thing last mentioned before it—when in the singular. As the last thing mentioned before "haute" (this) in Matthew 24:34, Mark 13:30, and Luke 21:32, is the new life and the sprouting of the fig tree (Israel—God's own fig tree of Joel 1:7) therefore we know for a surety that the generation here meant by "the generation, this generation"—He genea haute—is the generation which will be living when God's fig tree, Israel, is once again beginning to grow, leaf, and flourish in her own land of Palestine—OUR OWN GENERATION![52]

Another writer, Milton B. Lindberg, in his book *Is Ours the Closing Generation of This Age?,* stated:

> There are many able Bible teachers who believe that Jesus was speaking of the Jewish race, which should continue until the end of the age. It is, therefore a view worthy of careful examination, and disagreement, if any, must be without dogmatism.
> The word for generation in the Greek New Testament is genea, a feminine noun used forty-one times and invariably translated in the Revised Version as GENERATION.
> The word genos, on the other hand, is a masculine noun and in-

variably translated by certain words which have a meaning akin to race, such as, nation, kind, kindred, offspring, stock. Only once does the Authorized Version translate genos as generation (I Peter 2:9) but in this passage, also the revisers have rendered it as race. Judging by usage in the Greek Testament, therefore, genea and genos are not used interchangeably, but each has its distinctive meaning.

Not only is genea used in the passage under consideration (Matthew 24:34) but a careful scrutiny of its context demands that the translation be GENERATION. God has plainly declared that so long as times shall endure, the Jewish race shall not cease from being a nation before Him (Jeremiah 31:36, 37). But if Jesus were saying that the Jewish race should continue until after His return, he would be turning from the subject of His discourse which had to do with the SIGNS that should PRECEDE His coming. Says Francis Asa Wright concerning this passage: "The perpetuity of the Jews as a race is not Christ's theme, and could not be a sign, for how could their continuance show that He was "nigh, even at the door?'"

If Jesus were referring to the Jewish nation, His words would be tantamount to saying: "This race (a race that shall never pass away) shall not pass away, till all these things be accomplished." Such a truism is entirely unnecessary and would make of His discourse little more than a waste of words.[53]

Other Bible scholars say that "this generation" refers to the generation who will be living in the future when these signs are witnessed. Dr. Pentecost said concerning this view: "Others hold that the word has reference to the future, so that Christ is saying that those who witness the signs stated earlier in the chapter will see the coming of the Son of man within that generation. . . . such may be the interpretation."[54]

Robert J. Little, fomer Radio Pastor of WMBI, Chicago, Illinois, wrote in his book, *Here's Your Answer*:

A third view seems more acceptable. It is that the generation which sees the beginning of the final fulfillment of the prophecies uttered by the Lord will see the consummation of those prophecies. This does not mean that we can set a date for the time of our Lord's coming, which we are told no man knows (Mark 13:32). We have no way of knowing from what event we should begin the counting of the generation, nor are we told the precise length of the generation. But the implication is that when these events begin to take place, they will reach their completion in a swift succession of events."[55]

Theodore H. Epp writes: "The generation, then, that sees a great worldwide conflict followed by famine and pestilence and earthquakes and the rise of Jewish nationalism is the generation that will see the return of the Lord. . . ."[56]

He comments further on this topic in several issues of the *Back to the Bible Broadcaster:*

> It seems to us that the only interpretation that will fit this word generation in this passage is that it refers to a particular group of people living over a certain span of time. I could speak of my generation as the span of time from my birth until the time I die. It could also be an indefinite period, meaning 30 or 50 or 70 years, just as the life span is different in different areas. So our understanding of this passage is that some of the people at least, who live to see the beginning of these things mentioned in Matthew 24 will still be living when they are consummated. . . . [57]

> We have been investigating this subject: "Will this generation see the return of the Lord?" The raising of such a question may lay one open to the accusation of being a date-setter. This would not be true here, however, for we know not of the day nor the hour nor the year of our Lord's coming.
> We should, however, not be indifferent to this subject, for we are quite thoroughly informed in the Scriptures with regard to the signs of His coming. In writing to the Thessalonians Paul said, "But of the times and the seasons, brethren, ye have no need that I write unto you. For yourselves know perfectly that the day of the Lord so cometh as a thief in the night" (I Thessalonians 5:1, 2). This is how His coming will appear to unbelievers, for they will ignore the signs, "willfully" ignore them as Peter says in his second letter. But those of us who know the Lord "are not in darkness, that that day should overtake" us as a thief (I Thessalonians 5:4). . . .[58]

> I have no interest in setting the time whether it be the day or the year when Christ will come. I cannot do that. But neither can I hide the truth the Word of God gives. On several occasions, God gave explicit information concerning a certain generation that would see certain things come to pass. He told Abraham that in the fourth

generation, his descendants, the nation of Israel, would return from Egypt.

At a later time God made it very clear to Babylon that in the third generation of their kings, considering Nebuchadnezzar as the first generation, Babylon would fall.

The Lord made it very clear to certain ones in Israel that they would not die until they saw the Lord Jesus Christ come the first time.

During the time of His public ministry, our Lord warned the Israelites that many of those listening to Him would see the destruction of Jerusalem.

Let us not be surprised then, that He made it clear that a certain generation that sees certain signs on the earth will also see the coming of the Lord.

Concerning the time of that coming, our Saviour stated: "Heaven and earth shall pass away, but my words shall not pass away. But of that day and hour knoweth no man, no, not the angels of heaven, but my Father only." The day and the hour would not be known, but the nature of the times and seasons would be.[59]

Hal Lindsey, in an article in *Moody Monthly* entitled, "The Pieces Fall Together," after quoting Matthew 24:32-34, stated: "I believe we may be that generation. In the light of this conviction, I am convinced it is no time for 'business as usual.' Every New Testament reference to the 'blessed hope' carries with it an admonition for holy living. We must live and preach and witness not in a spirit of fear and panic, but in a spirit of obedience, confidence and urgency, knowing that times such as these provide our greatest spiritual opportunities."[60]

In a message entitled, "Has God Revealed The Generation of Christ's Coming?", Evangelist John Linton said, "In the unfolding of His divine plan for the ages, from the very beginning of human history, when one important era was to end and a new one begin, God revealed the generation of fulfillment."[61] Then he showed from the Bible that God revealed the generation of the flood in Noah's day; Israel's entrance into Canaan; the fall of Babylon; the fall of the Persian world empire; the destruction of Jerusalem; the first coming of Christ; and Christ's second coming. In the last part of his message he makes these statements:

Does the Bible contain any reference to a particular generation living in the end time just before the second coming of Christ? It does.

Does the Bible use the word generation in describing this end period? It does. It is found in my text where Jesus said, "This generation shall not pass, till all these things be fulfilled" (Matthew 24:34).

Does our Lord tell us when this particular generation will begin? He does. There would be no sense in referring to some particular generation unless He told us when it began.

Does Jesus use the word "beginning"? He does. He uses the word twice, once by Matthew (Ch. 24:8) and once by Luke (Ch. 21:28) so that we have two witnesses to confirm certainty. And not only so, but our Lord gives a fourfold sign to pinpoint this beginning, with four different elements in it, so that we cannot possibly mistake it. This sign is a great unprecedented world war, accompanied by famines, pestilence, and earthquakes, and all four disasters happening simultaneously. In answer to the disciples question regarding THE SIGN of His coming, Jesus said, "For nation shall rise against nation, and kingdom against kingdom: and there shall be famines, and pestilences, and earthquakes, in divers places. ALL THESE ARE THE BEGINNING OF SORROWS" (Matthew 24:7-8).

Has this fourfold sign been given? Has the beginning of sorrows commenced? I think I can prove to any open minded person that it has. The greatest war this world had ever known, the worst famines, the most destructive pestilence, and the greatest earthquakes ALL HAPPENED TOGETHER in the same decade of the world's history beginning with World War I, in 1914-1918.

Historical facts verifying the above are given in my book on this subject so I will make no further mention of it here.

Our Lord then goes on from this point of beginning, to describe other events in this end period leading up to and including His coming in verse 30. He then looks back to "the beginning of sorrows" and with this beginning in mind He says—By this definite revelation I am about to give, you are to know that my coming is right at the doors—"THIS GENERATION SHALL NOT PASS TILL ALL THESE THINGS BE FULFILLED."

Mark you there is no datesetting wrapped up in the word "generation." No time is set, no exact day, hour, month, or year is stated. But just as the generation of fulfillment was revealed in the past, so, when we see "all these things" described in the chapter, from verse 7, to His coming at verse 30, we are to know we have reached the last generation of this age of grace. . . .

The question will arise—How long is a generation? I reply, no one knows. It can be proven from the Bible that a generation is no definite period of years. When our Lord used the term it is reasonable to believe He meant a full generation. What my message implies is that some of the people living at the time of World War I, will not all have passed from the earth before Christ comes. Jesus gave the generation that crucified Him only 40 years of probation before the Romans and judgment came upon them. When I remember that it is now 50 years since the warning catastrophe known as World War I, took place, I tremble.

Surely this striking truth set forth in my message is a trumpet call from God to the men and women of this generation to repent and be saved from the coming judgment. When Peter preached on the day of Pentecost he cried to the men of his day—"Save yourselves from this untoward generation" (Acts 2:40). Peter had heard Christ's prophecy of Jerusalem's fall in that generation. He believed many of his hearers would die in that judgment. He told them they could be saved from among a nation that was doomed.

This actually happened! Josephus tells us that of the 1,100,000 who perished in the seige there was not one Christian among them. Warned by our Lord to flee to the mountains they did so before the Romans came. Thus they were saved, not only from their sins, but also from the disaster that befell their unbelieving generation several years later.

This should be the message of the church today to a generation marked out by God for judgment. This ought to be the loving warning every Christian should give to friends and loved ones unsaved. I am praying that God will use this message to that end. I pray that He will lead many of our readers to spread this startling truth among the unsaved. Show it to them in the Bible as I have shown you. It is Scriptural, it is startling, may it also be soulstirring for us all.[62]

I believe, with other Bible scholars, that many people living today will still be living when Jesus comes. No other generation has seen the signs which God has given this generation. When I preached some years ago that Christ would come in this generation, I was nicknamed by some of my friends, "This-Generation Johnson." I am more convinced than ever now that "this generation" will see the coming of Christ.

As I was closing this chapter, I was interrupted by a phone call from a lady hundreds of miles away who had heard me preach on the second coming of Christ about a month before. She told me that she remembered I had said that Jesus could come at any moment and she said, "I am afraid. I know I'll be left when He comes and will be lost forever." I had the privilege of telling her that she could repent of her sins and receive Jesus Christ as her personal Saviour (Lk 13:3; Jn 1:12), and be saved and ready for His coming, even look with real joy for His appearing (1 Jn 3:2, 3). I now plead with you, as Jesus does, "Therefore be ye also ready: for in such an hour as ye think not the Son of man cometh" (Mt 24:44).

Dr. Stephen Olford, in a message "The Coming of Christ," concluded:

> To illustrate the relevance of these happenings to the near return of our Lord, Harold Wildish tells a lovely story of a father who had to leave his home and go on a long journey. Just before he left, his little three-year-old son asked him, "Daddy, when will you be coming back?" Now, the father knew that he would not be back until the end of September. However, he realized it would be of little use to talk about times and seasons to his little boy, for he would not know the difference between them. The father said to the boy, "Now listen; when you see the leaves on the trees turning red and brown and beginning to fall to the ground, then you can be sure that Daddy is coming back very soon."
>
> The next day the father left home. During the months of July and August the little boy would go for walks with his nurse. On these walks he used to talk about his absent Daddy. Slowly the weeks went by until it came early September, and then mid-September. Although the boy did not notice it, the leaves on the trees were changing colors.
>
> Then one night there was a big windstorm and millions of leaves came down, filling the sidewalks and gutters. The next morning when the little fellow went out, he immediately saw them. Letting go his nurse's hand, he went among the leaves and began to kick them sky high. Then he began to shout, "Hurrah! Hurrah! Daddy is coming soon!"

Likewise, all over the world there is an expectation. The leaves are turning brown and they are beginning to fall. Jesus said, . . . when ye see these things," be gloomy? No, chins up! "Lift up your heads." The great future of every child of God may be dawning, "for the coming of the Lord draweth near."[63]

What If It Were Today?

Jesus is coming to earth again, what if it were today?
 Coming in power and love to reign, What if it were today?
Coming to claim His chosen Bride, All the redeemed and purified,
 Over this whole earth scattered wide, What if it were today?

Satan's dominion will then be o'er, Oh, that it were today!
 Sorrow and sighing shall be no more, Oh, that it were today!
Then shall the dead in Christ arise, Caught up to meet Him in the skies;
 When shall these glories meet our eyes? What if it were today?

Faithful and true would He find us here, If He should come today?
 Watching in gladness and not in fear, If He should come today?
Signs of His coming multiply, Morning light breaks in eastern sky;
 Watch, for the time is drawing nigh, What if it were today?

Glory, glory! Joy to my heart, 'twill bring,
 Glory, glory! When we shall crown Him King;
Glory, glory! Haste to prepare the way;
 Glory, glory! Jesus will come some day.

Mrs. C. H. Morris

6

THE RAPTURE—
When There Will Not Be One Christian on the Earth

SOMETIME IN THE FUTURE, it could be even today, millions of people will suddenly disappear from this earth. There will not be one Christian left when this takes place, because those millions of people who will suddenly disappear will be Christians. Every baby and every child who has not reached the age of accountability will also disappear at the same time. This will be when Christ descends from heaven to receive His own, and is called the rapture.

The word *rapture* is not found in the Bible, but is from *rapere*, found in the expression "caught up" in the Latin translation of 1 Thessalonians 4:17. Its Greek counterpart is *harpadzo*.

There are a number of different views among Christians concerning the rapture.

PARTIAL RAPTURE THEORY

In the last century, a small group of Christians arose who taught that only those who are faithful to the Lord will be raptured, and those who are not faithful will not be raptured until later, either in the tribulation period or at the end of the tribulation. They explained that Christians will be raptured in groups during the tribulation as they are prepared to go. Based upon Scriptural exhortations to watch for Christ's coming and be faithful, this teaching regards rapture as a reward. This view is limited to a few adherents.

I will not take the time in this chapter to refute the different theories, but in a later chapter I will write why I believe the Bible teaches the pretribulation rapture of the church.

POSTTRIBULATION RAPTURE THEORY

This is the theory, held by many, that the church will be raptured at the close of the tribulation; and those who teach and believe this say that the church must pass through this time of tribulation. This is the view of practically all amillenarians and postmillenarians, Roman Catholics and Greek Catholics, and many Protestants, conservatives as well as liberals.

MIDTRIBULATION RAPTURE THEORY

This theory, comparatively new, is held by only a small minority. Those who hold it teach that the church will be translated in the middle of the seventieth week of Daniel (Dan 9:27) and before the time of great tribulation.

THE PRETRIBULATION RAPTURE

This position is held by conservatives and teaches that Christ raptures His church before the tribulation period, and that His coming is imminent. This is the position held by the author and will be discussed further in a later chapter.

JESUS SPOKE OF THE RAPTURE

In John 14:3, Jesus promised His own: "And if I go and prepare a place for you, I will come again, and receive you unto myself; that where I am, there ye may be also." It is said that there are 318 references to the second coming of Christ in the New Testament, one verse in every twenty-five mentioning it.

PAUL SPOKE OF THE RAPTURE

One of the clearest passages in the New Testament concerning the rapture is 1 Thessalonians 4:15-18:

> For this we say unto you by the word of the Lord, that we which are alive and remain unto the coming of the Lord shall not prevent them which are asleep. For the Lord himself shall descend from heaven with a shout, with the voice of the archangel, and with the trump of God: and the dead in Christ shall rise first: Then we which

are alive and remain shall be caught up together with them in the clouds, to meet the Lord in the air: and so shall we ever be with the Lord. Wherefore comfort one another with these words.

Revelation. In verse 15, Paul reminds us: "For this we say unto you by the word of the Lord . . ." He wanted us to know that he was speaking, not by himself, but by the revelation of the Lord. What he is telling us in these verses that follow was revealed by the Lord Himself.

Return. "For the Lord himself shall descend from heaven . . ." The Lord Jesus Christ Himself, Who has been in Heaven for over nineteen hundred years, is going to return for His own. He does not come all the way to the earth at this time, but He calls the Christians to rise and meet Him in the air.

Resurrection. "And the dead in Christ shall rise first." Those who have put their trust in Christ and have died before He comes, will be resurrected. They will then get their glorified bodies and will be reunited with their souls and spirits, which have been with Jesus Christ since their death, and will go up to meet Him in the air.

Years ago, I heard Dr. James McGinley speak at a Bible conference. He told of the time he was at Winona Lake Bible Conference. One day, as he was reading a brochure of the Conference, saying that the world's greatest speakers were preaching at this conference (he was one of them), a lady approached him. She said, "Mr. McGinley, if God is no respecter of persons, will you tell me why on the day when Christ comes back for His Church the dead are given the preeminence over the living? Paul says, 'For the dead in Christ shall rise first.' Will you please reconcile this fact with the statement that God deals with all His children on the grounds of equality?"

Dr. McGinley continues the story: "In order to gain time and to give my brain a chance to work, I asked her to repeat the question. Then I repeated it, saying, 'You want to know why the dead in Christ shall rise first? Well, that is simple. They have six feet farther to come. Were God to call the dead and the living at the same time, then the living would be six feet ahead of the dead all the way up, but instead of that He raises the dead first. They come to the surface, and, together with the living, are caught up to meet Him in the air.'

"She gripped my hand, looked into my face, and said, 'Mr. Mc-Ginley, you are wonderful.' Now, can you imagine an intelligent woman fooling around with that kind of stuff?"

Rapture. "Then we which are alive and remain shall be caught up. . . ." Those Christians who are alive when Jesus returns in the air will be caught up (raptured, translated) without dying. God's Word throws light on this in 1 Corinthians 15:51, 52: "Behold, I show you a mystery; We shall not all sleep [die], but we [Christians] shall all be changed, in a moment, in the twinkling of an eye [Dr. A. T. Schofield, British scholar, said, "The term, 'twinkling of an eye,' means two-fifths of a second"], at the last trump: for the trumpet shall sound, and the dead [in Christ] shall be raised incorruptible, and we [the living Christians] shall be changed." This is why some Christians say, "I'm not waiting for the undertaker; I'm waiting for the Uppertaker!"

Some time ago, I was asked to speak on a TV program. In the course of the message, I mentioned the truth that there would be a generation of Christians who would not have to die. I told my audience, "Christians who are living when Christ comes again for His church will escape death. They will 'cheat the undertaker.' " When the program was finished, one of the men listening in the studio rushed to me and asked, "Man, do you know who sponsored this program?" I replied, "No, I don't. Who is the sponsor?" He said, "A local funeral home." Millions of Christians will be caught up without dying and will "cheat the undertaker."

Reunion. "Together with them. . . ." Those Christians who are raptured will have a reunion with their loved ones and friends who have been resurrected. Dr. M. R. DeHaan wrote: "Are you sure that you caught the implication of that wonderful phrase? Don't miss it. We shall be caught up *together—together with them.* First, we are brought together. *Then,* we rise to meet the Lord *together.* How Wonderful!"[1]

Reception. "To meet the Lord in the air: and so shall we ever be with the Lord." The Lord Jesus Christ will meet us in the air, will receive us to Himself as He promised in John 14:3, and we shall be with Him forever and be like Him (Phil 3:20, 21; 1 Jn 3:2, 3).

Refreshment. "Wherefore comfort one another with these words."

What a refreshment this is for us who belong to Him! What a joy to know that He may come today and take us who love Him to Himself.

Dr. Franklin Logsdon wrote concerning the rapture: "The meeting in the air is an exclusive appointment of the Lord with His Church. It looms on faith's horizon as the golden prospect. It furnishes an inspiration for vision, an inducement to purity, an incentive to patience, an impetus for witnessing, an expectation of deliverance, an anticipation of reunion, and the gateway to glory."[2]

THE TIME OF THE RAPTURE

It is clear from the study of the Bible that no one knows the day or the hour that Jesus will return, but there are many indications that His coming is near, even at the doors. Dr. Charles C. Ryrie wrote recently:

> The rapture of the Church can occur at any time. Nothing is yet unfulfilled which must take place before believers are caught up to meet the Lord in the air.
> By every indication which we can gauge, the Rapture seems near. Certainly each day that passes brings it 24 hours nearer, and each trend that develops points to its coming. God says that this is a blessed hope—at least it *will* be if we are ready to meet the Lord. If not, we should *get* ready and then know the joy of eagerly anticipating seeing Him whose coming will be "in the twinkling of an eye"![3]

Dr. M. R. DeHaan, in a message at Moody Founder's Week Conference in 1963, said, "I believe—you may disagree with me if you want to—but I believe that the rapture is past due. I believe we are living on borrowed time. I do not know of anything that has to happen before our Lord could come. I know a lot of things could happen and must happen before the second coming at the end of the tribulation, but I do not know of anything that must happen before the rapture."[4]

D. L. Moody, speaking of the second coming, said, "I have felt like working three times as hard since I came to understand that my Lord is coming again. I look upon this world as a wrecked vessel. God has given me a life boat, and said to me, 'Moody, save all you can.' God will come in judgment and burn up this world. This world is getting darker and darker; its ruin is coming nearer and nearer. If you have any friends on this wreck unsaved, you had better lose no time in getting them off."

May we who are Christians daily pray the last prayer of the Bible: "Even so, come, Lord Jesus" (Rev 22:20); may we "love His appearing" (2 Ti 4:8); and may we "abide in him; that when he shall appear, we may have confidence, and not be ashamed before him at his coming" (1 Jn 2:28).

May you who are lost hear and heed the words of Jesus Christ: "Therefore be ye also ready: for in such an hour as ye think not the Son of man cometh" (Mt 24:44). To be ready, you must repent and receive Jesus Christ as your personal Saviour (Lk 13:3; Jn 3:16). Do it now—tomorrow may be too late.

If Christ Should Come Tonight

If you could know that Jesus would appear
    Before another morn should give its light,
Oh, would your heart be filled with joy or fear,
    If you could know that He would come tonight?

The things you'd do, the words that you would say,
    Perchance the letter you had thought to write;
How many plans would have to change today,
    If you were sure that Christ would come tonight?

How many acts would then remain undone?
    How many wrongs would have to be made right,
If you should meet Him ere another sun,
    And knew for sure that He would come tonight?
How many things would you find time for then,
    Now crowded out or else forgotten quite—
The kindly deed, the hour of prayer again—
    Would aught be different, should He come tonight?
Some day that dawns will make all time as past;
    Then may we keep our lamps all trimmed and bright.
Oh, may we live each day as 'twere the last,
    And ready be if Christ should come tonight.

                                                    Unknown

7

THE JUDGMENT SEAT OF CHRIST
A Practical Prophetic Truth

EARLY IN MY CHRISTIAN LIFE, a book became mine which has meant very much to me. I learned from this book, *The Judgment Seat Of Christ* by Dr. L. Sale-Harrison, the importance of living "with eternity's values in view." I have since then read everything I can find on this very important subject, of which Dr. John F. Walvoord said, "There is no more practical prophetic truth than this simple pointed doctrine of the judgment seat of Christ."[1]

Dr. W. Myrddin Lewis, prophetic scholar of England, wrote of this judgment in these words: "Here too is a thought that should be the greatest inducement to holy living, greater than any other single thing."[2]

THE JUDGMENT SEAT OF CHRIST—WHAT?

The phrase "*the judgment seat of Christ,* appears only twice in the Bible, but it is referred to many times. The first direct use of the phrase is found in Romans 14:10: "But why dost thou judge thy brother? or why dost thou set at nought thy brother? for we shall all stand before *the judgment seat of Christ*" (ital. added). The second and only other use of this wording is in 2 Corinthians 5:10: "For we must all appear before *the judgment seat of Christ*; that every one may receive the things done in his body, according to that he hath done, whether it be good or bad" (ital. added). In these two passages, God is speaking of Christians, who *must* all stand or appear before this judgment. The "we" in 2 Corinthians 5:10 refers only to Christians, since this pronoun is used twenty-six times in this chapter and always refers to believers in Christ.

The words *judgment seat* are a translation of the Greek word *bema*, which is a raised platform. In Paul's day, outside the city of Corinth there was a large Olympic stadium containing a raised platform on which the judge of the contest sat and watched the contestants. When the contests were finished, the contestants would assemble before the *bema* to receive their rewards. The Bible speaks of the Christian life as a race (1 Co 9:24; Hebrews 12:1), and the judge, the Lord Jesus Christ, is watching every Christian; and when the race is finished, and the Lord Jesus returns for His own, each Christian will receive that which he has done in the body (1 Co 4:5; 2 Co 5:10).

This is not a judgment of the unsaved. Only Christians will be at this judgment; and the judgment will be of works done from the time the individual became a true Christian.

The Judgment Seat of Christ—When?

Paul tells us in 1 Corinthians 4:5: "Therefore judge nothing before the time, *until the Lord come*, who both will bring to light the hidden things of darkness, and will make manifest the counsels of the hearts: *and then* shall every man have praise of God" (ital. added). Here we are told that the hidden things of darkness will be brought to light, and counsels of the hearts will be made manifest (or exposed), when the Lord comes. Paul also instructs us: "Henceforth there is laid up for me a crown of righteousness, which the Lord, the righteous judge, shall give me at that day: and not to me only, but unto all them also that love his appearing" (2 Ti 4:8). The crowns will be given to faithful Christians "at that day," the day of "his appearing." Jesus also told us when He would judge the Christians and reward those who were faithful to Him: "And, behold, I come quickly; and my reward is with me, to give every man according as his work shall be" (Rev 22:12).

Dr. I. M. Haldeman, great prophetic preacher of some years ago, wrote: "According to the Word of God, the testimony of the Son of God, and the corroborative and unbroken testimony of the Apostles, there is not the thickness of tissue paper between us who are Christians and the Judgment Seat of Christ."[3]

In the light of the soon return of our Lord Jesus Christ and our appearing before Him to give an account of our Christian lives, these words of Dr. W. Myrddin Lewis should alert us: "We see every major prophecy of God's Word regarding our Lord's return fulfilled, including the great prophecy in Ezekiel 37, where God through the mouth of His servant foretold the uniting of the Jewish people into one nation, brought back from across the seven seas, and re-established in Palestine as a sovereign nation. With that now history, and with no other prophecy to be fulfilled that could possibly delay His coming, what manner of persons ought we to be, in the light of this truth that any minute now we shall be snatched from off this sinful, evil and wicked earth to stand in His presence before His Judgment Seat?"[4]

The Judgment Seat of Christ—Why?

I wish to make it very clear that this judgment is only for Christians, not the unsaved. Dr. J. Dwight Pentecost writes of this in these words: "The word translated 'appear' in 2 Corinthians 5:10 might better be rendered to be made manifest, so that the verse reads, 'For it is necessary for all of us to be made manifest.' This suggests that the purpose of the bema is to make a public manifestation, demonstration or revelation of the essential character and motives of the individual. Plummer's remark: 'We shall not be judged *en masse*, or in classes, but one by one, in accordance with individual merit,' substantiates the fact that this is an individual judgment of each believer before the Lord."[5]

In 2 Corinthians 5:10, Paul gives the reason for our appearing before the judgment seat of Christ: ". . . that every one may receive the things done in his body, according to that he hath done, whether it be good or bad."

In 1 Corinthians 3:10-15, God speaks of the judgment seat of Christ:

> According to the grace of God which is given unto me, as a wise masterbuilder, I have laid the foundation, and another buildeth thereon. But let every man take heed how he buildeth thereupon. For other foundation can no man lay than that is laid, which is Jesus Christ. Now if any man build upon this foundation gold, silver, precious stones, wood, hay, stubble; Every man's work shall

be made manifest: for the day shall declare it, because it shall be revealed by fire; and the fire shall try every man's work of what sort it is. If any man's work abide which he hath built thereupon, he shall receive a reward. If any man's work shall be burned, he shall suffer loss: but he himself shall be saved; yet so as by fire.

Here God says that there is only one foundation on which we should build our lives, and that is Jesus Christ, and He warns us in verse 10: "But let every man take heed how he buildeth thereupon." Then He speaks of the different kinds of materials a Christian can use in building: "gold, silver, precious stones, wood, hay, stubble." There is a distinct contrast in the materials: gold, silver, precious stones, or wood, hay, stubble. The gold, silver, and precious stones speak figuratively: of that which is permanent, in contrast to that which is perishing, represented by the wood, hay, and stubble; of worthiness, in contrast to worthlessness; of quality in contrast to quantity; of the Spirit in contrast to the flesh; of living for eternity in contrast to living only for time; of that which is done in the will of God in contrast to that which is done in the will of man; of that which is done for the glory of God in contrast to that which is done for the glory of man.

In verse 13 we are told that our works will be tried or tested by fire. Fire is a symbol of Deity: "For the LORD thy God is a consuming fire, even a jealous God" (Deu 4:24); "For our God is a consuming fire" (Heb 12:29). It is said of Jesus Christ in Revelation 1:14: "His eyes were as a flame of fire." The Word of God is spoken of as fire in Jeremiah 23:29: "Is not my word like as a fire? saith the Lord." The Holy Spirit of God is referred to as "the spirit of burning" in Isaiah 4:4. Putting these three thoughts together, they speak of this: When a holy God tests our works and service, only that which has been done according to the Word of God, and in the power of the Holy Spirit will be approved and rewarded.

REWARDS

The Christian who has lived in the Spirit and according to the Word of God will be rewarded—"he shall receive a reward" (1 Co 3:14). There are five crowns spoken of in Scripture which will be given to faithful Christians:

1) the Incorruptible Crown (1 Co 9:25-27), for running the Christian race well and keeping his body under subjection
2) the Crown of Rejoicing (1 Th 2:19, 20), for winning souls
3) the Crown of Righteousness (2 Ti 4:8), for loving the appearing of Jesus Christ
4) the Crown of Life (Ja 1:12; Rev 2:10), for enduring trials and loving the Lord, in spite of the trials, even to the point of death
5) the Crown of Glory (1 Pe 5:1-4), for being a faithful pastor and feeding the flock of God willingly and with a ready mind.

In Revelation 4:10, 11, we read of the time when the four and twenty elders cast their crown before the throne to give glory and honor and power to the Lord. Dr. E. Schuyler English said, "They represent, unless I am badly mistaken, the raptured church after her receipt of the awards given out at the *bema* of Christ."[6] Dr. Pentecost comments:

> In Revelation 4:10, where the elders are seen to be casting their crowns before the throne in an act of worship and adoration, it is made clear that the crowns will not be for the eternal glory of the recipient, but for the glory of the Giver. Since these crowns are not viewed as a permanent possession, the question of the nature of the rewards themselves arises. From the Scriptures it is learned that the believer was redeemed in order that he might bring glory to God (I Corinthians 6:20). This becomes his eternal destiny. The act of placing the material sign of a reward at the feet of the One who sits on the throne (Revelation 4:10) is one act in that glorification. But the believer will not then have completed his destiny to glorify God. This will continue throughout eternity. The greater the reward, the greater the bestowed capacity to bring glory to God. Thus in the exercise of the reward of the believer, it will be Christ and not the believer that is glorified by the reward.[7]

When Queen Victoria listened to the Hallelujah Chorus in London, in the Albert Hall, she instantly rose to her feet. When someone asked her why she did this, she replied: "My Lord is coming one day. I would love for Him to come now, so that I could, as Queen of Britain and Empress of India, take my crowns and lay them at His feet." She believed in Jesus Christ as her personal Saviour and Lord and anxiously waited for Him to return.

Dr. F. E. Marsh tells an interesting story about rewards:

> It is said that Ivan, of Russia, used sometimes to disguise himself, and go out among his people to find out their true character. One night he went, dressed as a beggar, into the suburbs of Moscow, and asked for a night's lodging, but he was refused admittance at every house, until at last his heart sank with discouragement to think of the selfishness of his people. At length, however, he knocked at a door where he was gladly admitted. The poor man invited him in, offered him a crust of bread, a cup of water, and a bed of straw, and then said, "I am sorry I cannot do more for you, but my wife is ill, a babe has just been given her, and my attention is needed for them." The Emperor lay down and slept the sleep of a contented mind. He had found a true heart. In the morning he took his leave with many thanks.
>
> The poor man forgot all about it, until a few days later, the royal chariot drove up to the door, and attended by his retinue, the Emperor stopped at his humble abode.
>
> The poor man was alarmed, and throwing himself at the Emperor's feet, asked, "What have I done?"
>
> Ivan lifted him up, and taking him by both his hands, said, "Done! You've done nothing but entertain your Emperor. It was I who lay upon that bed of straw, it was I who received your humble but hearty hospitality, and now I have come to reward you. You received me in disguise, but now I come in my true character to recompense your love. Bring hither your new-born babe." And as he brought him, he said, "You shall call him after me, and when he is old enough, I will educate him and give him a place in my court and service." Giving him a bag of gold, he said, "Use this for your wife, and if ever you have need of anything, don't forget to call upon the poor tramp that slept the other night in the corner."
>
> Something similar will happen when our Lord returns. For every cup of water given in His name, for every kindly word spoken for His sake, for every meal given out of love to Him, for every encouragement given to others, for every self-denying act to our brethren, there will be recognition and recompense from our Lord Jesus Christ.[8]

Dr. Marsh concludes his chapter entitled "The Worker's Rewards" with these encouraging words:

> Let us remember that not a single action done out of love to Christ

shall miss His commendation and reward in the day of His reckoning. Everything done for "His name's sake" is recorded for our reward. He records the ardent faith of a clinging soul (Matthew 15:28); the generous heart which gives its all, although it be but two mites (Luke 17:18, 19); the true confession of Himself is music in His ears, and calls forth His approbation (Matthew 16:17); He appreciates the breaking of the costly box of ointment over His person, and makes a lasting memorial of it (Matthew 26:13); He commends the earnest desire of David to build Him a temple, and puts the building down to His account, although he never placed a stone in it (II Samuel 7:2-7; I Chronicles 28:2); He is careful to give as much reward to the prophet's host, as He gives to the prophet himself (Matthew 10:41), and the cup of water given to one of His own is accepted as done to Himself (Mark 9:41).[9]

Jesus said, "Behold, I come quickly: hold that fast which thou hast, that no man take thy crown" (Rev 3:11). We are encouraged in 2 John 8, "Look to yourselves, that we lose not those things which we have wrought, but that we receive a full reward."

Charles C. Luther has written words that should stir our hearts:

Must I go, and empty-handed, thus my dear Redeemer meet?
　Not one day of service give Him, lay no trophy at His feet?
Not at death I shrink nor falter, for my Savior saves me now;
　But to meet Him empty-handed, thought of that now clouds my brow.
O the years in sinning wasted! Could I but recall them now,
　I would give them to my Savior—to His will I'd gladly bow.
O ye saints, arouse, be earnest, up and work while yet 'tis day;
　Ere the night of death o'ertake thee, strive for souls while still you may.
Must I go, and empty-handed? Must I meet my Savior so?
　Not one soul with which to greet Him—must I empty-handed go?

Loss

"If any man's work shall be burned, he shall suffer loss: but he himself shall be saved; yet so as by fire" (1 Co 3:15). Those works done by a Christian—which were not done according to the Word of God; which were not done in the power of the Holy Spirit, but in the flesh; which were not done because of love for the Lord, but love of self; which were not done for the glory of God, but to glorify man—will be burned up as "wood, hay, stubble," and the unfaithful Christian shall suffer loss. This does not mean the loss of the soul, because the verse goes on to say, "but he himself shall be saved; yet so as by fire." This has the thought of a man asleep in his house while his house catches fire. Someone comes along, sees the fire, rushes in, drags the man out through the fire, and brings him outside to safety. The house and everything in it is burned to the ground, but the man is saved "yet only as in passing through fire" (1 Co 3:15, Berkeley Version).

Dr. Lehman Strauss comments on the loss:

> We hear much preaching to Christians about the rewards they will get in heaven, but we hear very little preaching about those Christians who will "suffer loss." Of course, the latter subject is less popular. But my Christian friend, none of us can afford to be careless and indifferent, because it will make a big difference in the end. I do not know all that is meant by the words "suffer loss," but we may be certain they do not mean that we will enjoy our losses. What shame and regrets are suggested in this prospect![10]

Nor do I know all that is meant by the words "suffer loss," but in the rest of this chapter I want to share with you what I have found in my studies. I realize that all Christians do not share these views, but I pray that every Christian who reads this will be like the Bereans, of whom it was said, "they received the word with all readiness of mind, and searched the scriptures daily, whether those things were so" (Ac 17:11). I will quote quite extensively from a number of men of God of the past and present who have written concerning the judgment seat of Christ.

Dr. Keith L. Brooks:

> Some seem to think that if we are Christians, God is not going to bring up anything done in this life. It is all "under the blood." Put everything on Jesus and live any way you please. Surely that cannot be right.
>
> There has undoubtedly been too much emphasis on the "rewards for works" side of the teaching concerning the Judgment Seat of Christ (Romans 14:10; II Corinthians 5:10). It is of primary importance to understand that, while salvation is free through the grace of God (John 4:10; Romans 6:23; Revelation 22:17, etc.) if we have rewards, it will be because we have built up enduring works on the Foundation of Jesus Christ as our personal Saviour (I Corinthians 3:11-15; 9:24; Luke 19:17; Matthew 10:42, etc.).

Many Christians will see much of their "church work" go up as a puff of smoke—"wood, hay and stubble"—because it had nothing to do with the salvation of souls or edification of the saints, and was therefore without enduring quality. Even that could make one most uncomfortable standing before Christ's Judgment Seat.

But, there is another side, for the word "Bema" rendered "Judgment Seat," signifies a place where judgment is rendered and that judgment will have to do not only with our works, but our witness, our stewardship, our LIVING. The Christian's DOING will pass in review—will be exposed. All those matters never confessed and made right with man and God, will come up as on a great screen and it is quite possible that within a brief space of time, one might experience pangs of shame equal to years of mortal sorrows.

I John 2:28 says expressly that some will (lit.) "shrink in shame from Him." At His coming is the time and place where stubborn Christians will be caught up with for all those things never made right. It would appear that even those spirits coming with Him from the heavenly side after long waiting the day of the Judgment Seat, will be capable of having such matters drawn from their memories, for the judgment of all believers is represented as taking place at the same time—when He comes. Bear in mind that the spirits in heaven will not until that time receive their completed condition nor could their works until then be summed up.

Dr. Graham Scroggie, writing to a friend, once said: "I would rather go through the Great Tribulation than endure what I believe some Christians will go through at the Judgment Seat of Christ." In the white light of His glory, who can say what his capacity for a sense of mortification may be when faced with a moving picture of wrongs neither confessed nor straightened out? . . .

"He that doeth wrong shall receive for the wrong he hath done and there is no respect of persons" (Colossians 3:25). Christ will "bring to light the hidden things and will make manifest the counsels of hearts" (I Corinthians 4:5). We shall receive according to what we have done, "Whether it be good or bad" (II Corinthians 5:10).

Teachers of the Word are responsible to warn believers that while God may send them chastening in this life for many of their misdeeds (I Corinthians 11:31, 32; Colossians 3:25; Hebrews 12:7-9) there will still be a day of reckoning for matters left unadjusted at the time they are called out of this world.[11]

Dr. M. R. De Haan:

There is no question that if the average believer in the average church could be more conscious of the fact that every act and every moment, and every talent which he possesses is to pass before the Judgment Seat of Christ, an end would be made to much of the worldliness and sinfulness, and carelessness on the part of believers.

Before they can reign in righteousness with Him, a lot of things which are all wrong among believers now will have to be made right, first. If we do not make them right now, they will be made right at the judgment seat of Christ, and it will not be a pleasant experience for many to see their works burned up and they themselves saved so as by fire, and then consigned to a lower place in the Kingdom with loss of rewards and with many sad regrets.

If Jesus were to return today, I fear that He would find many, many believers quite unprepared for His coming. Those who are living in unconfessed sin and bitterness and pride; Christians who are carnal, selfish and worldly; Christians who are wasting their talents, opportunities, time and privileges. Do not imagine for a moment that these things will all be passed over in grace and forgotten when Jesus comes. Before we can reign with Him, we must be perfectly, spotlessly clean, and if we refuse it now, it will be done at the Judgment Seat of Christ. This is the purpose for this judgment of believers.[12]

Dr. Theodore H. Epp:

At the Judgment Seat of Christ, difficulties and inequalities among the saints will be ironed out. We have so many of these in our present day. All the injustices and misunderstandings of God's people among themselves will then be settled. Those of the saints who were humble, and who endured meekly and unresistingly accusation and malicious gossip for Christ's sake, even from fellow-believers, will be manifested in their true light. They will then be vindicated in the eyes of all, and cleared of all false charges.

We must not overlook the fact that those who in their pride have done and said wrong things, unless they have confessed these things to God and renounced them, will face the consequences of such conduct at the Judgment Seat of Christ by losing rewards.[13]

Dr. Lehman Strauss:

The Judgment Seat of Christ seems a necessity to the writer. Think of the believers, all members of the body of Christ, who are divided because of differences. In organizations, in churches, and in families I have seen Christians who are not on speaking terms. People who were at one time very close and intimate friends are now separated and a bitter feeling exists between them. Each blames the separation on the other, and they continue on, trying to serve the Lord, but their difference has not been adjusted. Now if our Lord returns before there is a reconciliation of such Christians here on earth, it is necessary that they get right with each other somewhere, for certainly they cannot continue on forever in holding hatred and animosity in their hearts. Heaven knows no such actions. Hatred and unforgiveness is sin. Yet there is no sin in Heaven. Hence the necessity of the Judgment Seat of Christ.[14]

Dr. Emery H. Bancroft: "There will be a vast amount of healthy work transacted at the judgment seat of Christ. . . . The mistakes of time will there be rectified; wrong judgments reversed, misunderstandings corrected; ungenerous attempts to impute falsehood or evil where such do not exist, exposed; and, in short, persons, ways, words, motives and acts shall then appear in their true light and character. It will be a clearing up moment. . . . Every difficulty and question between believers and God, and between brother and brother shall then be righteously adjusted."[15]

Dr. Isaac M. Haldeman:

> Each Christian must give an account to Him. You cannot give an account for me. I cannot give an account for you. You must give an account for yourself. I must give an account for myself. We will have to make our speech to Him, give a narrative of our lives as Christians. We shall have to give a reason for what we did and what we did not do. We shall have to tell Him why we neglected His Holy Word, the exercise of prayer, the house of God, and why again and again we refused to meet the responsibility of the profession we made or the service into which He called us. Everything will come out in that all-searching light. . . .
>
> At this Judgment Seat all things will be adjusted by the Lord. All things will be righted and regulated. . . .
>
> Confessed sins will not appear at the Judgment Seat of Christ. Unconfessed sins will be revealed and will weigh the scales of judgment in relation to our work and service.[16]

Dr. Donald G. Barnhouse:

> All our dealings with fellow Christians must be brought out at the

return of the Lord Jesus Christ. The innuendo, slander, backbiting, envy, jealousy, gossiping and lying among Christians is a first-class scandal. . . .

My mind has been very much occupied with thoughts that have grown out of my studies concerning our appearance before the judgment seat of God in Christ. Can we remain careless when we realize that all our deeds will be reviewed there? Unsettled accounts will be fully opened and settled. What we have done as Christians will face us there. . . .

The question is now asked: But if we confess our sins, do we not find forgiveness? Certainly. But after the sinner has found mercy, and after the saint has found forgiveness, several things remain to be dealt with. Do we think for one moment that the terrible words 'that shall he also reap' (Galatians 6:7) apply to this life alone? Shall not much of the reaping be done beyond the grave? Can we think for one moment that death is sufficient to wipe out the neglected duties, the lost opportunities, and the wasted times of this life? We may be sure that the consequences of our character will survive the grave and that we shall face those consequences at the judgment seat of Christ.[17]

Dr. W. H. Griffith Thomas: "While a genuine Christian who becomes a backslider will not be judicially condemned forever, there *will* be a very serious measure of personal and *practical condemnation* when such an one stands before the judgment seat of Christ to be dealt with according to works since conversion."[18]

Dr. W. Myrddin Lewis:

In I John 2:28 we read: "And now, little children, abide in him; that when He shall appear, we may have confidence, and not be ashamed before Him at His coming." Now, the words "not be ashamed" clearly suggest that the Judgment Seat of Christ will be a place where many of His people will be ashamed. They also suggest that it will be a place where many tears of shame will be shed by countless numbers of His people, who in their pilgrimage on earth, failed in their stewardship and thus were made unworthy of the crown which He had set aside for them the day that they were saved. . . .

It may be well if we again, in the light of His immediate appearing, examine ourselves so that no known sin or wrong is left unconfessed, for if we neglect this God-given, merciful exercise and arrive at the Judgment Seat with unconfessed wrongs and sins, then bitter indeed will be our tears as we stand before Him in the presence of all heaven and all His people. . . .[19]

Evangelist John Linton:

Scripture declares that God is keeping a record of the sinner's thoughts, words and deeds. Before an assembled universe at the great white throne in heaven, each man's record will be read out. When the unsaved man stands before God to have his record unfolded, will there be any tears shed there in heaven? What think ye?

But God is also keeping a record of certain sins of the saints. This record includes all unconfessed sin due to an unrepentant heart; all unforgiven sin due to an unforgiving spirit; and all unfaithful service due to an unsurrendered life. A backsliding Christian who dies in his unfaithfulness will face his record at the judgment seat of Christ. A Christian who had wronged his brother and has never repented of his sin before God and man, will have that unconfessed and unforgiven sin to face at the judgment seat of Christ. Question: When the record of his wrong-doing is read out before the whole assembled Church, will there be any tears of shame and regret shed there in Heaven. What think ye?

When the unfaithful Christian reads in the light of eternity the story of his unfaithfulness; when he realizes that the cause of Christ has sorely suffered by his indifference and neglect; when he sees that through him souls have been lost to hell who could have been won for heaven; when he fails to hear the "Well done" given to him that is given to the faithful servants, will that Christian be utterly unmoved by the revelation of his failure? No sorrow over a lost reward? No regret over despised opportunities? No tears of shame in Heaven? What think ye?

Here is a Christian man who has grievously wronged his brother. He never repents of that sin before God or man. He makes a general confession of what he calls "all my sins," but he never drags this particular sin out of its hiding place. He lives and dies unrepentant with that sin unconfessed. What will happen when that man stands before the judgment seat of Christ? The brother he wronged is standing there beside him. What will God do about that? Why, you say, that man will be changed in a moment into the likeness of Christ. He will know nothing but joy in Heaven. Salvation is by grace and all our sins are under the blood of Christ. God will welcome that man into heaven and never mention his sin, whether confessed or unconfessed. My friend, to make that statement is to construe the grace of God as license; is to impugn the holiness of God; is to ignore the fact of human responsibility and to deny the plainest teaching of the Bible. Jesus said, "If thou bring thy gift to the altar, and there rememberest that thy brother hath ought against thee: leave there thy gift before the altar and go thy way: first be reconciled to thy brother, and then come and offer thy gift." If that be required at the altar down here, will it not be required at the altar up yonder? Is the command "first be reconciled" true on earth, but not true once we get to heaven?

Yes, Christians will be brought face to face at the judgment seat with every alienated brother, with every unredressed wrong, with every unconfessed sin, with all unfaithful service.[20]

Alexander Patterson:

There is a searching process here which will be terrible to work done from wrong motives, or works left undone. The judgment of Christ is of persons as well as their works. "Saved as by fire" intimates a searching personal examination. Every secret thing not repented of and confessed, will be exposed, to the shame and mortification of the doer. Paul writes of issues to come up in this judgment: "Therefore judge nothing before the time, until the Lord come, who both will bring to light the hidden things of darkness, and will make manifest the counsels of the hearts: and then shall every man have praise of God." All wrong estimates of men will be set right and the result will be as Christ has said, "many that are first will be last, and the last will be first." All idle words, as Christ said, will be accounted for at the day of this judgment. All unsettled quarrels will be brought to account.[21]

Dr. H. H. Savage:

God's judgment seat is not anything to look forward to with anticipation if there is sin in your heart. It is a fearful thing for God's own children to face Him when He says, "Why weren't you doing what you ought to have done? Why weren't you living as you should have lived? Why weren't you as true to Me as you should have been? Why weren't you?" For we shall all stand before the judgment seat of Christ. . . .

Those at the Judgment Seat of Christ are going to have to confess before Him the things that still need to be confessed. Those who are critics, those who are fault-finders, those who are character assassins, those who are doing everything they can to bring about schisms and difficulties in the church will have to report to Him. They have to confess to Him what sort of influence they have had on earth.[22]

Dr. L. Sale-Harrison:

The seriousness of a Christian's life of failure is clearly outlined in many portions of God's Word, for the life lived outside God's will suffers a dual loss. It has a serious effect on his earthly life in loss of power, joy and communion with God; but the loss revealed at the Judgment Seat of Christ is even more tragic. . . .

Sin must be judged. God cannot condone it. If He does, then He is approving of unrighteousness. This He cannot do. God's grace so marvellously manifested to a Christian cannot be an excuse for sin. If we are not willing to judge ourselves after the Holy Spirit convicts us, then it must be judged at the Judgment Seat of Christ. It must be judged either here, or there; but it must be judged. . . .

Read again I John 1:9: "If we confess our sins, He is faithful and just to forgive us our sins, and to cleanse us from all unrighteousness." Therefore if we do not confess our sins, that unrighteousness —which has not been cleansed—must be manifested (exposed) at the Judgment Seat of Christ. . . .

May we be led by the Spirit of God to examine ourselves and seek the removal of all things which mar fellowship with the Lord; for some do not realize how serious a sin it is to trifle with our opportunities, and to walk out of fellowship with Him.[23]

John R. Rice:

But return again to the Scripture, II Corinthians 5:9-11. Saved people are to receive according to things done in the body, "whether it be good or bad." Those who have done good will have joy and praise from Christ. Do you think those who are reproved for having done bad will not be sad? There, no doubt, will flow some tears!

In fact, to face Christ at that time will be a terror to those who have failed to do His bidding after they were saved. I say "terror"— that is exactly what Paul wrote of that time, by inspiration of God: "Knowing therefore the terror of the Lord," Paul says after describing that judgment of Christians, "we persuade men." I once thought that verse was speaking of the terror with which lost men will face Christ, but it is not so. Knowing the terror that will fall on saved people, saints in Heaven after the rapture who face Christ after a wasted life, Paul went about persuading other Christians to do as he did, laboring that he might be acceptable to Christ when he should stand before the Saviour! In Heaven it will be terrible to face Christ who saved you and keeps you, in your shame over your wasted life! Tears in Heaven!

Paul urged Timothy to be "a workman that needeth not to be ashamed" (II Timothy 2:15), and doubtless spoke of this same time when saints in Heaven will be ashamed and sad as they face Jesus their Saviour. I am not speaking of punishment now, but of tears, of shame and sadness. Surely there will be tears in Heaven over our failure and wasted opportunities.[24]

Dr. S. Franklin Logsdon:

It is a solemn engagement indeed to project our thoughts toward this day when, on bended knees before the fiery eyes of Omniscience, we face the record. Yet the prevailing thought, if any consideration at all is given to it, is that Christ will be a mild-mannered examiner of deeds, and the careless believer continues in his self-centeredness, singing all the while, "That will be glory for me." . . .

We find a number of these pointed warnings regarding the Judgment Seat of Christ, couched in terse, incisive language. They are warnings which, admittedly, we have not taken very seriously. We either ignore them completely or relegate them to other people or transfer their application to another dispensation. Let us briefly allude to three.

The Vengeance of the Lord. "The Lord shall judge his people" (Heb. 10:30, last line). This statement is concise and clear. There can be nothing ambiguous about it. The term "my people" rules out the unbeliever and the Great White Throne Judgment. Its position in the context rules out the Old Testament Jewish saints, for the statement stands in contradistinction to Moses' law in verse 28. The verb is of emphatic future tense, and what other judgment for New Testament believers could be in view if not the Judgment Seat of Christ? It speaks of those who are "sanctified" but who have "done despite to the Spirit of grace." There is to be a time of reckoning for this type of unspiritual behavior.

Now, the disturbing feature of this whole revelation is the immediate statement that "It is a fearful thing to fall into the hands of the living God" (Heb. 10:31). We make no attempt to interpret this, but we do remind the reader with much solemnity that, whatever its sobering content, it is directly connected to the information that "the Lord shall judge his [own] people."

The Terror of the Lord. In seeking to register with the people the seriousness of the inevitable confrontation with Christ at the bema, Paul immediately added this, "Knowing therefore the terror of the Lord, we persuade men" (II Cor. 5:11). Again, we will attempt no explanation, for neither did the apostle. Anticipating the reactions to this outburst of concern, he said, "For if we are beside ourselves (mad, as some would say), it is for God and concerns Him; if we are in our right mind, it is for your benefit" (II Cor. 5:13, Amplified).

An Appropriate Retribution. The Spirit of God has gone to great pains to detail character and conduct for believers, making clear their responsibilities both to God and to man. According to Hebrews 2:1, there is a tearful tendency toward flagrant carelessness, letting such practical truths slip by. The next verse clearly warns that, for every violation and disobedience, there will be an appropriate penalty. How can it be otherwise since God is just? And, further, "How shall we escape (appropriate retribution) if we neglect and refuse to pay attention to such great salvation?" (Heb. 2:3, Amplified).[25]

Dr. F. E. Marsh:

The light of the Lord's presence will illuminate our life, and reveal every secret of our heart; for the counsels of the heart will be revealed, and the hidden things will be seen in the light. What a revelation it will be! Ambitions, not of the Lord, will be seen. Black bitterness against others will be detected. Covetousness of the heart will be unmasked. Deviations from the truth will be discovered. Envyings of others will be revealed. Fault-finding with our brethren will be discerned. Grumblings and murmurings will be disclosed. Heart backslidings and secret faults will be made known. Indulgings of the flesh and selfishness will be unearthed. Judging of others wrongfully will be unfolded. Love of money, ease, and the world will be decried. Mixed motives in work for Christ will be ferreted out. Opportunities lost for doing good and confessing Christ will be shown up. Perverseness of heart, and pleasures not of God will be apparent. Quarrellings, backbiting, anger, and malice will be seen.

Rebelliousness and repinings under God's chastening hand will be distinguished. Selfishness, slanderings, and self-will will be observed. Tremblings before the world will be palpable. Uncleanness of heart will be recognized. Wilfulness and wanderings will be visible. Yearnings for the flesh pots of Egypt will be evident; and zealousness to be had in honor of men will be made plain.[26]

Dr. Robert I. Ketcham:

The question of what happens to the believer whose works are all burned up has been a vexing one. Does he go into the millennial reign as a sort of "silent partner"? Since he has no crown of reward, what position *does* he hold in the reign?

Scripture says the reigning is contingent upon the suffering. II Timothy 2:12: 'If we suffer, we shall also reign with him: if we deny him, he also will deny us.' What about the believer who has never really 'suffered' with Christ? What is his status in the reign? . . .

I do not think the worldly believer will share in the millennial reign.[27]

Then Dr. Ketcham writes in his sermon, "The Carnal Christian At The Judgment Seat Of Christ," telling in a very convincing way why he believes the Scriptures teach that those who do not suffer with Christ, those who do not surrender to Christ and serve Him faithfully, will not reign with Him during the millennium. Then he continues:

Let us put it into an understandable picture. The millennial reign is now on. Day after day King Emmanuel sends His co-reigning bride to the ends of His universe to carry out His biddings. When all the assignments are made for the day, I find myself sitting alone and unassigned. I ask the Lord what *I* am to do in His kingdom today. He replies, "Nothing." I cry out, "Why, Lord, am I not allowed to do something for You today?" He will reply, "Because you were content to do nothing for Me before you arrived here!" Believe me, dear reader, *that* would be "outer darkness" enough for me! Just to see others of my friends and fellow Christians with whom I associated down here going out day after day in responsible co-reigning with my Lord and I am denied that privilege because I took the easy way here will be enough to cause me to weep and sorrow. Just to see others going here and there for Him and with Him and I must remain behind would be "outer darkness" enough! I want none of it. . . .

The general attitudes concerning the matters discussed in this chapter are: First: There will be rewards for faithfulness in various lines of Christian living. Second: The believer does sin, and, as a consequence, receives chastisement, but it is confined to this life only. Third: Some believers will have no reward at the Judgment Seat of Christ, but because chastisement ends with this life, there will be none there.

The difference between this common conception and the view set forth in this chapter is simply this: The principle of chastisement remains the same; the difference is in the extent to which it is to be carried. One halts the process at the Judgment Seat of Christ; the other allows its continuance for those who did not submit to its benefactions here. I have searched in vain for a single Scripture to prove the discontinuance of this principle at the Lord's return. On the other hand a great mass of Scripture, the most of which I have not mentioned here, seems to indicate the awful and soul-searching truth that there is such a thing as corrective discipline when we see Him face to face.

We have been surprised to discover that many teachers have had a conviction that this was the teaching of Scripture, such men as Lange, Dean Alford, Stanley, Goebel, and Govett. And when we read the following from the pen of G. G. Trumbull, editor of The Sunday School Times, are we not led to believe he had some convictions along this line? Writing of the parable of the talents, he said: "If the servant (who is cast into outer darkness) is not a believer, but a mere professor, then we have in this parable nothing to represent the Christian who fails in faithfulness."[28]

Dr. Herbert Lockyer, in an excellent article "The Advent and Youth," agrees that believers must experience the judgment seat of Christ before they are qualified to serve Him in the kingdom. He sees as a prime function of the *bema* the restoration of broken or damaged fellowship among believers. "As the judgment seat of Christ is not a criminal court, but a court of inquiry, it is logical to assume that the Lord and His own are to be alone as all disputes are settled, and all relationships harmonized."[29] In this light, Dr. Lockyer urges the settling of differences now, rather than waiting to experience the shame of adjusting them in front of Christ.

As one of the many Bible teachers who teach that our place and position in the coming world will be decided at the judgment seat, Dr. Lockyer observes, "What the great majority of Christians lose sight of is the fact that they are presently developing themselves for

future positions in Christ's coming kingdom."[30] He urges greater
loyalty to the Lord and the Word, greater service, that we may have
"an abundant entrance" into the Lord's presence.

Evangelist Kenneth F. Dodson:

> The words, "suffer loss" have a far greater significance than many
> believers realize. Both the Lord Jesus and the Apostle Paul point
> out that the greatest reward for the victorious, overcoming child
> of God will be the privilege of sitting upon the throne with the Lord
> Jesus and reigning with Him over this earth for a thousand years.
> The Lord Jesus said, "To him that overcometh will I grant to sit
> with me in my throne" (Rev. 3:21a). (See also Rev. 20:4.) Paul
> said, "If we suffer, we shall also reign as kings together with him:
> if we deny him, he also will deny us the privilege of reigning with
> him" (II Tim. 2:12—[a] literal [translation of the] Greek).
>
> Actually, for the Christian, the judgment seat of Christ is God's
> gateway into the Millennial Kingdom of the Lord Jesus Christ. It
> is there that every Christian's position in the thousand year reign
> will be determined on the basis of God's just evaluation of the
> Christian's life in this sinful world. According to Paul's peerless
> philosophy of life expressed in Romans 8:28, 29, everything in the
> Christian's daily life is designed of God to make the Christian worthy
> of reigning with the Lord Jesus, so that "He may be the first-born
> among many brethren," in His glorious kingdom. Did not the Lord
> Jesus, Himself, say that some would reign with Him over ten cities
> and some would be "unprofitable servants," stripped of every re-
> ward? (Luke 19:11-26).
>
> So, the Christian who is not willing to take his stand for Christ
> "in this wicked and adulterous generation," and accept the per-
> secution which is bound to come (II Tim. 3:12), will really "suffer
> loss" for a thousand years. He will see some other Christian who
> was willing to be either a "living martyr" (Rom. 12:1, 2) or a
> "dying martyr" (Rev. 20:4) sitting with the Lord Jesus in the place
> of honor which might have been his. He will see what a fool he
> was for spending his time and energy for the gadgets and material
> baubles of a twentieth century civilization instead of "seeking first
> the Kingdom of God and His righteousness" (Matt. 6:33). He will
> not lose his salvation, but he will have a "so-as-by-fire entrance" in-
> stead of an "abundant entrance into the everlasting kingdom of our
> Lord and Saviour, Jesus Christ" (II Peter 1:11).
>
> Since the "kings" of the millennial earth bring their "honor and

glory" into the heavenly city on "the earth" (Rev. 21:24) the Christian's foolish preoccupation with "the things which are seen" may cost him the loss of the greatest possible reward for all eternity —the privilege of reigning with the Lord Jesus Christ over "the principalities and powers" of all interstellar space "unto the ages of the ages." How many of God's born-again children are living realistically in the light of the eternal consequences of every thought, word and deed of their lives?

Paul makes it very clear that there will be real judgment of Christians' unconfessed, unforsaken sins at the judgment seat of Christ. To the Colossian Christians he wrote, "Whatsoever ye do, do it heartily, as to the Lord, and not unto men; knowing that of the Lord ye shall receive the reward of the inheritance: for ye serve the Lord Christ. But he that doeth wrong shall receive for the wrong which he hath done, and there is no respect of persons" (Col. 3:23-25). To the Corinthians, he wrote, "For we walk by faith and not by sight. We are confident, I say, and willing to be away from home in the body, and to be at home with the Lord. Wherefore, we are ambitious, that whether at home or away from home, we may be well pleasing to Him. For we must all be exposed to view before the judgment seat of Christ; that every one may receive the things done in his body, according to that he hath done, whether it be good or evil. Knowing therefore the terror of the Lord, we persuade men" (II Cor. 5:7-11, in a literal translation of the Greek).

One very well-read teacher in a large church was very much disturbed at the thought of a Christian facing actual judgment for sins at the judgment seat. She was quite sure that the passage in Colossians must refer to the judgment of Christians' unconfessed sins in this life, until she was asked where and when the victorious Christian will "receive the reward of the inheritance." This she had to admit would be received at the "judgment seat of Christ," so whatever he receives "for the wrong which he hath done," must also be at the bema-seat. Then, with regard to the passage in Corinthians, she said that the judgment was to be for "bad works" and not "sins." When she was asked to give a Scriptural distinction between "bad works" and "sins," she could not do so. Christians are constantly searching for some method of explaining away Paul's teaching concerning the judgment seat of Christ, but it cannot be done. "For we must be exposed to view before the judgment seat," and "there is no respect of persons."[31]

I have purposely quoted many Christian scholars. They have said that the loss at the judgment seat of Christ will be much greater than most of us have thought, not only at the time of the judgment itself, but extending through the millennial reign of Christ.

After speaking of the judgment seat of Christ in 2 Corinthians 5:10, Paul immediately says in the next verse: "Knowing therefore the terror [fear] of the Lord, we persuade men. . . ." I personally know the fear of God and I persuade them to trust the Lord, love Him, honor Him, obey Him, and serve Him faithfully, so that when we meet Him, we will not be "ashamed before Him at His coming" (1 Jn 2:28), but that we shall hear Him say to us: "Well done, thou good and faithful servant: thou hast been faithful over a few things, I will make thee ruler over many things: enter thou into the joy of thy lord" (Mt 25:21).

Give heed to the words of evangelist John Linton:

> In conclusion, I urge every saved man and woman to get right with man. If there is a wrong to be righted, do it dear friend, while yet there is time. If there is a sin unconfessed, confess it this side of the judgment seat. Don't spoil that first interview with Christ by having to be rebuked for unfaithfulness. Give to the blessed Saviour the joy of saying to you, 'Well done.' Begin to live for that day and that world. If you have crossed over the line of separation, turn back this very hour. Cut loose from the things that are sinful or even questionable. If your giving has not been worthy of Christ, start giving sacrificially and in real earnest before death calls you hence. Start today laying up treasure in heaven. You will be there a long time to enjoy it. Give in the light of the judgment seat; forgive as you would be forgiven; live for eternity. And may He present you and me unblamable and unreprovable in His sight.[32]

8

THE TRIBULATION PERIOD
The Darkest Time in Human History

ACCORDING TO THE BIBLE, the time is coming when more than one-half of the world's population will be killed in a short time. This period is called the tribulation and will take place between the rapture of the church and the revelation (or return) of Jesus Christ, a period seven years in length, also known as Daniel's seventieth week. Jesus Christ said of this time: "For then shall be great tribulation, such as was not since the beginning of the world to this time, no, nor ever shall be. And except those days should be shortened, there should no flesh be saved: but for the elect's sake those days shall be shortened" (Mt 24:21, 22).

The word *tribulation* comes from the Latin word *tribulum*, which means a flail, an instrument used in beating out the grains of wheat from the chaff. God is going to beat out sin and judge this Christ-rejecting world.

Three times in the Bible we are told that it will be a time of suffering beyond comparison with anything in previous human history: "And there shall be a time of trouble, such as never was since there was a nation even to that same time" (Dan 12:1); "A day of darkness and of gloominess, a day of clouds and of thick darkness . . . there hath not been ever the like, neither shall be any more after it, even to the years of many generations" (Joel 2:2); "For then shall be great tribulation, such as was not since the beginning of the world to this time, no, nor ever shall be" (Mt 24:21).

Its Characteristics

This seven-year period will be divided into equal parts of three and a half years each, the latter three and a half years called the great tribulation. It is referred to as:

1) "the day of the LORD"—Is 2:12; 13:6, 9; Eze 30:3; Joel 1:15; 2:1, 11, 31; 3:14; Amos 5:18, 20; Ob 15; Zep 1:7, 14; Mal 4:5; Ac 2:20; I Th 5:2; 2 Th 2:2; 2 Pe 3:10
2) "a destruction from the Almighty"—Is 13:6
3) "the indignation"—Is 26:20; 34:2
4) "the time of Jacob's trouble"—Jer 30:7
5) "a time of trouble"—Dan 12:1
6) "a day of darkness and of gloominess, a day of clouds and of thick darkness"—Joel 2:2
7) "a day of wrath, a day of trouble and distress, a day of wasteness and desolation"—Zep 1:15
8) "the great day of his wrath"—Rev 6:17

The character of this period is one of severe judgments on the inhabitants of the earth, both Jews and Gentiles.

The Jews will experience God's judgment because of their national sin and unbelief. God will purge out the rebels from among them (Eze 20:33-38), and two-thirds of them will be killed in "the time of Jacob's trouble" (Zec 13:8, 9). God promises to bring "the third part through the fire." This will be the believing remnant of Israel, of whom Paul writes in Ro 11:26: "And so all Israel shall be saved."

The Gentiles will also experience God's wrath and judgment. God will judge the world because of its wickedness and ungodliness. This judgment will come on all the world. Isaiah declares:

> Howl ye; for the day of the Lord is at hand; it shall come as a destruction from the Almighty. . . . Behold, the day of the Lord cometh, cruel both with wrath and fierce anger, to lay the land desolate: and he shall destroy the sinners thereof out of it. . . . And I will punish the world for their evil, and the wicked for their iniquity. . . . (Is 13:6, 9, 11).
>
> The earth also is defiled under the inhabitants thereof; because they have transgressed the laws, changed the ordinance, broken the everlasting covenant. Therefore hath the curse devoured the earth, and they that dwell therein are desolate: therefore the inhabitants of

the earth are burned, and few men left. Fear, and the pit, and the snare, are upon thee, O inhabitant of the earth. And it shall come to pass, that he who fleeth from the noise of the fear shall fall into the pit; and he that cometh up out of the midst of the pit shall be taken in the snare: for the windows from on high are open, and the foundations of the earth do shake. The earth is utterly broken down, the earth is clean dissolved, the earth is moved exceedingly. The earth shall reel to and fro like a drunkard, and shall be removed like a cottage; and the transgression thereof shall be heavy upon it; and it shall fall, and not rise again. And it shall come to pass in that day, that the Lord shall punish the host of the high ones that are on high, and the kings of the earth upon the earth. (Is 24:5, 6, 17-21).

Other Old Testament passages which also look ahead to this judgment are Isaiah 26:20, 21; 34:1, 2; Jeremiah 25:29-33; 30:23, 24; and Zephaniah 1:17, 18. From the New Testament comes the following passage: "And the kings of the earth, and the great men, and the rich men, and the chief captains, and the mighty men, and every bondman, and every free man, hid themselves in the dens and in the rocks of the mountains; and said to the mountains and rocks, Fall on us, and hide us from the face of him that sitteth on the throne, and from the wrath of the Lamb: For the great day of his wrath is come; and who shall be able to stand?" (Rev 6:15-17).

Not only is the tribulation a time of severe divine judgment, but it will also be a time of salvation for a great multitude. God uses two witnesses and the ministry of the 144,000 servants of God—12,000 each from twelve tribes of Israel (Rev 7:1-8). As a result of their ministry, we are told that "a great multitude, which no man could number, of all nations, and kindreds, and people, and tongues, stood before the throne, and before the Lamb, clothed with white robes, and palms in their hands" (Rev 7:9). When the question was asked, "Who are these people in the white robes?" the answer was given: "These are they which came out of great tribulation [the Greek reads 'tribulation, the great one'], and have washed their robes and made them white in the blood of the Lamb" (Rev 7:13, 14).

When these 144,000 Jews experience conversion after the rapture, persecution will also come on them, pressuring them to scatter through the world, similar to the early church. They too will go "every where preaching the word" (Ac 8:4).

In addition to using the two witnesses and the 144,000 servants, God will also send an angel, "having the everlasting gospel to preach unto them that dwell on the earth, and to every nation, and kindred, and tongue, and people, saying with a loud voice, Fear God, and give glory to him; for the hour of his judgment is come: and worship him that made heaven, and earth, and the sea, and the fountains of waters" (Rev 14:6, 7).

William R. Newell comments on this:

> Now we find an *angel* flying in mid heaven proclaiming this eternal gospel. This should not astonish us. It is then no longer the Church age, when the gospel of reconciliation through the blood of the Cross is being proclaimed for simple faith. (How astonishing that any Christian should *dream* that the true *Church* is on earth at the time we are considering!) Angels warned Lot in Sodom and rescued him from doom. The Law on Sinai was ministered by angels (Acts 7:53; Galatians 3:19) and especially by one—possibly Michael (Exodus 23:20-23; 33:2).[1]

The message which will be preached during the tribulation period will be the gospel of the kingdom, the same message that was preached by John the Baptist, Jesus, and His disciples: "Repent ye: for the kingdom of heaven is at hand" (Mt 3:2; 4:17; 10:7). In the tribulation they will preach that the kingdom will soon be established by the return of Jesus Christ to the earth.

Besides the great multitude which will be saved during the tribulation and martyred (Rev 7:9-17), there will be many more who will be saved but escape martyrdom and come to the close of the tribulation. Jesus referred to them as "sheep" (Gentiles) and "my brethren" (Jews) as recorded in Matthew 25:31-46; and to them Jesus will say: "Come, ye blessed of my Father, inherit the kingdom prepared for you from the foundation of the world" (Mt 25:34).

Dr. Herman A. Hoyt writes of these two groups: "With these two saved companies of people—living Israelites and living Gentiles—the millennial kingdom will be populated. In these two companies of the saved God will make a new departure during the period of the kingdom in order to fulfill His eternal purpose."[2]

There will be at least five companies of Jews saved in the tribulation: 1) the 144,000 (Rev 7:1-8); 2) those Jews who will be in the multitude out of every nation, kindred, people, and tongue (Rev

7:9-17); 3) those who flee into the wilderness and are under God's protection (Rev 12:6, 13, 14); 4) the remnant back in the land who has the testimony of Jesus Christ (Rev 12:17); and 5) those Jews who will confess Jesus Christ as their Saviour and Messiah when He appears to them at His revelation (Zec 12:10; 13:8, 9).

Hearing that many will be saved during the tribulation, people sometimes ask: "Will an unbeliever have a second chance to be saved during that time?" Though there will be a great multitude saved during this period, I believe the Bible teaches that those who have heard the gospel before the rapture and have rejected Jesus Christ will not have another opportunity to be saved after Christ comes for His own. Paul speaks of those who "received not the love of the truth, that they might be saved. And for this cause God shall send them strong delusion, that they should believe a lie: That they all might be damned who believed not the truth, but had pleasure in unrighteousness" (2 Th 2:10-12).

Its Course

The tribulation begins with the signing of a covenant between the Antichrist and the Jews for a period of seven years (Daniel's seventieth week, Dan 9:24-27). This treaty will guarantee protection to Israel so that she may rebuild her temple and reestablish her ancient religious rituals of Judaism. The Antichrist will attempt to settle the Arab-Israeli dispute and will side with Israel in her claim to the land of Palestine.

There will be three series of judgments in the tribulation: the seven seal judgments; the seven trumpets judgments; and the seven vials judgments, all of them referred to in Revelation 6-19.

The seven seal judgments

These judgments are the first judgments of the tribulation and will probably occur early in the period.

The First Seal Judgment (Rev 6:1, 2). A white horse represents the Antichrist who comes to conquer.

The Second Seal Judgment (Rev 6:3, 4). A red horse represents bloodshed; peace is taken from the earth at this time.

The Third Seal Judgment (Rev 6:5, 6). A black horse represents famine; a day's wages will buy only one-eighth the normal supply of food.

The Fourth Seal Judgment (Rev 6:7, 8). A pale horse represents death, when one-fourth of the world's population will be killed. Today there are approximately three and one-half billion people on the earth. When the Lord Jesus comes for His own at the rapture, it is estimated that only 2 percent of the population of the world will be removed. If we would take the figure of three billion as those left after the Rapture, this judgment may mean that 750 million people will be killed at this time.

The Fifth Seal Judgment (Rev 6:9-11). This speaks of those who will be martyred in the tribulation period for "the word of God, and for the testimony which they held."

The Sixth Seal Judgment (Rev 6:12-17). At this time there will be drastic physical changes in the earth and sky, which will produce terror in the hearts of people; and they will try to hide from God and from Christ, knowing that "the great day of his wrath is come."

The Seventh Seal Judgment (Rev 8:1). When this seal is opened, there is silence in heaven for half an hour. Newell comments on this: "Again, on the other hand, this is an ominous silence! It is the calm before the storm. God, the Lamb, the four living ones, the twenty-four elders, the seraphim of Isaiah 6, the hundred million and millions of angels, the Church, the martyrs beneath the altar—all *silent*. Meditate on this scene: it greatly grows upon your soul!"[3]

THE SEVEN TRUMPET JUDGMENTS

When the seventh seal is opened, the seven trumpet judgments are introduced.

The First Trumpet Judgment (Rev 8:7). At this time, there will be hail and fire mingled with blood; one-third of the trees and all green grass will be burned. Clarence Larkin says of this judgment, "There is no need to spiritualize this. It means just what it says"; and Newell says, "But it will occur, literally!"

The Second Trumpet Judgment (Rev 8:8, 9). When this second trumpet sounds, what appears to be a great mountain is dropped into the sea; one-third of the sea becomes blood, one-third of the sea creatures die, and one-third of all ships are destroyed.

The Third Trumpet Judgment (Rev 8:10, 11). A burning star falls on a third of all rivers and springs of water, making them bitter, and many die because of the poisoned water.

The Fourth Trumpet Judgment (Rev 8:12, 13). This judgment affects the sun, moon, and stars, and the day-night cycle, so that the day and night are shortened by one-third. This perhaps means that the twenty-four-hour cycle will be shortened to sixteen hours.

The Fifth Trumpet Judgment (Rev 9:1-12). This is also the first of three "woes," and out of the bottomless pit, literally the "abyss," come locusts upon the earth which will torment men for a period of five months. They are creatures like locusts, but demonic in nature; and their torment is like a scorpion's sting. It has been said that the pain from the sting of a scorpion, though not generally fatal, is possibly the most intense of any wound inflicted by an animal. The torment will be so severe that men will try to commit suicide to escape their suffering, but God will not permit them to take their lives.

The Sixth Trumpet Judgment (Rev 9:13-21). This is the second woe, in which a large army of 200 million horsemen will kill one-third of the population. It seems that these will be supernatural horsemen, although some commentators say that these will be the armies of the Orient as they march to Armageddon. It is interesting to note that, according to an Associated Press release, April 24, 1964, in China alone in 1961, there were an estimated 200 million armed and organized militiamen.

In two judgments in the tribulation, one-half of the world's population will be killed. Under the fourth seal judgment, one-fourth will be killed (Rev 6:8), and under the sixth trumpet judgment, one-third will be killed.

The Seventh Trumpet Judgment (Rev 11:15-19). The sounding of the seventh trumpet announces the end and includes all that happens in the rest of the period. The announcement is preliminary to all of the great events that are yet to come, including the last seven vial judgments. This is also the third woe.

THE SEVEN VIAL JUDGMENTS

This is the third series of judgments, called the seven last plagues, in which "is filled up the wrath of God" (Rev 15:1). They are also called the "vials of the wrath of God" (Rev 16:1), that is, the judgments of the bowls of God's wrath.

The First Vial Judgment (Rev 16:2). This brings a sore described as "noisome and grevious" upon the men who had the mark of the beast and who worshipped his image. These sores will be malignant, horrible in appearance, and very painful.

The Second Vial Judgment (Rev 16:3). The sea becomes as the blood of a dead man, and every animal or fish in the sea will die. Think of 72 percent of the earth's surface becoming blood, and the stench and disease caused by all these creatures dying!

The Third Vial Judgment (Rev 16:4-7). Here the rivers and the springs of waters become blood; and it is said of those living in that day that they deserve this, because they had shed the blood of the saints and prophets.

The Fourth Vial Judgment (Rev 16:8, 9). The heat is intensified and men are scorched with great heat. In spite of this, they blaspheme the name of God, and do not repent.

The Fifth Vial Judgment (Rev 16:10, 11). This plague will bring darkness over the earth, and men will gnaw their tongues because of the pain; but they will continue to blaspheme God and refuse to repent.

The Sixth Vial Judgment (Rev 16:12-16). This causes the river Euphrates to dry up, so that the kings of the east (China, Japan, India) can cross it and march to the Battle of Armageddon. Kipling wrote:

> Oh East is East and West is West,
> And never the twain shall meet,
> Till earth and sky stand presently
> At God's great judgment Seat.

But Kipling didn't know that one day East and West will come together in a great meeting to oppose God and Jesus Christ, more than a thousand years before "God's great judgment seat."

The Seventh Vial Judgment (Rev 16:17-21). This seventh vial covers the whole period from the time it is poured out until Christ returns to the Mount of Olives. Under this judgment six "great" things are mentioned: 1) "a *great* voice" (v. 17); 2) "a *great* earthquake" (v. 18), so great that it is described as one "such as was not since men were upon the earth"; 3) "the *great* city" (v. 19), which is broken into three parts by the earthquake; 4) "*great* Babylon"

(v. 19); 5) "a *great* hail" (v. 21), of which each hailstone weighs about a hundred pounds; and 6) "*great* plague" (v. 21).

In a leaflet by Dr. Charles E. Fuller, the course of events in the tribulation is summarized very well:

Events of First 3½ Years	1. The Jews will return to Their Land in Unbelief. Isaiah 43:5-7.
	2. The Temple Will be Rebuilt. Revelation 11:1-2.
	3. The Anti-Christ Will Appear. II Thessalonians 2:3.
	4. Israel Will Enter Into a Covenant With The Anti-Christ. Daniel 9:27.
	5. Testimony of the Two Witnesses. Revelation 11:3.
Events of Second 3½ Years	6. At the End of 3½ Years Anti-Christ is Revealed in His True Character. Daniel 9:27.
	7. Anti-Christ Kills the Two Witnesses. Revelation 11:7.
	8. He Stops the Daily Sacrifices. Daniel 9:27; 11:31; 12:11.
	9. His Image Set Up for Worship. Matthew 24:15; II Thessalonians 2:4; Revelation 13:14.
	10. The Devil Cast to the Earth. Revelation 12:7-12.
	11. The Holy City Trodden Down. Daniel 9:26; Revelation 11:2.
	12. The Judgments of the Tribulation. Jeremiah 30:7; Daniel 12:1; Matthew 24:21; Revelation 13:14, 17. Seals, trumpets, vials of Revelation 6-16.
	13. Death for Defiance of Anti-Christ. Revelation 13:15.
	14. The Mark of the Beast. Revelation 13:16-17.
	15. Armageddon. Revelation 16:14-16, 17:14; Zechariah 14:1-5.

Events
which conclude
and immediately
follow the
Tribulation

16. Christ and His Glorified Saints Return. Jude 14; Revelation 1:7, 19:11-16; II Thessalonians 1:7.
17. Israel Delivered. Revelation 17:14; Zechariah 12:9.
18. Beast and False Prophet Destroyed. Revelation 13:16-17.
19. Satan Bound. Revelation 20:2-3.
20. Tribulation Martyrs Raised. Revelation 20:4.[4]

ITS CLIMAX

This tribulation period is climaxed by the second coming of Jesus Christ to this earth, when He "cometh with clouds; and every eye shall see him" (Rev 1:7). Heaven will open and Christ, the rider on the white horse will appear, leading the armies of heaven (Rev 19:11-14). The nations of the world will be gathered against Jerusalem and "then shall the Lord go forth, and fight against those nations, as when he fought in the day of battle. And his feet shall stand in that day upon the mount of Olives" (Zec 14:3, 4).

The Antichrist, the world rulers, and their armies will gather together to fight against Christ and His army. The Antichrist and false prophet will be taken and thrown alive into the lake of fire; the rest of the armies of earth will be slain by Jesus Christ and left for the carrion birds to gorge themselves (Rev 19:19-21). This is the Battle of Armageddon which will be spoken of in another chapter. Thus, the tribulation comes to a close with Jesus Christ and His armies triumphant over Satan and his armies.

If you are a Christian, you can thank God that you will never be exposed to these awful judgments, because God's Word promises deliverance for His own from that period of trouble. (*See* chapter 9, The Church Will Not Go Through the Tribulation—Seven Reasons Why.") Christ will come and take away at one time all who are His before these judgments fall upon the earth.

If you are not a Christian, I pray that you will right now repent of your sins, receive Jesus Christ as your own personal Saviour and Lord, and then you will be able "to escape all these things that shall come to pass, and to stand before the Son of man" (Lk 21:36). Do it now, because it will be too late one second after the rapture when Jesus comes.

9

THE CHURCH WILL NOT GO THROUGH THE TRIBULATION
Seven Reasons Why

A FEW YEARS AGO I was in Michigan for a week of meetings in a church. About the middle of the week, the pastor of the church asked me, "Carl, you wouldn't press your views of eschatology on everybody, would you?" I immediately answered, "No, I wouldn't press them, but I would preach them." He said, "But I don't agree with you. I believe the church will go through the tribulation." "You don't have a leg to stand on," I replied.

For the rest of the week we discussed in a friendly way what we thought the Bible taught concerning this subject. At the close of the week he said to me, "You know, Carl, now I believe the church could be raptured in the middle of the tribulation."

I said to him, "I talk to you for a few days and you move back three and a half years." He replied, "Since I have moved back three and a half years, why don't you move up three and a half years?" I told him, "No, I know what I believe and why I believe it. I believe the church will be raptured before the tribulation."

I shared with him what I had read in a message given by Dr. Vance Havner. Speaking of the need to know what the Bible teaches concerning God's plan, Dr. Havner said, "Scholarship doesn't have the answer. When it comes to understanding the future of this world, the meaning of history and the secret of destiny, unless a man understands God's plan and purpose, a Ph.D. just means phenomenal dud!"[1]

135

About a year later, I was back in the same church for meetings. He was no longer the pastor there, but he did come with his family for one of the services. I was invited to his home after the service. We talked for awhile, then he asked me, "Carl, have you changed your views on eschatology since I saw you?" I again said to him, "No, I know what I believe and why I believe it." He then said, "Carl, how could a man of your ability still believe like that?"

Once again we had a friendly discussion, and after a few more minutes he said, " I believe Christ could come today." I quickly said to him, "Good—let's shake hands and drop the discussion right here."

I have been taught from the beginning of my Christian life that the church would not pass through the tribulation. Although I have found in my studies that many people believe and teach otherwise, I am more convinced than I have ever been that Christ will rapture His church before the awful tribulation period which is coming upon the earth, when more than half of the world's population will be killed.

Many Bible students of prophecy believe that the Word of God teaches a pretribulation rapture of the church.

Dr. John F. Walvoord has given fifty arguments for the pretribulation rapture of the church in his book *The Rapture Question.*[2] I want to give only seven reasons why the church will not go through the Tribulation.

By the church I mean every born-again believer, every person who has received Jesus Christ as his own personal Saviour and Lord during this age of grace, the true body of Christ, the true bride of Christ.

By the tribulation I mean the seven-year period of intense trouble which is yet to come upon the earth, described in the Olivet discourse, the book of the Revelation, and elsewhere in the Bible, in fulfillment of the prophecy of Daniel's seventieth week (Dan 9:24-27).

The Church Is Promised Deliverance

In a message to John, Jesus promised the church in Philadelphia (an ancient city in what is now Turkey), "Because thou hast kept the word of my patience, I also will keep thee from the hour of temptation, which shall come upon all the world, to try them that dwell upon the earth" (Rev 3:10). There are some who say that this promise is only to the Philadelphian church in the first century, but the language of the promise goes beyond a local persecution of that church.

These seven letters to the seven churches in Revelation 2 and 3 were written to the churches of the world during any period of church history, for individual Christians at any time during the church age; and they give a prophetic forecast of the entire church age. Philadelphia represents the true church at the end of the age, and to this true church was given the promise of being kept from "the hour of temptation." Notice, this verse speaks of the "hour of temptation, which shall come upon *all the world*," thus indicating a worldwide time of temptation, or trial. The promise is to "keep from" not to "keep in," as Thiessen states: "We should note that the promise is not merely to be kept from the *trial*, but from the *hour* of trial, i.e., it holds out exemption from the period of trial, not only from the trial during that period."[3]

Dr. Gerald B. Stanton comments, " 'The hour of temptation' is to fall on 'earth dwellers,' a designation which occurs constantly throughout the Tribulation portion of the book of Revelation but which never suggests a heavenly people (Rev. 6:10; 8:13; 11:10; 12:12; 13:8, 12, 14; 14:6; 17:2, 8)."[4]

THE CHURCH IS NOT APPOINTED TO WRATH

"For God hath not appointed us to wrath, but to obtain salvation by our Lord Jesus Christ" (1 Th 5:9). Paul is speaking here of the wrath that is to come upon the unsaved at the end of this age, the wrath and anguish of the great tribulation. To prove that he is promising that the church is not appointed to wrath, he repeats what he had already said to them concerning the rapture, "Wherefore comfort yourselves together" (1 Th 5:11; cf. 4:18). Compare "Jesus died and rose again" (4:14) with "Jesus Christ Who died for us" (5:9, 10); "we which are alive . . . them which are asleep" (4:17, 13) with "whether we wake or sleep" (5:10); "caught up together . . . to meet the Lord in the air" (4:17) with "we should live together with him" (5:10).

In these two chapters, I Thessalonians 4 and 5, Paul taught that the rapture would be God's method of escape from the wrath of the tribulation.

One posttribulation writer said, "It is a blunder that the Great Tribulation consists of God's wrath."[5] All we need do to refute this is to look at some Scripture verses, such as Revelation 6:16, 17; 11:18; 14:10, 19; 15:1, 7; 16:1, 19; 19:15.

God saves His own from divine wrath. He saved Rahab out of Jericho before the city was destroyed (Jos 6:25); Lot was removed from Sodom before God's wrath was poured out on that city (Gen 9:14-24); Enoch was translated before the judgment of the flood (Gen 5:24); and thank God, those who are His when Jesus returns for His own at the rapture will be saved from the wrath of the tribulation.

THE CHURCH IS NOT MENTIONED DURING THE TRIBULATION

The book of Revelation is divided by Jesus Christ into three distinct parts, according to Revelation 1:19: 1) "the things which thou hast seen" (chapter 1), 2) "the things which are" (chapters 2 and 3), and 3) "the things which shall be hereafter" (chapters 4-22). The word *church* is mentioned seven times in chapters 1-3; the word *churches* is mentioned twelve times in chapters 1-3; but neither word is mentioned again in chapters 4-19, the chapters which describe the tribulation judgments. "The things which shall be hereafter" speak of those things which follow "the things which are" (things referring to the church in chapters 2 and 3). The church is seen in Revelation 4 already in heaven, represented by the twenty-four elders.

THE CHURCH IS TO WATCH FOR THE IMMINENT RETURN OF CHRIST

Imminent means that it may occur at any moment, that it is overhanging, that it is impending; and as applied to the coming of Christ, it means that He may come at any moment, that no one knows the time, and that the church should be in a constant state of expectancy, looking and watching for His return.

It is very evident as you read the New Testament that the first-century Christians expected Christ to return at any moment. Paul said, "We shall not all sleep, but we shall all be changed, in a moment, in the twinkling of an eye, at the last trump" (1 Co 15:51, 52); "For our conversation is in heaven; from whence we look for the Saviour, the Lord Jesus Christ" (Phil 3:20); "ye turned to God from idols to serve the living and true God; and to wait for his Son from heaven" (1 Th 1:9, 10).

Dr. H. C. Thiessen comments: "Paul . . . does not ask us to look for the Tribulation, or the Antichrist, or for persecution and martyrdom, or for death, but for the return of Christ. If any of these events must precede the Rapture, then how can we help looking for them rather than the Lord's coming? Such a view of the coming of the Lord can at best only induce a very general interest in the 'blessed hope.' "[6]

James wrote, "Be ye also patient; stablish your hearts: for the coming of the Lord draweth nigh" (Ja 5:8). John wrote, "He which testifieth these things saith, surely I come quickly. Amen. Even so, come, Lord Jesus" (Rev 22:20).

These promises were given to the entire church, for the entire age, and are so worded that Christians in any generation could and should expect Christ in their day and be blessed and comforted by "that blessed hope" (Titus 2:13).

Not only did the first-century Christians expect Christ at any moment, but Christians in other centuries also have believed in His imminent return. Jesse Forest Silver, in his book, *The Lord's Return: Seen in History and in Scripture as Premillennial and Imminent*, says concerning the ante-Nicene Fathers: "By tradition they knew the faith of the Apostles. They taught the doctrine of the imminent and premillennial return of the Lord."[7]

William R. Newell, in *The Book of the Revelation*, writes:

> Who have been the teachers and preachers of Christ's imminent coming? We have such men as John Darby, who was probably the greatest interpreter of Scripture since Paul, with such early Brethren as C. H. Mackintosh, J. G. Bellett, Wm. Kelly, and the rest, a marvelous coterie. Then you have C. H. Spurgeon. It is idle to claim that he was not looking for Christ's coming. He split no hairs such as the post-tribulationalists do, but boldly and constantly proclaimed the second coming of Christ as an actual and a daily possibility. D. L. Moody was a wonderful witness to any truth God revealed to him; and his sermon on "The Second Coming of Christ" is a classic. He was looking for the Lord's coming. George C. Needham, beloved Irishman; Wm. E. Blackstone, whose life has been to look for his Lord; James H. Brookes, a mighty warrior, now

with the Lord; A. B. Simpson, of whom Moody said, "Everything
he says reaches my heart." All these were looking for Christ's appearing. It was the hope of their lives. H. M. Parsons, of Toronto,
and Dr. Weston . . . faithful witnesses alike. Grand old I. M. Haldeman, of New York, as well as J. Wilbur Chapman, now with Christ.
A. T. Pierson, of wonderful penetration in the meaning of Scripture;
A. J. Gordon; George E. Guille . . . devoted, gentle, sane, yet a con-
tender for Christ's imminent coming; our Brother Ironside, whose
praise is among the real churches of Christ; Lewis Sperry Chafer at
Dallas; A. C. Gaebelein, of New York, Editor of Our Hope, perhaps
the most persistent, faithful witness for over fifty years to the imminent return of our Lord . . . James M. Gray, late President of the
Moody Bible Institute of Chicago . . . a host of faithful witnesses to
Christ's imminent coming, in Great Britain, Scandinavia, the mission
fields, and Australasia.[8]

Evangelist John Linton states it well: "Put the Church through the
Tribulation and Christ cannot come for years. Destroy the immi-
nence of the coming and the many Scriptures declaring an unan-
nounced advent would present hopeless contradiction. Every injunc-
tion to daily watchfulness for Christ's return loses its significance if
several years of tribulation precedes the Rapture."[9]

Dr. Gerald B. Stanton speaks of the imminency of Christ's return:

> For these many years, believers have been looking and watching
> for their Lord from glory. They have believed that, while His
> coming might not be immediate, nor necessarily in their lifetime,
> His coming could be very soon. Weary from the presence of sin or
> in pain from the presence of sickness, in the morning they have said,
> "Perhaps today!" and in the evening they have whispered, "Perhaps
> tonight!" They have "loved his appearing," viewing it as imminent,
> and so have watched for the return of the Saviour. Yet, with it all,
> they have lived in accord with that other most practical exhortation,
> "Occupy till I come." As Blackstone well says:
>
> "True watching is an attitude of mind and heart which would joy-
> fully and quickly turn from any occupation to meet our Beloved,
> rapturously exclaiming 'this is the Lord; we have waited for Him.'"
>
> Needless to say, the posttribulation view discredits and robs the
> Biblical exhortations to watchfulness of any real significant mean-
> ing.[10]

The Church Is to be Judged and Married Between the Rapture and the Revelation

Homer Duncan, in his excellent booklet, *An Outline Of Things to Come,* clearly speaks: "There must be an interval between the Rapture and the Revelation. Christ cannot come for His own and with His own at the same time. . . . it is logical to believe that there will be an interval of some kind. It is reasonable to believe that the tribulation on earth and the Judgment Seat of Christ and the Marriage supper of the Lamb will take place during this interval."[11]

The judgment seat of Christ and the marriage supper of the Lamb are literal events and will not be fulfilled in a fleeting moment, as some posttribulational writers teach. One of these writers, James R. Graham, Jr., states: "On the same 'day' and probably only a few moments apart, He comes for His saints, and with His saints (I Thessalonians 4:16, 17). The dead and living go up to meet Him as He descends, join His train and accompany Him back as He stands on the Mount of Olives and destroys Antichrist and his armies."[12] It will take more than "a few moments" to review the lives of all the Christians, to give the rewards, and to celebrate the Marriage Supper.

Dr. Stanton has written logically:

> From this point, a quick review of the nature of the Church and the character of the Tribulation, of promises which exempt the Church from any wrath poured out by God, of the shift in viewpoint from earth to heaven at Revelation 4:1, revealing crowned and glorified elders who worship Christ and sing the song of the redeemed—such a review should convince any candid mind that the place of the rapture in the chronology of the Revelation and in the order of prophetic events is clearly pretribulational. On the other hand, since intervening events require a marked interval between the rapture and the revelation, the whole posttribulational idea that these two phases of our Lord's return are only moments apart, if not simultaneous, is demonstrated to be utterly untenable.[13]

The Church Is to Be Removed Before the Antichrist Is Revealed

Some were teaching in Paul's day that the day of the Lord had already come ("day of Christ" in 2 Thessalonians 2:2 is better translated "day of the Lord"), so Paul writes in this chapter to give them, and us, some clear teaching concerning the rapture and the day of the Lord which follows. He gives assurance that this day will not come until "there come a falling away [or apostasy] first, and that man of sin be revealed, the son of perdition [the Antichrist]" (v. 3). Then he speaks of a restrainer or one who "withholdeth" (v. 6), who will be "taken out of the way" (v. 7).

Many are the views of those who attempt to identify the restrainer. Some say the Roman Empire (Alexander Reese), the Jewish state (B. B. Warfield), human government (C. F. Hogg and W. E. Vine), Satan (Mrs. George C. Needham), Paul himself (Schott), a collection of saints at Jerusalem (Wieseler), the succession of Roman emperors (Wordsworth), the church, etc.[14]

It is believed by many excellent prophetic scholars that the restrainer is none other than the Holy Spirit: E. Schuyler English, J. Dwight Pentecost, John F. Walvoord, William K. Harrison, and Charles C. Ryrie, to name a few. A typical comment comes from Herman Hoyt:

> A careful exegesis of II Thessalonians 2:6-8 indicates that a Restrainer will be removed. This restrainer must be the Holy Spirit (Gen. 6.3). He has been responsible for restraining evil through all of human history, and He has performed this function through the people of God. In this dispensation the people of God are the church. By rapture the church will be caught away and in that sense the Spirit will be removed. This opens the way for the Antichrist to appear on the scene, make his covenant with Israel (Dan. 9:27), and usher in the period of tribulation which runs concurrently with the seventieth week of Daniel.[15]

H. C. Thiessen asserts "that which 'withholdeth' (neuter, ver. 6) and 'he who letteth' (hindereth) (masculine, ver. 7), is none other than the Holy Sipirit."[16] Gerald Stanton, after also identifying the restrainer as the Holy Spirit, concludes: "The removal of the Spirit takes place before the Wicked One shall be revealed, and this removal sets the time for the rapture of the Church. Thus II Thessalonians 2:6, 7 adds a considerable weight of evidence to the teaching of other Scriptures that the rapture of the Church is clearly pretribulational."[17]

These men—and many more could be quoted—are in agreement that the restrainer is the Holy Spirit. The Holy Spirit indwells the true Christians, who make up the true church. As long as the Holy Spirit is resident in the church, His restraining work will continue, and the Antichrist cannot be revealed. When the church is removed, His restraining ministry ceases and the Antichrist will be revealed. (The Holy Spirit does not cease His ministries when the church is removed, nor does He cease to be omnipresent, but the restraining ministry ceases). Therefore, since the Antichrist appears at the beginning of Daniel's seventieth week, which is equivalent to the tribulation, and the Holy Spirit is taken out of the way before the Antichrist appears, the church, which is the temple of the Holy Spirit, must be removed before the tribulation begins.

The Church Is Made up of "Ambassadors for Christ"

Christians are called "ambassadors for Christ" (2 Co 5:20), and are to represent our country, heaven, in a foreign country, earth. We are to speak the Word of heaven's King, and work as led by Him. As ambassadors, we are to beg men in Christ's behalf to be reconciled to God.

Before a nation declares war on another nation, it calls its ambassador home. Before God pours out His wrath and judgments on this earth, He will call His ambassadors home to heaven. "Even so, come, Lord Jesus." As we wait for Him, look for Him, love His appearing, may we be encouraged and exhorted by the words of James H. Brookes:

> If we heartily and practically believe that the Lord may come for His people at any moment, it must separate from the world, and kill selfishness, and blast the roots of personal ambition, and increase brotherly love, and intensify zeal, and deepen concern for the salvation of the lost, and give comfort in affliction, and put us in a state of preparedness for the great interview, like a bride arraying herself to meet her bridegroom. Oh, there is no truth in the Bible that can bring greater blessing to the soul, when received in the power of the Holy Ghost, but this blessing is largely hindered if we are taught to expect that our gathering together unto Him lies beyond the appalling tribulation that shall come upon all the world.[18]

After giving seven very good and strong points as to why the church will not pass through the tribulation, in his book *Will The Church Pass Through The Tribulation?*, Dr. Henry C. Thiessen concluded:

> From all this we conclude that the doctrine of the Pre-Tribulation Rapture is not the invention of man, whether early or late in the history of the Church, but the clear teaching of the sure word of prophecy.
>
> We may then comfort one another with the thought that the Church will not pass through the Tribulation. The "blessed hope" is not some distant event that has little practical value for the believer, but an imminent prospect. Our Lord may come at any time and receive us to Himself. Therefore let us look for Him at all times, purify ourselves as He is pure, and labor for the salvation of others until He shall actually appear.[19]

10

WHEN RUSSIA INVADES THE MIDDLE EAST

DAILY WE READ OR HEAR of the Middle East. Recently, I checked some of the titles of articles in news magazines: "Is the Middle East about to Explode Again?"; "Why War Threatens Again in the Middle East"; "Can Mideast War Be Averted?"; "Zero Hour for the Middle East"; "The Mideast: Another Step Closer to Explosion"; "President's Warning on Mideast: 'More Dangerous than Vietnam' "; "Mideast: Alarm Signals for U. S. and Russia"; "Russia's Gamble in the Mideast"; "Why Moscow Risks New Mideast War"; "Russia's Menacing New Challenge in the Middle East."

According to the Bible, Russia will one day march upon the Middle East to the nation of Israel. The complete description of this is found in two chapters in the Bible, Ezekiel 38 and 39. General Moshe Dayan said in 1968, "The next war will not be with Arabs, but with the Russians."[1]

THE PARTICIPANTS IN THE INVASION

In Ezekiel 38:1-6, God names five nations which will come with Gog and Magog against the nation of Israel: Persia (Iran), Ethiopia (Cush), Libya (Put), Gomer, and Togarmah.

There are some people who believe these two chapters in Ezekiel do not speak of Russia. They say that Bible scholars try to twist Bible passages to fit into the current picture. For those who are not sure Russia is referred to in this prophecy, I want to show why many Bible scholars believe she is.

The footnote for Ezekiel 38:2 in the Scofield Bible declares: "That

145

the primary reference is to the northern (European) powers, headed up by Russia, all agree. . . . 'Gog' is the prince, 'Magog,' his land. The reference to Meshech and Tubal (Moscow and Tobolsk) is a clear mark of identification."

Magog was the second son of Japheth (Gen 10:1, 2), who was one of the three sons of Noah. His descendants seemed to have inhabited the region of the Caucasus and northern Armenia. The word *Caucasus* means "Gog's fort." During World War II, England received fifty thousand lead pencils from Russia with this imprint upon them: "Gog of Magog."[2]

The *New Schaff-Herzog Encyclopedia of Religious Knowledge* says: "A stricter geographical location would place Magog's dwelling between Armenia and Media, perhaps on the shores of Araxes. But the people seem to have extended farther north across the Caucasus, filling there the extreme northern horizon of the Hebrews."[3]

The learned and devout Bishop of London, Robert Lowth, more than two hundred years ago, wrote: "Rosh, taken as a proper name in Ezekiel, signifies the inhabitants of Scythia, from which the modern Russians derived their name."[4]

The eminent scholar Gesenius, whose Hebrew Lexicon has never been surpassed, says, " 'Gog, is undoubtedly the Russians." He also identified Mescheck as Moscow, and Tubal as Tobolsk.[5]

Dr. Wilbur M. Smith writes: "Probably Magog was intended to include all of this great territory north of Syria, of which Gomer, Tubal, and Mescheck were a part. One thing is certain: all these names as understood 2500 years ago, refer to territory either now included within the boundaries of, or immediately adjacent to, what is now Asiatic Russia. What the northern powers stood for then is what Russia stands for today in world events."[6]

Three times in these two chapters it is said that the armies come from the north (38:6, 15; 39:2). Dr. M. R. DeHaan comments on this:

> In all these passages, Gog is said to be north of Palestine. Right here we would remind you that directions in the Bible are always given in relation to Palestine. Palestine is the geographic center of the earth's surface, and all directions start in this land, so that south in the Bible *always* means south of Palestine, north is always north of Palestine, and so with east and west. In the Bible, Gog and the land

of Magog are located as *north* of Palestine, and can refer to nothing else than Russia and her allies. If you draw a straight line from Jerusalem to the North Pole on your world map or globe, this line will pass right through the city of Moscow.

Both Moscow and Jerusalem are located in the same meridian, just a few seconds west of the fortieth meridian. The northern armies, who will meet their waterloo when they invade Palestine in the latter days, can be none else than the communistic block under the leadership of Russia.[7]

A professor of history at Oklahoma University confirms that history during this twenty-six-hundred-year period offers no record of an invasion of the Holy Land by a major world power from the north. Russia, who has come on the scene as a world power in the last few years, is the first nation that could fulfill the prophecy in Ezekiel 38 and 39.

In Ezekiel 38:5, 6, five nations are mentioned which will take part in the invasion of Israel. Persia's name was changed to Iran in 1935. Ethiopia is next named. This evidently does not refer to the Ethiopia in Africa. Young, in his *Analytical Concordance*, lists the word *Ethiopia* in the Bible nine times as referring to "the country to the south of Egypt," but in eleven other places in the Bible Ethiopia is listed separately "to denote the people who occupied the land of Cush." Cush, in Ezekiel's prophecy, was most likely located in the region of Babylon adjoining the land of Iran.

Libya is the third nation mentioned and is also known as Put, which refers to a country adjacent to Iran and Cush. Libya apparently does not refer to the Libya of North Africa. John D. Davis, in his dictionary of the Bible, said that Put lay south or southeast of Cush.

Gomer is mentioned in verse 6. Gomer has been identified as the people of Germany. Richard DeHaan writes: "Gomer is almost universally among Jewish historians looked upon as present-day Germany, at least the eastern part."[8] Gibbon, in *The Decline and Fall of the Roman Empire*, says, "Gomer is modern Germany."[9]

Togarmah is the last nation mentioned. This refers to Turkey. Dr. V. Raymond Edman, former president of Wheaton College, studied hours on this word, Togarmah, and concluded it speaks of Turkey. O. E. Phillips, in his booklet *Russia and the World Crisis,* writes: "There is rather general agreement among scholars that Gomer is Germany and Togarmah is Turkey."[10]

In verse 6, the statement is added, "and many people with thee." This expression probably refers to other groups of smaller nations which have become allied with the countries mentioned. It refers to the multitudes of the people who will invade the Middle East.

To sum up, the nations which will invade the Middle East are these: Russia; Iran; Cush and Put, nations adjacent to Iran; Germany; Turkey; "and many people with thee."

In the November 1970 issue of *Moody Monthly*, Dr. Louis Goldberg, a member of the faculty of Moody Bible Institute, who has spent the past three summers in Israel and the Middle East, made this statement:

> I saw a recent article in one of Jerusalem's Hebrew dailies in which a secular reporter went into the very religious quarter and questioned some of the rabbis and leaders as to "where we are today from God's point of view." Some of the rabbis answered by turning to Ezekiel 38:1-4. "There you have a clear hint that in the days of Gog, which are near to those of Messiah, those who hate Israel will be drawn to leave their land and lay siege to the land of Israel and here they shall fall." One rabbi went on to say, "It is known that the Holy One, blessed be He, shall save Israel at the war of Gog and Magog after a number of years of affliction." And an old man added, "Do these words not fit our day? We have but to wait for the Messiah and to longingly look for the redemption." Of course these views are not shared by Israel's masses. It is significant, however, that there is this air of expectancy among the most pious of Jewry.[11]

In 1854, a Bible scholar named Walter Chamberlain, in his book *The Natural Resources and Conversion of Israel*, wrote: "From all which I should infer, the coming restoration of Israel will at first be gradual and pacific; a restoration permitted, if not assisted and encouraged or protected. They will return to occupy the whole land, both cities and villages; they will be settled there, become prosperous and increasing in wealth, before this great confederacy of northern people will be formed against them."[12]

THE REASONS FOR THE INVASION

One reason given in Ezekiel 38:12, 13 for this invasion is "to take a spoil, and to take a prey, . . . to carry away silver and gold, to take away cattle and goods, to take a great spoil."

In *The Evangel*, this article appeared recently:

Israel has recently been found to be a land of fabulous wealth. Gordan Gaskill (*Reader's Digest*, July 1966) writes that there is an estimated forty-five billion tons of unprocessed chemicals in the Dead Sea. Besides common table salt which has been taken from the Dead Sea since earliest times, there is: sodium, chlorine, sulphur, potassium chloride (potash), calcium, magnesium and bromine. Israel's goal is to export one million tons of potash (plant food) a year which is about equal to the world's need per year. At this rate, Israel could supply the world's need for potash for the next two hundred years. Some scientists believe that the Jordan River is pouring mineral wealth into the Dead Sea as fast as they are taking it out.

This indicates that the Dead Sea alone will prove to be a perpetual source of wealth to the power that controls it. Moreover, the celebrated German geologist, Blanchenhorn, has made an exhaustive exploration of the mineral resources of Israel, and has published his findings in a learned book. In this book he writes that more than 300 square miles of the Dead Sea region offers an unusually high percentage of oil-bearing sands. These findings have since been corroborated by other eminent geologists, and they speak of petroleum pools lying near the surface, and to get these pools, vast beds of mineralized potash of colossal monetary wealth must be penetrated.

It now appears that no land in all the world is near so rich in minerals as the little land of Israel. It is really the "Jewel Box" of the world.

There is no more speculation. These are facts gathered from reports given by some of the world's most eminent scientists. These facts have not been kept secret, but have been made a matter of general information to all nations.

Can we wonder, then, that the tide of battle is rolling toward Israel as the center of conflict? War is a very expensive enterprise—war requires resources. These warring nations are rapidly exhausting their resources in a supreme effort to win the war. Could we be far wrong in saying that Israel, with all she has to offer the conqueror, may be regarded as the prize of war?

Does it not really appear that Israel is the big, juicy plum that most of these nations are trying to pluck?

We believe this in itself gives sufficient explanation of the present magnetic power of Israel over the nations and earns for her this new title— "Vortex of the Nations."[13]

George T. B. Davis, in his book, *Rebuilding Palestine According To Prophecy*, wrote: "One is almost staggered by the computed wealth of the chemical salts of the Dead Sea. It is estimated that the potential value of the potash, bromine, and other chemical salts of its water is one trillion, two-hundred and seventy billion dollars— $1,270,000,000,000.00."[14]

We are told that the wealth that lies in the earth at the Dead Sea is worth more than all the gold that has been dug from the bowels of the earth since it was created.

There is a one-thousand-mile oil line from Aqaba to Haifa carrying 700 thousand barrels of oil daily—70 percent of the world's output. To the east of the land of Israel are large oil reserves. One of the largest and richest oil fields in the world is in the Middle East. President Nixon, in a television speech in July, 1970, said:

I think the Middle East now is terribly dangerous—it is like the Balkans before World War I—where the two superpowers, the United States and the Soviet Union, could be drawn into a confrontation that neither of them wants. . . .

It isn't just a case of Israel versus the Arab states, but the Soviet Union is now moving into the Eastern Mediterranean. The Mideast is important. We all know that 80 per cent of Europe's oil and 90 per cent of Japan's oil comes from the Mideast. We know that this is the gateway to Africa, it's the gateway to the Mediterranean, it's the hinge of NATO. And it's also the gateway through the Suez Canal down into the Indian Ocean.

Another reason for the invasion is the geographic significance of the Middle East, which makes the Russians want to have it under her control. The Middle East is a hub between three major continents, Europe, Asia, and Africa; and any country that wants to dominate the world would want to control this area. Israel, in Ezekiel 38:12, is said to be "in the midst of the land." One version translates this phrase, "the navel of the earth." Webster says that the navel is the central part or point of anything. In Ezekiel 5:5 we read, "Thus saith the Lord God; This is Jerusalem: I have set it in the midst of the nations and countries that are round about her."

Still another reason for the invasion is that Russia is against God and against the Jews; and she wants to wipe out all knowledge of God and completely destroy all the Jews. Zenovieff, one of the chief exponents of Communism, said, "We will grapple with the Lord God of heaven in due season. We shall vanquish him from his heaven, and wherever he seeks refuge, we shall subdue him forever."[15]

The *Manifesto* of 1848 says, "Communism abolishes eternal truths, it abolishes all religion and all morality."

In his book called *Religion*, Lenin makes his famous statement, "Religion is the opiate of the people." He views religion as an "intoxicant" used by the capitalistic system to make the slave-worker lose his desires for a better existence. Lenin states that because communism is based on a scientific and materialistic world conception, it necessarily involves the propaganda of atheism.

The leader of the anti-God movement, Yoroslavsky, in his book, *Religion in the U.S.S.R.* echoed Lenin's thoughts, comparing religion to a bandage over the eyes of a man, preventing him from seeing the real world. His job, he felt, is to tear off that bandage.

In 1932 Stalin, then in power in Russia, signed the following: "On May 1, 1937, there must not remain on the territory of the Union of Soviet Socialist Republic a single house of prayer to God; and the very concept of God will be banished from the Soviet Union."[16] There exists a manual for young atheists now being distributed in the Soviet Union. It has its own "Ten Commandments," which include exhortations to remember that the clergy is communism's foremost enemy and should always be shunned. The propagation of antireligious magazines is urged, as well as generous donations to the cause of "missionary atheism" outside of Russia. These young atheists are reminded that only a devoted atheist can be a faithful communist upon whom the state can rely.

In the August, 1970, issue of *The Reader's Digest*, Joseph Alsop, in an article entitled, "Russia's Menacing New Challenge in the Middle East," wrote:

> Why should the Soviets wish to aid the destruction of Israel, which is, I believe, their aim? Simply put, Israel's destruction, with Russian aid, would surely cause Saudi Arabia, the Gulf coast sheikdoms and both Jordan and Libya to fall completely under Soviet influence; the backwash can easily topple the Shah of Iran; and all

but Soviet power would then be utterly excluded from the entire Middle East. A greater prize than this can hardly be imagined. For Western Europe and Japan are 80 to 90 percent dependent on Middle Eastern oil today, making the Kremlin's power of blackmail really past calculating.

The second question is whether the Soviet leaders are sufficiently cold-blooded to contemplate so horrible an act as Israel's destruction. The answer lies in the Soviet Union's own history: directly or indirectly, by execution, by hunger or by the cruelties of the labor camps, no less than 20 million Russians were sent to their deaths in the pre-World War II years of Stalin's terror. All 11 members of today's Politburo collaborated in, or benefited from, that terror. This is not the sort of government likely to boggle at a little genocide of Israelis if that would richly serve its purposes. . . .

We are therefore confronted with a challenge in the Middle East that is the most perilous of the entire cold war. What the United States should do about that challenge is a complex subject. All I shall do here is lay down one principle. Our aces in this highly dangerous game are the shining courage, the extraordinary and fully proven military proficiency of the Jews of Israel.

"We don't ask you to pay with your lives," Prime Minister Golda Meir said to me. "We only ask you to give us the means to fight for our lives; we will do the fighting, and the God of Hosts will decide."[17]

The final reason I give for the invasion is that God may be magnified and known by the nations of the earth. In Ezekiel God says, "Behold, I am against thee, O Gog . . . And I will turn thee back, and put hooks in thy jaws, and I will bring thee forth . . . that the heathen may know me, when I shall be sanctified in thee, O Gog, before their eyes . . . Thus will I magnify myself, and sanctify myself; and I will be known in the eyes of many nations, and they shall know that I am the LORD. . . . So will I make my holy name known in the midst of my people Israel; and I will not let them pollute my holy name any more: and the heathen shall know that I am the LORD, the Holy One in Israel. . . . And I will set my glory among the heathen, and all the heathen shall see my judgment that I have executed, and my hand that I have laid upon them. So the house of Israel shall know that I am the LORD their God from that day and forward" (38:3, 4, 16, 23; 39:7, 21, 22). God will show to Russia and to the world who is the Almighty One. He will put a hook in this great northern bear's jaw and lead him around, make a fool out of him, and then destroy him. When He destroys Russia and the other nations who come with her, the people of the world will realize that He is the living God with all power; and the Jews will realize that the prophetic Scriptures are being fulfilled, and many of them will turn to the God of their fathers. God will be magnified and glorified in the eyes of both Jews and Gentiles through this invasion. "Surely the wrath of man shall praise thee: the remainder of wrath shalt thou restrain" (Ps 76:10).

THE TIME OF THE INVASION

There are a number of schools of thought as to the time when this invasion occurs. Some scholars say that it occurs before the tribulation. Others say it occurs at the close of the tribulation. Still others are convinced that it occurs at the beginning of the millennium, while some say that it will occur at the close of the millennium.

God's Word says that Russia will invade Israel in the "latter years," or "latter days" (Eze 38:8, 16). The latter years and latter days of Israel's history will not begin until after the rapture of the church, at which time God will deal in a direct and supernatural way with Israel again. Dr. Arthur W. Kac, in his book *The Rebirth of the State of Israel*, comments: "The phrase 'latter days' always refers in the Old Testament to the time of Israel's final and complete national restoration and spiritual redemption."[18]

The Bible also makes it clear that this invasion will be after Israel has returned to the land of Palestine, and is dwelling safely there. "In the latter years . . . *they shall dwell safely all of them.* And thou shalt say, I will go up to the land of unwalled villages; I will go to *them that are at rest, that dwell safely,* all of them dwelling without walls, and having neither bars nor gates" (Ezekiel 38:8, 11, ital. added). Surely Israel is not dwelling safely now. She is in constant jeopardy because she realizes there are millions of Arabs in neighboring nations who would love to attack her and completely annihilate her. She will dwell safely during the millennium but the Bible makes it clear that there will be no war during the millennium (Is 2:4).

There is only one period in the future that seems to fit the description of Ezekiel, and that is the first half of the tribulation. After the rapture of the church, there will come on the scene a confederacy of

ten nations, and out of that confederacy will come the Antichrist.
He is called "the prince that shall come" in Daniel 9:26; and he will
enter into a covenant with Israel for a period of seven years (called
"one week" in Daniel 9:27, and referring to seven years instead of
seven days in this passage). This covenant will give Israel the right
to rebuild her temple, restore her sacrificial worship as prescribed in
the Old Testament, and her borders will be guaranteed. In the
middle of the week (after three and one-half years of the tribulation), the Antichrist will break his covenant and cause the sacrifices
to cease (Dan 9:27), and will demand that people worship him
(2 Th 2:3, 4—"man of sin" and "son of perdition" refer to the Antichrist). The Jews will refuse to worship him and will have to flee
for their lives (Rev 12). Millions of Jews will be killed during this
period, called in the Bible "the time of Jacob's trouble" (Jer 30:7).

A number of prophetic scholars concur in this:

Theodore H. Epp, writing in his booklet *Russia's Doom Prophesied*, remarks: "The question arises, when will this battle of Palestine
take place? I say boldly again that, as I understand the Scriptures,
it will take place during the Tribulation, not before or after, but during the Tribulation. The Church of Jesus Christ will not be here
when this happens. We who are true believers shall not see the final
conflict of Russia in Palestine. We shall see the preparations only,
in fact, we are seeing them today."[19]

Dr. Charles C. Ryrie, in his book *The Bible and Tomorrow's News*,
answers the question, "When will this happen?" by answering, "This
is not an easy question to answer, but it is probable that the conquest
of Egypt and the defeat of Russia will both occur just before the
middle of the Tribulation."[20]

William H. Walker, in his book, *Will Russia Conquer the World?*
concludes that 1) Israel will not be completely safe until she makes
a treaty with the powerful prince or Antichrist; 2) after the treaty is
broken, persecution will replace the peace and security; and 3) therefore, since the first half of the tribulation is the only time when Israel
will be at peace in the land, it is the predicted time of invasion from
Russia.[21]

Dr. John F. Walvoord, in the book *The Prophetic Word In Crisis
Days*, comments: "Under that covenant, Israel will be able to relax,
for their Gentile enemies have now become their friends, and have

apparently guaranteed their borders and promised them freedom. During the first three and one-half years, we have the one time when Israel is at rest and secure. Apparently Russia will invade the land of Israel during that period, possible toward the close, and this Scripture will be fulfilled."[22]

In *Prophecy For Today,* Dr. J. Dwight Pentecost writes: "This suggests to me the following sequence of events. After the head of the Federated States of Europe gives the land of Palestine to Israel, Russia is going to want that land. But she will do nothing about it for probably three years. Then in the middle of the Tribulation period, Palestine is going to be invaded by Russia and his allies. It is at that time, in the middle of the Tribulation period, that God will wipe out Russia and Russian Communism with all of her allies."[23]

Dr. Richard DeHaan, in his book, *Israel and the Nations in Prophecy,* remarks: "Therefore, inasmuch as this attack will come from the north when 'they [Israel] shall dwell safely, all of them . . . dwelling without walls, and having neither bars nor gates . . .' (Ezekiel 38:8, 11), it must occur sometime *after* the Beast [Antichrist] makes this covenant with Israel and *before* he turns against them. This places it during the first half of the tribulation period, Daniel's seventieth week. . . . Therefore, we conclude that Russia and her allies will be utterly defeated by the hand of God in the middle of the seventieth week of Daniel."[24]

Dr. M. R. DeHaan, in his book *Signs of the Times,* stated: "Now the pattern becomes clear. The king of the north will attack Palestine only after Israel is apparently safe and at rest under the protection of the federated western nations, led by the superman, the antichrist. According to II Thessalonians, chapter 2, this superman will not be revealed until after the Church, the body of Christ, indwelt by the Holy Spirit, has been taken out of the way. With the stage so clearly set, how near must be the coming of the Lord!"[25]

THE RESULTS OF THE INVASION

As I have studied Ezekiel 38 and 39, I have found at least seventeen results of this invasion.

SOME NATIONS WILL PROTEST

When Russia invades the Middle East, some nations will protest their invasion. We read in Ezekiel 38:13: "Sheba, and Dedan, and the merchants of Tarshish, with all the young lions thereof, shall say unto thee, Art thou come to take a spoil? hast thou gathered thy company to take a prey? to carry away silver and gold, to take away cattle and goods, to take a great spoil?" *The International Standard Bible Encyclopaedia* and *The New Schaff-Herzoz Encyclopaedia of Religious Knowledge* agree that Sheba is the name of an Arab people, located probably in southern or southwest Arabia. Dedan was a commercial people of Arabia living in the area of Edom, according to *Davis' Dictionary of the Bible*. Tarshish has been variously identified, but I believe with Dr. David L. Cooper that "when all the historical statements are examined thoroughly, it seems that the evidence is in favor of identifying Tarshish as England."[26] Theodore H. Epp agrees:

TARSHISH. There are many who believe that the Tarshish here refers to Great Britain and that, as one of the young lions, the United States is included. Moreover, much has been said and written about this, and we shall take a little time to identify this nation. . . .

Just which nation exists today that fits into Ezekiel's description of this great western nation with many ships? . . . That is the nation known today as England, or Great Britain. No other nation seems to fit the description of the land of many ships.

Furthermore, this land will be one that has a particular interest in Palestine, and certainly this is true of Great Britain today. It will be a power of enough importance to lift a protesting finger against the mighty hordes of the north. . . .

In addition to these characteristics, this nation must have the lion as a familiar symbol. While it is true that several nations have used the lion as a symbol, yet the British lion is best known. "The Lion of England" and "The British Lion" are familiar expressions.

This nation must be the mother of strong, healthy cubs, or young lions, as Ezekiel calls them, which will be strong enough in that day to dare show their teeth and join in the growl of displeasure in the face of the prince of the north. Great Britain's young lions, such as Canada, Australia, New Zealand, the African colonies, and the United States, are strong enough to make an exhibit of disfavor in that day.

Tarshish, therefore, must represent England and all her colonies. America is the strongest one at the present time.[27]

Sheba, Dedan, Tarshish, "with all the young lions thereof" will issue a protest, but it is not said that they do any fighting. They only ask some questions. Nations through the years have sent protests to other nations, which for the most part have been ignored, and the matter has been dropped after diplomatic representation was made to the government involved. So it will be in this instance.

GOD'S WRATH WILL THEN BE SHOWN

When Russia invades the Middle East, terrible judgments will fall on her and her allies. God says, "And it shall come to pass at the same time when Gog shall come against the land of Israel, saith the Lord GOD, that my fury shall come up in my face" (Eze 38:18). The American Standard Version renders this last phrase 'my wrath shall come up into my nostrils," which "describes the vehement breathing (inhalation and exhalation) of an angry man through his nose."[28] No one can mistreat the Jew and go unpunished, for God very distinctly declares that He will "curse him that curseth thee" (Gen 12:3), referring to those who curse the Jews. God warned people against mistreating the Jews "for he that toucheth you [the Jews] toucheth the apple of his eye" (Zec 2:8). As we read the history of the nations that came into contact with Israel we see very clearly that God avenges Himself to all who persecute the Jews.

THERE WILL BE A GREAT EARTHQUAKE

"Surely in that day there shall be a great shaking in the land of Israel" (Eze 38:19). A great earthquake will occur which will be so great that the fishes and birds, the animals, ground creatures, and all men will shake at this manifestation of God's presence; and the mountains, steep places, and walls shall fall to the ground (v. 20). In the past God has used earthquakes to forward His plans and purposes (Amos 1:1; Zec 14:5; Nahum 1:5-6; Ac 16:26), and in the future He will use them again (Rev 6:12-17; 11:13; 16:17-21).

GOD'S SWORD WILL BE CALLED FOR

"And I will call for a sword against him throughout all my mountains, saith the Lord God" (Eze 38:21). This is God's graphic way of saying that He will slay these armies by mountains, rocks, and walls. In Deuteronomy 32:40, 41, God warns: "For I lift up my hand to heaven, and say, I live for ever. If I whet my glittering sword, and mine hand take hold on judgment; I will render vengeance to mine enemies, and will reward them that hate me."

THERE WILL BE FIGHTING AMONG THEMSELVES

"Every man's sword shall be against his brother" (Eze 38:21). The invading armies will be thrown into such utter confusion that they will kill each other. God has caused men in the past to kill each other. In Judges, chapters 7 and 8, we are told of 135 thousand Midianites who had gathered against Israel. Gideon and his three hundred men, under the direction of God and through the power of God, threw the enemy into consternation and confusion and we read: "And the three hundred blew the trumpets, and the Lord set every man's sword against his fellow, even throughout all the host" (Judg 7:22), and "Thus was Midian subdued before the children of Israel" (8:28). In 1 Samuel 14:20, 23, again we are told that God did a similar thing: "behold, every man's sword was against his fellow, and there was a very great discomfiture. So the Lord saved Israel that day." Also, in 2 Chronicles 20:20-25, the Bible records an instance when an invading army of the Moabites and Ammonites was destroyed by God, and "every one helped to destroy another."

THERE WILL BE PESTILENCE AND BLOOD

"And I will plead against him with pestilence and with blood . . ." (Eze 38:22). Four times in his book Ezekiel links pestilence with blood (5:17; 14:19; 28:23; 38:22). This perhaps will include diseases and sickness of all kinds. A note at Ezekiel 5:17 on blood in the Pilgrim Edition Bible says: "BLOOD. This stood for every kind of unnatural death," and a comment in *The Pulpit Commentary* says, " 'blood' probably points to some special form of plague, possibly dysentery (Acts 27:8, Revised Version), or carbuncles, like Hezekiah's boil (Isaiah 38:21)." There will be many of the invading army who will die because of this judgment.

THERE WILL BE FLOODS

"And I will rain upon him, and upon his bands, and upon the many people that are with him, an overflowing rain." God will send an overflowing rain which will produce floods, and many of the enemy will be drowned. Matthew Henry commented: "He comes like a storm upon Israel, v. 9. But God will come like a storm upon him."[29] When Deborah and Barak fought against their enemies, led by Sisera, God sent an overflowing rain and we read: "The kings came and fought . . . They fought from heaven; the stars in their courses fought against Sisera. The river of Kishon swept them away" (Judg 5:19-21).

GREAT HAILSTONES WILL FALL

"And great hailstones . . ." God will send great hailstones upon Russia and her allies. When Joshua and Israel, together with the Gibeonites, fought against the Amorites, "the LORD discomfited them before Israel, and slew them with a great slaughter at Gibeon. . . . And it came to pass, as they fled from before Israel, and were in the going down to Beth-horon, that the LORD cast down great stones from heaven upon them unto Azekah, and they died; they were more which died with hailstones than they whom the children of Israel slew with the sword" (Josh 10:10, 11). A note at verse 11 in the Pilgrim Edition Bible reads: "Hailstones in Palestine, as big as a man's two fists, are known to have killed men and animals." In Revelation 16:21, we have a prediction of hailstones falling upon men during the tribulation period weighing about a talent, which is about one hundred pounds.

THERE WILL BE FIRE

As seen in verse 22, God will also rain down fire from heaven upon Israel's enemies, as He did when He brought the seventh plague upon Egypt: "And Moses stretched forth his rod toward heaven: and the LORD sent thunder and hail, and the fire ran along upon the ground; and the LORD rained hail upon the land of Egypt" (Ex 9:23).

THERE WILL BE BRIMSTONE

"And brimstone . . ." Brimstone is sulfur which, when it is burned, gives off suffocating fumes. The *International Standard Bible Encyclopaedia* says of brimstone: "That the inhabitants of the land had experienced the terrors of burning sulfur is very probable. Once one of these deposits took fire it would melt and run in burning streams down the ravines spreading everywhere suffocating fumes such as come from the ordinary brimstone match. No more realistic figure could be chosen to depict terrible suffering and destruction."[30] When God destroyed Sodom and Gomorrah we read, "Then the LORD rained upon Sodom and upon Gomorrah brimstone and fire from the LORD out of heaven" (Gen 19:24). In Psalm 11:6 David says, "Upon the wicked he shall rain snares, fire and brimstone, and an horrible tempest: this shall be the portion of their cup." In Revelation 20:10 and 21:8, God reveals the final lake of fire and brimstone into which every unsaved person will be finally cast.

J. D. Davies, in *The Pulpit Commentary*, discerningly wrote:

> God's army is composed of unexpected forces. In ancient times God has employed winds, storms, hail, fire, to defeat the enemies of Israel. The sea was God's triumphant army against Pharoah. He sent the hornet to drive out the Canaanite. Locusts have been once and again employed as His invading regiment. Flakes of snow have done His destructive work. Pestilence has often served as His light brigade. Hailstones have been irresistible artillery. He has turned back an army by the spectre of its own superstitious fears. Fire overthrew the cities of the plain. The eruption of Vesuvius did a deadly work. Every force in nature is a servant of the living God, and in a moment can be made a soldier, armed to the teeth. Men are slowly discovering that God's forces stored in nature are mightier than the brawn of the human arm. . . .[31]

ALL OF THE INVADERS WILL BE KILLED

For years I have believed that five-sixths of the invading army would be killed, because of Ezekiel 39:1: "And I will turn thee back, and leave but the sixth part of thee." Most all of the commentators I have read who have written on this passage say that five-sixths of the invaders will be killed, although a few do say that all will be killed. Dr. William W. Orr, in his booklet, *What Will God Do With Russia*, says: "How many million are dead we do not know. But evidently none escape along with their blasphemous leader, Gog."[32] Dr. Walvoord says, "In other words, this army is completely destroyed."[33] A note at Ezekiel 39:11 in the Amplified Bible reads: "The number of dead bodies left, after the great catastrophe which God will send upon Gog and his hosts, as here described, would necessarily amount to several millions. . . . And not some, but 'all' of

Gog's multitude will die then (39:4, 11); before they have had a chance to use their weapons they will be struck from their hands (39:3). That one-sixth of the horde from the north will be left alive, as the King James Version says (39:2), is without noted exception conceded to be a mistaken translation by all authorities of modern times." As I have made this study very recently, I have come to the conclusion that all of the people of the Northern Confederacy will be killed. The rendering in the margin of "leave but the sixth part of thee" is "strike thee with six plagues" (viz., pestilence, blood, overflowing rain, hailstones, fire, and brimstone, Ezekiel 38:22); or "draw thee back with an hook of six teeth" (Eze 38:4), the six teeth being those six plagues just mentioned. Plumptre, who wrote the exposition of Ezekiel for the *Pulpit Commentary*, says it could be translated, "I will six thee," i.e. "afflict thee with six plagues," viz., those mentioned in verse 22. Then Plumptre comments, "The latter derivation, presumably the more correct, is adopted by the LXX, the Vulgate, the Revised Version ('I will lead thee on'), and by modern expositors generally."[34] In Ezekiel 39:4 God says, "Thou shalt fall upon the mountains of Israel, thou, and all thy bands, and the people that is with thee"; and in chapter 39:11 we are told, "and there shall they bury Gog and all his multitude." So it looks as if all the people who invade the land of Israel will be killed by the Lord.

THEY SHALL FALL UPON THE MOUNTAINS AND FIELD

"Thou shalt fall upon the mountains of Israel, thou, and all thy bands, and the people that is with thee" (39:4); "Thou shalt fall upon the open field" (39:5).

THEY WILL BE GIVEN TO THE BIRDS AND BEASTS

"I will give thee unto the ravenous birds of every sort, and to the beasts of the field to be devoured" (v. 4, *see also* vv. 17-20).

FIRE WILL BE SENT ON RUSSIA AND OTHERS

"And I will send a fire on Magog, and among them that dwell carelessly in the isles" (v. 6). Not only will there be fire sent upon the invaders, but fire will also be sent upon the land of Russia (Magog), and upon those who live securely on islands or along coastlands. Possibly these are Gog's sympathizers, supplying forces for his armies.

WEAPONS WILL BE BURNED

"And they that dwell in the cities of Israel shall go forth, and shall set on fire and burn the weapons, both the shields and the bucklers, the bows and the arrows, and the handstaves, and the spears, and they shall burn them with fire seven years" (Eze 39:9). There is speculation about these weapons. Some Bible scholars have suggested that the arms we now use in warfare will be abandoned in the future, and there will be a reversion to the use of primitive weapons. Others say that because modern missiles seek out metal, it will be necessary to abandon the large use of metal weapons and substitute wood. In a recent issue of *Christian Victory* there was an article entitled, "Fuel For History's Greatest Fire," in which another possibility was reported:

> There is a Dutch invention by the name of LIGNOSTONE, invented by a man in Terapel, Netherlands. It is stronger than steel and very elastic. The Russians are using this invention for their weapons of war. It is being used for the cogs of wheels. The Dutch are using lignostone in their gas works, and the Russians are using it for their weapons of war, and the material burns with great heat. The Jews will be burning these weapons on their fires, and will not need to go to the forests to cut down any wood for seven years. It will be the greatest fire in all history. This is fantastic! Everything is getting in readiness. The clock of prophecy is moving rapidly. Everything points to the near return of Christ.[35]

Perhaps the most satisfying explanation is that Ezekiel described the weapons in language familiar to himself and his contemporaries. He spoke of the weapons as they appeared in his day. The counterpart today would be mechanized vehicles and offensive weapons. The wood spoken of could correspond to fuel which men use today to run their vehicles. Dr. Donald G. Barnhouse says of this: "Likewise Ezekiel saw this army of the future and recorded it in the vocabulary of his day." Dr. David L. Cooper wrote: "I am of the firm conviction that one must take the language of Ezekiel as referring to the weapons that will be used in the future but he expressed his thought in terms with which his audience was familiar."[36]

ALL OF THE INVADING ARMIES WILL BE BURIED

"And it shall come to pass in that day, that I will give unto Gog a place there of graves in Israel, the valley of the passengers on the east of the sea: and it shall stop the noses of the passengers: and there shall they bury Gog and all his multitude: and they shall call it The valley of Hamongog" (Eze 39:11). The Jews will bury the invaders, which will take seven months (v. 12). After that time, searchers will be sent to find if any bodies have been missed, placing a sign by any bones they find, so that the ones doing the burying will find the body (v. 14, 15). "Thus shall they cleanse the land" (v. 16).

GOD WILL BE GLORIFIED

In Ezekiel 39:13 God says: "Yea, all the people of the land shall bury them; and it shall be to them a renown the day that I shall be glorified, saith the Lord GOD." In chapter 38:16, 23 God says: "I will bring thee against my land, that the heathen may know me, when I shall be sanctified in thee, O Gog, before their eyes"; "Thus will I magnify myself, and sanctify myself; and I will be known in the eyes of many nations, and they shall know that I am the LORD." (*See also* 39:7, 21, 22).

The nations of the earth, when they see God's destruction of Russia and her allies, will be made to realize His greatness and holiness, and they shall know that He is the sovereign ruler. Matthew Henry wrote: "God, in all this, will be glorified. The end He aimed at (v. 16) shall be accomplished (v. 23): *Thus will I magnify myself and sanctify myself.* Note, In the destruction of sinners God makes it to appear that He is a great and Holy God, and He will do so to eternity. And, if men do not magnify and sanctify Him as they ought, He will magnify Himself; and this we should desire and pray for daily, *Father glorify thy own name.*"[37]

Israel will understand from that day forward that God has been righteous and just in His past dealings with them in His punishing them because of their sins and in His scattering them among the nations. This will be the beginning of a turning to God by the Jews, and at the close of the tribulation, perhaps about three and one-half years later "all Israel shall be saved" (Ro 11:26). Two-thirds of them will be killed during the tribulation (Zec 13:8), when God purges out the rebels (Eze 20:33-44), and the other one-third will look upon

Jesus Christ when He reveals Himself to them and they will be converted.

I do not know of a more appropriate conclusion to this chapter than the words by Dr. Jack Van Impe, in his message, "The Coming War With Russia":

> We are coming to that point right now as we read the papers daily, where there is so much tension in the middle East and the Mediterranean area is already full of Russian vessels and missile-bearing submarines, that the stage is being set for what could explode into World War III at any moment. I'll tell you, friend, if I ever believed as a Bible evangelist that the coming of Jesus Christ was near, I believe it more tonight than I have ever believed it. . . . All the propaganda of the Middle East is building up this fear, hatred and anti-Semitism for the Jew and is going to unleash one of these hours, sooner than most of us think. But the strange thing of it is that none of these details, none of the circumstances, from the text we are preaching tonight, ever, ever happened as they are happening right now. We are living, for the first time in world history, when this could explode immediately. Listen. Do you know that the Jew was not even in Jerusalem until 1948, as far as a nation? For 1900 years, the Jew was homeless, so Russia couldn't go down to Jerusalem to get the Jew in his own land in 1946, because he wasn't there. But, your Bible says, when they come down from the north, they are going down to the Jew's own land. This could only have happened since 1948. Let me say it again. Jesus Christ is coming soon. . . .
>
> I believe I am preaching the most serious message that you will ever hear tonight, and it is so close. All you need to do is go home and pick up your newspaper tonight. The front page again. . . . It is full of the Middle East. The tension is growing by the hour. Before it all breaks, we Christians are gone. He is coming soon. Is Christ in your heart? Are you saved? Can you say, if Jesus comes tonight, 'I'll be there'? How about some of you folks who are backslidden? Listen! Some of you have been so busy making money, building homes, buying furniture, making payments, that you don't have time for God, time for church, time for your family.
>
> I am going to ask you to get saved tonight. I am going to ask others to get right with God. You who are backslidden—away from God—you who have been playing with the world—do you want Jesus

to come and find you in the places you have been? Do you want Him to find you where you have been this last week, or do you want to be living for Him when He returns? He is coming soon! Be ready![38]

11

ARMAGEDDON
The World's Greatest War

IN SEPTEMBER 1961, former President Dwight D. Eisenhower said, "Nuclear-tipped missiles place all of us—even in Chicago—but 30 minutes from Armageddon—tonight, every night, every hour of every day." Theodore Roosevelt declared at the convention of the Progressive Party, "We stand at Armageddon, and we battle for the Lord."

Newspaper and magazine writers, authors, speakers, commentators, and others write and speak of Armageddon as a synonym for any great crucial issue or decisive conflict. They have applied it to World War I, World War II, and other wars or battles. Some think of it as the end of the world or total destruction by a thermonuclear war.

There have been famous battles fought, such as Bunker Hill, Valley Forge, Waterloo, Gettysburg, Iwo Jima, the Battle of the Bulge, and many others; but none compares with this conflict of Armageddon. This is a very unique war, and in this chapter the Biblical view of it will be presented.

THE LOCATION OF THE WAR

The word *Armageddon* is mentioned only once in the Bible, in Revelation 16:16: "And he gathered them together into a place called in the Hebrew tongue Armageddon." The Hebrew word *harmageddon* means the mount of Megiddon. *Har* means mount, and *megiddon* means slaughter; so the meaning of Armageddon is

Mount of Slaughter. Megiddo was an ancient city west of the Jordan River in north central Palestine, some ten miles south of Nazareth, northeast of Carmel, overlooking a vast plain called the Plain of Esdraelon. J. McKee Adams, an authority on Biblical geography, said of this area:

> Properly regarded, Esdraelon is triangular in shape, its lines being roughly drawn from the following points: from Mt. Tabor in the north, by way of the slopes of Little Hermon (the Hill of Moreh), to the foothills of Mt. Gilboa; from Gilboa to the base of Mt. Carmel, where the low hills of Galilee form a narrow pass at the entrance to the plain of Acre; and from Carmel, by way of the southern Galilean steppes, to Mt. Tabor. These lines, of course, are irregular, but in general they represent the limits of the plain. From Tabor to Gilboa, the distance is about 14 miles; from Gilboa to Carmel, 24 miles; and from Carmel to Tabor, 14 miles. The area thus inclosed is justly regarded as one of the most beautiful plains in the world. In fertility it compares most favorably with the delta sections of the Tigris-Euphrates, the Nile, and the Mississippi. In strategic importance, Esdraelon lay across the path of all approaches to central and southern Canaan from the north. The position of Esdraelon in the land of Canaan assured to its possessors a practical domination over the lower parts of the country. Through the heart of this territory passed all of the Old World caravan routes, the connecting highways between the Orient and the Levant. . . . Sufficient here to state that Esdraelon lay at the door of Canaan; once beyond its fortified outposts, the invader was virtually master of the land, particularly of its middle portion.[1]

Frederick L. Brooks, in his book *Prophetic Glimpses*, speaks of the battles fought there: "Here many of the most noted military generals have fought. Thothmes fought here 1500 B.C.; Rameses, 1350 B.C.; Sargon, 722 B.C.; Sennacherib, 710 B.C.; Nebuchadnezzar, 606 B.C.; Antiochus Epiphanes, 168 B.C.; Pompey, 63 B.C.; Titus 70 A.D.; Khosru, the Persian King, 614 A.D.; Omar, 637 A.D.; the Crusaders under St. Louis of France, 909 A.D.; Saladin, who conquered Richard the Lionhearted in 1187 A.D.; the Ottoman Forces, 1516 A.D."[2] It was also the place where Barak won the victory over the Moabites (Judg 4, 5); Gideon was victorious over the Midianites (Judg 7); the Israelites were defeated by the Philistines, and Saul and his sons were killed (1 Sa 31); King Josiah was slain by the king of Egypt (2 Ki 23:29,

30); and General Allenby, British officer, in 1917, turned the Turkish army and saved the Near East for the Western allies. For this achievement, he was given the title Lord Allenby of Megiddo. Napoleon called this plain the world's greatest battlefield.

As we study the Bible, we find there are a number of geographical locations involved in this war other than Megiddo or the Plain of Esdraelon. Jerusalem is seen at the center of the conflict (Zec 12:2-11; 14:2-5, 12).

The first eight verses of Isaiah 34 clearly refer to this great battle, and in this passage another place is mentioned: "For the indignation of the LORD is upon all nations, and his fury upon all their armies: he hath utterly destroyed them, he hath delivered them to the slaughter . . . for the LORD hath a sacrifice in Bozrah, and a great slaughter in the land of Idumea" (vv. 2, 6). Idumea refers to Edom; Bozrah was its ancient capital. Edom lies south and east of Jerusalem, below the Dead Sea. The first six verses of Isaiah 63 also look ahead to this final conflict, and again there is mention of Edom and Bozrah: "Who is this that cometh from Edom, with dyed garments from Bozrah? this that is glorious in his apparel, traveling in the greatness of his strength? I that speak in righteousness, mighty to save" (v. 1).

The third chapter of Joel adds a third location to the picture: "I will also gather all nations, and will bring them down into the valley of Jehoshaphat, and will plead with them there for my people and for my heritage Israel, whom they have scattered among the nations, and parted my land . . . Let the heathen be wakened, and come up to the valley of Jehoshaphat: for there will I sit to judge all the heathen round about" (vv. 2, 12). The location here is the Valley of Jehoshaphat, which was that portion of Palestine that went from Jerusalem over to the east of the Jordan River and then northward.

When all these locations are put together, we find that this war begins on the Plain of Esdraelon, or Megiddo, goes down through the Valley of Jehoshaphat, through Jerusalem, and then to Edom on the south. A. Sims, in his book, *The Coming War and the Rise of Russia*, comments on this:

> It appears from Scripture that this last great battle of that great day of God Almighty will reach far beyond Armageddon, or the Valley of Megiddo. Armageddon appears to be mainly the place

where the troops will gather together from the four corners of the earth, and from Armageddon the Battle will spread out over the entire land of Palestine. Joel speaks of the last battle being fought in the Valley of Jehoshaphat, which is close by Jerusalem, and Isaiah shows Christ coming with blood-stained garments "from Edom," and Edom is south of Palestine. So the battle of Armageddon, it seems, will stretch from the Valley of Megiddo in the north of Palestine, through the Valley of Jehoshaphat, near Jerusalem, and on down to Edom at the extreme southern part of Palestine. And to this agree the words of the prophet Ezekiel that the armies of this great battle will "cover the land." The book of Revelation also says the blood will flow to the bits of the horse bridles for 1,600 furlongs, and it has been pointed out that 1,600 furlongs covers the entire length of Palestine. But Jerusalem will no doubt be the center of interest during the battle of Armageddon, for God's Word says: "I will gather all nations against Jerusalem to battle."[3]

The Armies of the War

The "battle" of Armageddon referred to in Revelation 16:14 could more correctly be called the "war" of Armageddon. It is a series of battles, or a campaign. The Greek word translated battle in the Scripture above is *polemos*, and signifies a war or campaign, whereas the Greek word *machē* signifies a battle, sometimes a single combat. Pentecost says: "This distinction is observed by Trench, and is followed by Thayer and Vincent. The use of the word 'polemos' in Revelation 16:14 would signify that the events that culminate on the gathering at Armageddon at the second advent are viewed by God as one connected campaign."[4]

There is much confusion about who will be the armies in this conflict. Some Bible scholars say that Armageddon will be a conflict between the Roman Empire and Russia. There are a number of differences between this war and the invasion of the Middle East by Russia.

In the battle of Gog, Russia and at least five other nations are involved (Eze 38:2-6). In the battle of Armageddon, all the nations of the world are involved (Joel 3:2; Zec 14:2).

In the battle of Gog, the invaders will come from the north (Eze 38:6, 15; 39:2). In the battle of Armageddon, the armies come from the north, south, east, and west (Dan 11:40-45; Zec 14:2; Rev 16:12-16).

In the battle of Gog, the purpose of the armies is to "take a spoil, and to take a prey" (Eze 38:12). In the battle of Armageddon, the purpose is to annihilate the Jews and to fight Christ and His army (Zec 12:2-3, 9; 14:2; Rev 19:19).

In the battle of Gog, there will be a protest by certain nations against Russia's invasion (Eze 38:13). In the battle of Armageddon, there will be no protesting nations. All nations will be against Jerusalem (Zec 14:2).

In the battle of Gog, Russia will be the leader of the nations ("be thou a guard unto them," Eze 38:7). In the battle of Armageddon, the beast, or Antichrist, will be the leader (Rev 19:19).

In the battle of Gog, God defeats the northern invaders with pestilences, blood, an overflowing rain, great hailstones, fire, and brimstone (Eze 38:22). In the battle of Armageddon, the armies are defeated by the word of Christ ("a sharp sword," Rev 19:15, 21).

In the battle of Gog, the enemies will fall upon the mountains of Israel and the open field (Eze 39:4-5). In the battle of Armageddon, the slain of the Lord will be from one end of the earth to the other end (Jer 25:33).

In the battle of Gog, the dead will be buried—not a bone will be left unburied (Eze 39:12-15). In the battle of Armageddon, the dead will not be buried but totally consumed by the birds (Jer 25:33; Rev 19:17-18, 21).

After the battle of Gog, war will continue with other nations involved during the remainder of the tribulation (Rev 13:4-7). After the battle of Armageddon, swords and spears will be beaten into plowshares and pruning hooks (Is 2:4).

Other Bible scholars say this will be a conflict between the Roman Empire and the kings of the East. Others say it will be a conflict between God and all nations. Some say it will be between the Roman Empire, Russia, and the powers of Asia.

As we compare portions of the Bible with one another, we find that a number of armies will be involved. First will arise the man of sin, as shown in Daniel 11, whose power and conquests are depicted in the latter part of this chapter of Daniel: "The king shall do according to his will; and he shall exalt himself, and magnify himself above every god, and shall speak marvellous things against the God of gods, and shall prosper till the indignation be accomplished: for that that is determined shall be done" (v. 36). The Bible scholars are in agreement that this refers to the Antichrist, the beast of Revelation 13. "And at the time of the end shall the king of the south push at him" (11:40). This power is possibly Egypt and Africa, which will "push at him," the Antichrist. In verse 40 we also read: "The king of the north shall come against him like a whirlwind, with chariots, and with horsemen, and with many ships; and he shall enter into the countries, and shall overflow and pass over." Quite a number of Bible scholars say this is Russia. This interpretation presents a real problem, as Russia will be destroyed by God about the middle of the tribulation period, and Armageddon occurs at the close of that period. Dr. Walvoord, in his recent book *Daniel,* sees this problem and writes:

> A natural question is the relation of this struggle to the battle described in Ezekiel 38-39, where a great military force coming from the north attacks the land of Israel. The context in Ezekiel describes the time as a period of peace for Israel (Eze. 38:8, 11, 14), which probably is best identified as the first half of Daniel's seventieth week when Israel is in covenant relationship with the Roman ruler and protected from attack. This period of peace is broken at the midpoint of the seventieth week when the Roman ruler becomes a world ruler, and the great tribulation begins with its persecution of Israel.
>
> The chronology of Daniel 11:36-39 refers to the period of world rule, and, therefore, is later than Ezekiel 38 and 39. Hence it may be concluded that the battle described here, beginning with verse 40, is a later development, possibly several years later than the battle described in Ezekiel. . . . In any event, this battle is quite different from that of Ezekiel as, according to the Ezekiel prediction, the invader comes only from the north, whereas in this portion, the Holy Land is invaded both from the north and south, and later from the east.[5]

The "tidings out of the east and out of the north" that "shall trouble him" refer to an alliance of nations that will come from the east. Revelation 16:12 says, "And the sixth angel poured out his vial upon the great river Euphrates; and the water thereof was dried up, that the way of *the kings of the east* might be prepared" (ital. added). The invasion of the Holy Land described in Revelation 9:13-21 shows an army of two hundred million coming across the Euphrates River, which, according to Revelation 16:12, will be dried up miraculously by God to permit this large army from the east to march to Armageddon. This river forms the eastern boundary of the ancient Roman Empire and has long been an important geographic barrier. These people from the east will possibly include a number of nations of the Orient east of the Euphrates River—China, India, Japan, and others. Revelation 16:14, 16 speaks of "the spirits of devils, working miracles, which go forth unto the kings of the earth and of the whole world, to gather them to the battle of that great day of God Almighty . . . And he gathered them together into a place called in the Hebrew tongue Armageddon." Today, Red China alone boasts of a militia numbering two hundred million.

Although the details of all the movements of all the armies taking part in this war of Armageddon are not clear, there are obvious facts: There will be the Antichrist and his army, the king of the south and his army, the king of the north and his army, and the kings of the east and their army. So there will be an invasion of the Holy Land from the north, south, east, and west. But included in the armies at Armageddon will be an invasion from heaven by the Lord Jesus Christ and His armies.

"And I saw heaven opened, and behold a white horse; and he that sat upon him was called Faithful and True, and in righteousness he doth judge and make war. His eyes were as a flame of fire, and on his head were many crowns; and he had a name written, that no man knew, but he himself. And he was clothed with a vesture dipped in blood: and his name is called The Word of God. And the armies which were in heaven followed him upon white horses, clothed in fine linen, white and clean" (Rev 19:11-14). The Lord Jesus Christ leads His armies, which will include His saints and His angels.

Zechariah, in speaking of Armageddon, said, "and the LORD my God shall come, and all the saints with thee" (Zec 14:5). Paul spoke of "the coming of our Lord Jesus Christ with all his saints" (1 Th 3:13). "And to you who are troubled rest with us, when the Lord Jesus shall be revealed from heaven with his mighty angels . . . When he shall come to be glorified in his saints, and to be admired in all them that believe (because our testimony among you was believed) in that day" (2 Th 1:7, 10). Jude wrote, "Behold the Lord cometh with ten thousands of his saints, to execute judgment upon all" (vv. 14, 15).

Jesus Christ spoke of His return to the earth and said: "When the Son of man shall come in his glory, and all the holy angels with him, then shall he sit upon the throne of his glory" (Mt 25:31). "Whosoever therefore shall be ashamed of me and of my words in this adulterous and sinful generation; of him also shall the Son of man be ashamed, when he cometh in the glory of his Father with the holy angels" (Mk 8:38). Jesus will return not only with his saints but with angels.

THE RESULTS OF THE WAR

God says in Zephaniah 3:8: "Therefore wait ye upon me, saith the LORD, until the day that I rise up to the prey: for my determination is to gather the nations, that I may assemble the kingdoms, to pour out upon them mine indignation, even all my fierce anger: for all the earth shall be devoured with the fire of my jealousy." A note at this verse in the *Pilgrim Edition* of the Bible reads: "The ancient Jewish copyists made a note of the fact that all the letters of the Hebrew alphabet are found in this verse, and they took that to mean that the whole purpose of God for the earth is told in it." Yes, God in this war has determined to gather the nations, assemble the kingdoms, and pour out upon them His indignation and fierce anger. He says,

And in that day will I make Jerusalem a burdensome stone for all people: all that burden themselves with it shall be cut to pieces, though all the people of the earth be gathered together against it. . . . And it shall come to pass in that day, that I will seek to destroy all the nations that come against Jerusalem. . . . For I will gather all nations against Jerusalem to battle. . . . And this shall be the plague wherewith the LORD will smite all the people that have fought against Jerusalem; Their flesh shall consume away while they stand upon their feet, and their eyes shall consume away in their holes, and their tongue shall consume away in their mouth. And it shall come to pass in that day, that a great tumult from the LORD shall be among them; and they shall lay hold every one on the hand of his

neighbour, and his hand shall rise up against the hand of his neighbour (Zec 12:3, 9; 14:12, 13).

Notice in these verses God says that the people will be "cut in
pieces"; He will "seek to destroy" them, will "smite" them; and "their
flesh shall consume away while they stand upon their feet, and their
eyes shall consume away in their holes, and their tongue shall consume away in their mouth"; and "a great tumult from the LORD shall
be among them."

When Jesus Christ returns to earth with His armies from heaven
"out of his mouth goeth a sharp sword [His word, His voice], that
with it he should smite the nations: and he shall rule them with a rod
of iron: and he treadeth the winepress of the fierceness and wrath of
Almighty God" (Rev 19:15). "The winepress of the fierceness and
wrath of Almighty God" is spoken also in Isaiah 63:2, 3, 6: "Wherefore art thou red in thine apparel, and thy garments like him that
treadeth in the winefat? I have trodden the winepress alone; and of
the people there was none with me: for I will tread them in mine
anger, and trample them in my fury; and their blood shall be
sprinkled upon my garments, and I will stain all my raiment . . .
And I will tread down the people in mine anger, and make them
drunk in my fury, and I will bring down their strength to the earth."
Again in Revelation 14:20: "And the winepress was trodden without
the city [Jerusalem], and blood came out of the winepress, even unto
the horse bridles, by the space of a thousand and six hundred furlongs [200 miles]." Hengstenberg said, "As in the winepress the
grapes are crushed to nothing, so are the heathen by the wrath of
God." The spurting of the grape juice from under the bare feet of
those who trod the grapes in the winepress is compared to the spurting of blood of the enemies of Christ. Josephus says that when the
Romans destroyed Jerusalem in A.D. 70, the Roman soldiers "ob-
structed the very lanes with dead bodies; and made the whole city
run down with blood, to such a degree that the fire of the houses
was quenched with these men's blood."[6]

In Isaiah 34:1-8, referring to Armageddon, God says, "The mountains shall be melted with their blood. . . . The sword of the LORD is
filled with blood . . . and their land shall be soaked with blood. . . .
For it is the day of the LORD's vengeance."

Fowls will be called, "Come and gather yourselves together unto the supper of the great God; that ye may eat the flesh of kings, and the flesh of captains, and the flesh of mighty men, and the flesh of horses, and of them that sit on them, and the flesh of all men, both free and bond, both small and great" (Rev 19:17,18). William R. Newell speaks of this: "Flesh, flesh, flesh, flesh, flesh!—five times over! They chose to walk after the flesh spiritually and now their flesh must be devoured literally!"[7] What a supper! In a preceding verse, God speaks of another supper—"the marriage supper of the Lamb" (v. 9), which the Church and invited guests will attend along with the Lord Jesus Christ.

Dr. Louis T. Talbot, in his book, *An Exposition on the Book of Revelation,* wrote about these suppers:

> There are four suppers mentioned in the Bible. God invites you to the first three, but not to the fourth. If you accept His invitation to the first, you may go to the second, and you will be at the third, but not at the fourth. But if you refuse the invitation to the first, even though you dare present yourself at the second, you will have no place at the table when the third supper is set; but you will be at the fourth.
>
> Do you know what the first supper is? "A certain man made a great supper"; but only "the maimed, and the halt, and the blind" were persuaded to attend (Luke 14:16-24). That supper was used to typify the supper of salvation. It comes in this age. And why is it called "supper" instead of "dinner," or "breakfast," or "lunch"? Because supper is the last meal of the day, even as "the great supper of God" will be the last meal of that coming day. We eat our supper; the sun goes down; night falls; the shadows lengthen. So also, when this age of grace, this supper of salvation, is over, the night will descend upon the world.
>
> The second supper is the Lord's Supper, where the believer partakes of the emblems which represent the broken body and the shed blood of the Son of God. If you have accepted the invitation to the first supper, you have a right to sit at the table when the second supper is served. And if you are a Christian, you will surely be at the third, which we have already described, "the marriage supper of the Lamb."
>
> "And what is the fourth? Ah, it is that dreadful feast, to which the

angel "standing in the sun" invited the "fowls that fly in the midst of heaven."

"My friend, you do not want to be at that dreadful supper. But you will, unless you "believe on the Lord Jesus Christ." God Almighty says that every unregenerated man who eats of the sacred emblems at the Lord's Table, and drinks the wine, drinks and eats condemnation to himself. If you reject the invitation to the first, the supper of salvation, going to the second will avail you nothing; you will not be present at the third, the marriage supper of the Lamb; but you will surely be at the fourth, the last and dreadful "supper of God."[8]

A young girl at a Christian camp where I was speaking on this passage commented to the group as we were discussing these two suppers, "You can be *at* the supper [marriage supper] or be a *part of* the supper [the judgment supper]."

The beast and the false prophet will be cast alive into the lake of fire (Rev 19:20). One thousand years later they are still there (Rev 20:10), proving very definitely that the punishment of hell is eternal. Two men in the Old Testament, Enoch and Elijah, were taken into heaven alive; but these two men of tribulation days, enemies of God, will be cast alive into hell. Walter Scott, in his book *Exposition of the Revelation of Jesus Christ*, comments:

> Who can paint in words the horror of such a doom? Literally, actually this is the predetermined punishment of two individuals, one a Jew and the other a Gentile, and *perhaps* both on the earth at this moment! These two men are not killed, as their deluded followers are. Physical death in their own persons they will never know, but grasped by the hand of Omnipotence, seized red-handed in their crimes, they are at once cast into the lake of fire—a collection of agonies unutterable. They do not proceed, nor are driven onward to their fearful doom, but are *cast* alive into it, as you would throw aside that which is worthless. A thousand years afterwards Satan joins them in the same awful place. The lake of fire is never at rest. Fire and brimstone denote unspeakable torment (Isa. 30:33). The lake, not of water, but of fire, is the eternal place of punishment for the devil and for lost men and fallen angels. It is a *place*, and not a condition. And is it not significant that the phrase, which has rightly become crystallised in our minds from earliest years as the expression of all that is dark and agonising, should be mentioned here for

the *first* time? Perhaps the first inhabitants of the lake may be those two men.[9]

After the beast and the false prophet are cast alive into hell, their followers are dealt with: "And the remnant [the rest of the men in the armies] were slain with the sword of him [Christ] that sat upon the horse, which sword proceeded out of his mouth: and all the fowls were filled with their flesh" (Rev 19:21). All of the enemies of Christ in these armies will be killed by Him.

The question is asked in Job 9:4: "Who hath hardened himself against him [God], and hath prospered?" Then in verses 12 and 13 of the same chapter, Job says: "Behold, he taketh away, who can hinder him? who will say unto him, What doest thou? If God will not withdraw his anger, the proud helpers do stoop under him."

This confederation of nations against Christ and His armies is the literal fulfillment of Psalm 2. The kings and rulers of the nations set themselves against God and Christ, and they boast, "Let us break their bands asunder, and cast away their cords from us" (v. 3). Then we read, "He that sitteth in the heavens shall laugh: the Lord shall have them in derision. Then shall he speak unto them in his wrath, and vex them in his sore displeasure. . . . Thou shalt break them with a rod of iron; thou shalt dash them in pieces like a potter's vessel" (vv. 4, 5, 9). God promises in verse 6, "Yet have I set my king upon my holy hill of Zion." This refers to the time after Armageddon, when Jesus Christ will be recognized as King of kings and Lord of lords, and "The kingdoms of this world are become the kingdoms of our Lord, and of his Christ; and he shall reign for ever and ever" (Rev 11:15).

Ford C. Ottman, in his book, *The Unfolding of the Ages,* wrote:

> There is no quiet and gradual merging of things into the peaceful reign of the Messiah. The kingdoms of this world must be cast into the winepress of the fierceness and wrath of Almighty God. Judgment only, and judgment of the most unsparing kind, falling on principalities and powers of evil, can drive from the heavens the stormwind of iniquity. The wrath and judgment of God can alone do this, and establish the kingdom of Christ in everlasting righteousness over the earth,—and failure to see this must come from the refusal to accept the reality of the final rebellion that shall fill up the cup of iniquity, and fit the world for the just judgment of God.[10]

In closing, let me give the reader the invitation which God gives to the people of this earth: "Be wise now therefore, O ye kings: be instructed, ye judges of the earth. Serve the LORD with fear, and rejoice with trembling. Kiss the Son, lest he be angry, and ye perish from the way when his wrath is kindled but a little. Blessed are all they that put their trust in him." I pray that you will "be wise," "be instructed," will "serve the Lord with fear," and will "rejoice with trembling"; that you will "kiss the Son" (which means receive Him as Saviour and Lord, worship Him, honor Him, love Him, obey Him); and put your trust in Him.

12

PEACE AND PROSPERITY
For One Thousand Years

THERE IS AN UNENDING SEARCH by man for a time of peace and prosperity on this earth. There have been, and still are, plans and programs to bring this about. We have heard about the five-year plan, the ten-year plan, and some time ago, Hitler's One-Hundred-Year Plan for World Peace and Prosperity. There was the League of Nations to bring war to an end and peace to this world. The slogan after World War I was "Make the world safe for democracy." During World War II, the slogan was "The war to end all war." For some years now we have had the United Nations, attempting to bring peace to a warring world.

Today people are praying for peace, marching for peace, wearing peace symbols and signs, even dying for peace, but there is no peace in the world. In an index of European wars made by Professor Pitirim A. Sorokin, of Harvard University, and Nicholas N. Golovin, a former lieutenant general in the Imperial Russian Army, they learned that wars grew in number from 2,678 in the twelfth century to 13,835 in the first twenty-five years of the twentieth century. In their opinion, their findings refute completely the theory that wars tend to decrease with the progress of civilization.[1]

Dr. Harry Hager wrote about the many wars and lack of peace:

> In 3,358 years from 1496 B.C. to 1862 A.D. there were 227 years of peace and 3,130 years of war. Within the last three centuries there have been 286 major and minor wars in Europe. From the year 1500 B.C. to 1860 A.D. more than 8,000 treaties of peace, meant to re-

179

main in force forever, were negotiated. The average time they remained in force was two years. The statistics of the Society of International Law at London, corroborating those of Novikow, declare that during the last 4,000 years there have been but 268 years of peace despite more than 8,000 treaties. . . .

Under the inspiring leadership of Frank B. Kellogg of the United States, and M. Briand of France, fifteen governments in 1928 ratified the celebrated Pact of Paris. By 1934 sixty-three governments had signed and ratified it. President Nicholas Murray Butler wrote of that time "Many of us then thought that the end of war was in sight." He then expressed his disillusionment in these words: "We little realized the faithlessness of the signatory governments and that they would at once begin to prepare for war on an unprecedented scale of expenditure." We think of Hegel's word: "We ask men to study history. The only thing that man learns from the study of history is that men have learned nothing from the study of history."[2]

In spite of all the talk about peace, the teaching of the Bible can be clearly seen everywhere: "There is no peace, saith my God, to the wicked" (Is 57:21); "The way of peace they know not" (Is 59:8).

The Bible predicts that there is coming a time of peace and prosperity on this earth lasting for one thousand years. This golden age is called the millennium. Although there are some who say that Christ will never rule on this earth and that there will never be a millennium, God speaks much about this period. Pentecost says, "A larger body of prophetic Scripture is devoted to the subject of the millennium, developing its character and conditions, than any other one subject."[3]

George Marshall once said, "If man ever does find the solution for world peace, it will be the most revolutionary reversal of his record we have even known." There is a solution for world peace, and God tells us about it in His Word.

THE COMMENCEMENT OF THIS PERIOD

The thousand-year period is called the millennium, which is a Latin word compounded of two words: *mille,* a thousand, and *annus,* a year. Though the word *millennium* is not found in the Bible, the truth is found in many scripture passsages. The word *trinity* is not found in the Bible, but the existence of the trinity is there.

There are at least four views of the millennium:

POSTMILLENNIALISM

This is the view that the world will gradually improve from a lower state of society to a higher state. It teaches that through the church the world will grow better and better until the kingdom of God is brought in; and after a thousand years of peace, Christ will come and judge the world at a general judgment after a general resurrection. The prefix *post* means after, and this means that Christ will come after the millennium.

AMILLENNIALISM

This view teaches that there will not be a millennium. It does not accept the thousand years as a literal period but maintains that the thousand-year period runs through the entire New Testament, and that the Christians are now reigning upon earth. The prefix *a* is negative and *amillennium* means no millennium.

PROMILLENNIALISM

This is a new view which I have just heard of. Those who hold it are not sure whether there will be a millennium, but if there is one, they are all for it. (*Pro* means for).

PREMILLENNIALISM

This view teaches that Christ will come before the millennium (*pre* means before) and ushers it in. It teaches that through the church, God is gathering a group of people to represent Him (Ac 15:14), and when this number is completed, Christ will return for His church and then rule for one thousand years on this earth. There is no doubt in my mind that the Scriptures teach this view.

Dr. M. R. DeHaan writes about this golden age:

> The Bible is replete with prophecies of a coming age of peace and prosperity. It will be a time when war will be utterly unknown. Not a single armament plant will be operating, not a soldier or sailor will be in uniform, no military camps will exist, and not one cent will be spent for armaments of war, not a single penny will be used for defense, much less for offensive warfare. Can you imagine such an age, when all nations shall be at perfect peace, all the resources of earth available for enjoyment, all industry engaged in the manu-facture of the articles of a peaceful luxury? Can you imagine a

golden age when all the hospitals will be shut down, when all doctors and nurses will be out of a job, and medicines will be worthless and uncalled for? Can you imagine with me an age when there will be no poverty, when children will never die, when everybody will have all needs supplied, and when violence and crime will be practically unknown? Can you imagine a time when there will be no wastelands, no storms, no droughts, no crop failures, no floods, and when even the wild animals will be tame and harmless, and will cease devouring one another? . . .

If you ask me where we find any such information, you have but to read your Bible, the Word of the living God, for it is full of that glorious coming age of full redemption, and creation's restoration. We could spend hours reading from the Word of God alone, foretelling and describing this glorious future golden age of redemption.[1]

This period of a thousand years will commence immediately following the return of Jesus Christ. Christ will come in glory and will defeat Antichrist and his armies at Armageddon. After the beast and false prophet are cast alive into the lake of fire and their followers are slain (Rev 19:20-21), Satan will be imprisoned in the bottomless pit for a thousand years (Rev 20:1-3). Then the Old Testament saints and the tribulation saints will be resurrected, bringing the first resurrection to its conclusion, and they along with the church saints, will reign with Christ for a thousand years (Rev 20:4-6).

Jesus spoke of His coming in glory and His reign, "When the Son of man shall come in his glory, and all the holy angels with him, then shall he sit upon the throne of his glory" (Mt 25:31).

In Zechariah 14 we read of this return of Jesus Christ. In verses 3 and 9 the prophet says: "Then shall the LORD go forth, and fight against those nations, as when he fought in the day of battle. . . . And the LORD shall be king over all the earth: in that day shall there be one LORD, and his name one."

When Christ returns to set up His kingdom for a thousand years, part of the Lord's prayer will finally be answered (Mt 6:10). J. Vernon McGee comments:

> The Millennium is God's answer to the prayer, "Thy kingdom come." This is the kingdom promised to David (see II Samuel 7:12-17 and 23:5). God took an oath relative to its establishment (Psalm 89:34-37). This is the kingdom predicted in the Psalms

(Psalm 2; 45; 110) and in the prophets (Isaiah 2:1-5; 11:1-9; 60; 61:3-62; 66; Jeremiah 23:3-8; 32:37-44; Ezekiel 40–48; Daniel 2:44, 45; 7:13, 14; 12:2, 3; Micah 4:1-8; Zechariah 12:10-14:21; also all of the Minor Prophets point to the kingdom). These are but a few of the manifold Scriptures that speak of the theocratic kingdom.[5]

THE CHARACTERISTICS OF THIS PERIOD

During this period, the vegetable kingdom, the animal kingdom, and the human kingdom will experience amazing changes. When sin entered the world, all three of these kingdoms came under the curse; and all three will be affected during Christ's reign.

CHARACTERIZED BY PEACE

When Christ rules on the earth, that which the world has longed for so long will become a reality. Then the angel's message of "on earth peace" will be fulfilled. Of Christ it is predicted: "He maketh wars to cease unto the end of the earth; he breaketh the bow, and cutteth the spear in sunder; he burneth the chariots in the fire" (Ps 46:9). A note at this verse in the *Pilgrim Bible* says: "*Breaketh the bow; cutteth the spear; burneth the chariot*, are expressions to prove that in the rule of Christ, the Prince of Peace, all man-made implements of mechanized warfare will be eliminated. . . ." Speaking of the Messiah's reign in Psalm 72, David says: "In his days shall the righteous flourish; and abundance of peace so long as the moon endureth" (v. 7).

Isaiah 2:4 contains the same promise: "And he shall judge among the nations, and shall rebuke many people: and they shall beat their swords into plowshares, and their spears into pruninghooks; nation shall not lift up sword against nation, neither shall they learn war any more."

Isaiah attributes to the Messiah many names, one of them being "Prince of Peace," and declares, "Of the increase of his government and peace there shall be no end" (9:6, 7). The effect of His rule is also described in Isaiah: "And the work of righteousness shall be peace; and the effect of righteousness quietness and assurance for ever. And my people shall dwell in a peaceable habitation, and in sure dwellings, and in quiet resting places" (Is 32:17, 18).

Zechariah too spoke of this worldwide peace, "and he shall speak peace unto the heathen: and his dominion shall be from sea even to sea, and from the river to the ends of the earth" (Zec 9:10).

CHARACTERIZED BY PROSPERITY

The material prosperity promised for the millennium is almost beyond belief for a world which at present is so full of poverty.

> And I will make them and the places round about my hill a blessing; and I will cause the shower to come down in his season; there shall be showers of blessing. And the tree of the field shall yield her fruit, and the earth shall yield her increase, and they shall be safe in their land (Eze 34:26, 27).
>
> I will call for the corn, and will increase it, and lay no famine upon you. And I will multiply the fruit of the tree, and the increase of the field, that ye shall receive no more reproach of famine among the heathen. . . . And the desolate land shall be tilled, whereas it lay desolate in the sight of all that passed by. And they shall say, This land that was desolate is become like the garden of Eden (Eze 36:29, 30, 34, 35).
>
> Fear not, O land; be glad and rejoice: for the LORD will do great things. Be not afraid, ye beasts of the field: for the pastures of the wilderness do spring, for the tree beareth her fruit, the fig tree and the vine do yield their strength. . . . And the floors shall be full of wheat, and the vats shall overflow of wine and oil. And ye shall eat in plenty, and be satisfied, and praise the name of the LORD your God, that hath dealt wondrously with you (Joel 2:21, 22, 24).
>
> The plowman shall overtake the reaper, and the treader of grapes him that soweth seed; and the mountains shall drop sweet wine, and all the hills shall melt. And I will bring again the captivity of my people of Israel, and they shall build the waste cities, and inhabit them; and they shall plant vineyards, and drink the wine thereof; they shall also make gardens, and eat the fruit of them (Amos 9:13, 14).
>
> But they shall sit every man under his vine and under his fig tree; and none shall make them afraid (Mic 4:4).
>
> For the seed shall be prosperous; the vine shall give her fruit and the ground shall give her increase, and the heavens shall give their dew; and I will cause the remnant of this people to possess all these things (Zec 8:12).

As we read these promises, we notice that God says He will give abundant and timely rainfall; trees will bear fruit; the earth will be very fertile; people will no longer die from hunger and malnutrition; there will be no more famine; grain will be increased; formerly desolate land will become so productive that it will be compared to the Garden of Eden; the threshing floor of the granaries will be full of wheat; wine and oil will fill the vats to overflowing; people will have more than sufficient to eat; they will plant gardens and eat from them; each man will have his own fruit orchard and vineyard to enjoy; the planted seed will always produce; and the skies will be noted for dew rather than scorching heat or bitter cold.

CHARACTERIZED BY RIGHTEOUSNESS

Those entering the kingdom age will be righteous people; the unrighteous will be purged out before the millennium begins (Mt 25: 34, 41, 46). Only those looking for the Messiah will survive to see Him: "But unto you that fear my name shall the Sun of righteousness arise with healing in his wings" (Mal 4:2). Of Israel at that time it is written: "Thy people also shall be righteous: they shall inherit the land for ever, the branch of my planting, the work of my hands, that I may be glorified" (Is 60:21). "For Zion's sake will I not hold my peace, and for Jerusalem's sake I will not rest, until the righteousness thereof go forth as brightness, and the salvation thereof as a lamp that burneth. And the Gentiles shall see thy righteousness, and all kings thy glory" (Is 62:1, 2). "In his days shall the righteous flourish" (Ps 72:7).

Jerusalem shall be called "the city of righteousness, the faithful city" (Is 1:26).

Of Christ Isaiah said, "Behold, a king shall reign in righteousness, and princes shall rule in judgment" (Is 32:1). "But with righteousnes shall he judge the poor, and reprove with equity for the meek of the earth. . . . And righteousness shall be the girdle of his loins, and faithfulness the girdle of his reins" (Is 11:4, 5).

The psalmist wrote concerning Christ, "Say among the heathen that the LORD reigneth . . . he shall judge the people righteously" (Ps 96:10). "The LORD reigneth; let the earth rejoice; let the multitude of isles be glad thereof . . . righteousness and judgment are the habitation of his throne" (Ps 97:1, 2).

In this period it will be true, as Isaiah predicted, "The Lord GOD will cause righteousness and praise to spring forth before all the nations" (Is 61:11).

CHARACTERIZED BY HOLINESS

Holiness means not only separation from evil, but also being specially set apart for use by God. During the millennium, a new level of moral purity will characterize the earth. In addition, certain persons, places, and things will belong to God in a special way.

Christ will reign on the earth only after "his right hand, and his holy arm, hath gotten him the victory" (Ps 98:1), for the Bible says, "The LORD hath made bare his holy arm in the eyes of all the nations; and all the ends of the earth shall see the salvation of our God" (Is 52:10).

Christ will sit upon a throne representing His holiness: "For God is King of all the earth: sing ye praises with understanding. God reigneth over the heathen: God sitteth upon the throne of his holiness" (Ps 47:7, 8).

The region of His temple will be holy: "This is the law of the house. Upon the top of the mountain the whole limit thereof round about shall be most holy. Behold, this is the law of the house" (Eze 43:12).

Jerusalem shall be holy: "So shall ye know that I am the LORD your God dwelling in Zion, my holy mountain: then shall Jerusalem be holy, and there shall no strangers pass through her any more" (Joel 3:17).

Those who are left of the Jewish nation shall be holy: "And it shall come to pass, that he that is left in Zion, and he that remaineth in Jerusalem, shall be called holy, even every one that is written among the living in Jerusalem" (Is 4:3).

People shall be taught holiness: "And they shall teach my people the difference between the holy and profane, and cause them to discern between the unclean and the clean" (Eze 44:23).

Even bells and pots shall be holy: "In that day shall there be upon the bells of the horses, HOLINESS UNTO THE LORD; and the pots in the LORD's house shall be like the bowls before the altar. Yea, every pot in Jerusalem and in Judah shall be holiness unto the LORD of hosts" (Zec 14:20, 21).

CHARACTERIZED BY JOY

Israel's song during the millennium will be: "O LORD, I will praise thee: though thou wast angry with me, thine anger is turned away, and thou comfortedst me. Behold, God is my salvation; I will trust, and not be afraid: for the LORD JEHOVAH is my strength and my song; he also is become my salvation. Therefore with joy shall ye draw water out of the wells of salvation" (Is 12:1-3).

This is God's promise during this period: "He will swallow up death in victory; and the Lord GOD will wipe away tears from off all faces; and the rebuke of his people shall he take away from off all the earth: for the LORD hath spoken it. And it shall be said in that day, Lo, this is our God; we have waited for him, and he will save us: this is the LORD; we have waited for him, we will be glad and rejoice in his salvation" (Is 25:8, 9).

"Break forth into joy, sing together, ye waste places of Jerusalem: for the LORD hath comforted his people, he hath redeemed Jerusalem" (Is 52:9).

"But be ye glad and rejoice for ever in that which I create: for, behold, I create Jerusalem a rejoicing, and her people a joy. And I will rejoice in Jerusalem, and joy in my people: and the voice of weeping shall be no more heard in her, nor the voice of crying" (Is 65:18, 19).

"I will turn their mourning into joy, and will comfort them, and make them rejoice from their sorrow" (Jer 31:13b).

"Sing, O daughter of Zion; shout, O Israel; be glad and rejoice with all the heart, O daughter of Jerusalem. The LORD hath taken away thy judgments, he hath cast out thine enemy: the king of Israel, even the Lord, is in the midst of thee: thou shalt not see evil any more. The Lord thy God in the midst of thee is mighty; he will save, he will rejoice over thee with joy; he will rest in his love, he will joy over thee with singing" (Zep 3:14, 15, 17).

CHARACTERIZED BY TRUTH

Christ promises Israel: "Behold, I will save my people from the east country, and from the west country; And I will bring them, and they shall dwell in the midst of Jerusalem: and they shall be my people, and I will be their God, in truth and in righteousness" (Zec 8:7, 8).

Again He says, "I am returned unto Zion, and will dwell in the midst of Jerusalem: and Jerusalem shall be called a city of truth; and the mountain of the LORD of hosts the holy mountain" (Zec 8:3).

"And in mercy shall the throne be established: and he shall sit upon it in truth in the tabernacle of David, judging, and seeking judgment, and hasting righteousness" (Is 16:5).

CHARACTERIZED BY THE CURSE REMOVED

Because of sin the curse has been upon all creation; the ground was cursed, animals were cursed, and mankind was cursed (Gen 3:17).

During the millennium, the curse upon the ground and the animals will be removed.

"The wilderness and the solitary place shall be glad for them; and the desert shall rejoice, and blossom as the rose. It shall blossom abundantly, and rejoice even with joy and singing, . . . for in the wilderness shall water break out, and streams in the desert. And the parched ground shall become a pool, and the thirsty land springs of water" (Is 35:1, 2, 6, 7).

The curse will be removed from the animal kingdom during this period:

> The wolf also shall dwell with the lamb, and the leopard shall lie down with the kid; and the calf and the young lion and the fatling together; and a little child shall lead them. And the cow and the bear shall feed; their young ones shall lie down together: and the lion shall eat straw like the ox. And the sucking child shall play on hole of the asp, and the weaned child shall put his hand on the cockatrice' den. They shall not hurt nor destroy in all my holy mountain: for the earth shall be full of the knowledge of the LORD, as the waters cover the sea (Is 11:6-9).

CHARACTERIZED BY SICKNESS AND DEFORMITY REMOVED

"And in that day shall the deaf hear the words of the book, and the eyes of the blind shall see out of obscurity, and out of darkness. . . . And the inhabitant shall not say, I am sick: the people that dwell therein shall be forgiven their iniquity. . . . Then the eyes of the blind shall be opened, and the ears of the deaf shall be unstopped. Then shall the lame man leap as an hart, and the tongue of the dumb sing" (Is 29:18; 33:24; 35:5, 6).

"For I will restore health unto thee, and I will heal thee of thy wounds, saith the LORD; because they called thee an Outcast, saying, This is Zion, whom no man seeketh after" (Jer 30:17).

CHARACTERIZED BY LONG LIFE

During this period, God predicts:

> But ye be glad and rejoice for ever in that which I create: for, behold, I create Jerusalem a rejoicing, and her people a joy. And I will rejoice in Jerusalem, and joy in my people: and the voice of weeping shall be no more heard in her, nor the voice of crying. There shall be no more thence an infant of days, nor an old man that hath not filled his days: for the child shall die an hundred years old; but the sinner being a hundred years old shall be accursed. And they shall build houses, and inhabit them; and they shall plant vineyards, and eat the fruit of them. They shall not build, and another inhabit; they shall not plant, and another eat: for as the days of a tree are the days of my people, and mine elect shall long enjoy the work of their hands (Is 65:18-22).

According to these verses we find that life will be lengthened so that a child will not mature until he is at least a hundred years old. At one hundred years of age if the person rebels openly against the rule of Christ, he will be accursed. Verse 20 in the Amplified Bible says: "There shall no more be in it an infant that lives but a few days, or an old man who dies prematurely, for the child shall die a hundred years old, and the sinner who dies when only a hundred years old shall be [thought only a child; cut off because he is] accursed." Of course, during the millennium children will be born of parents with natural bodies, not glorified bodies. The law of death which now works in our bodies will be overcome by the changed condition of the earth. Perhaps conditions in this period will be such that there will be no death except for those who are killed under the judgment of God.

Robert J. Little was asked the question: "What is meant by a child dying at a hundred years old (in Isaiah 65:20) and a sinner being accursed at that age?" He answered:

This passage is a prophecy concerning conditions that will prevail during the millennial kingdom of Christ. In the first part of this verse, we read: "There shall be no more thence an infant of days, nor an old man that hath not lived out his days." We take this to mean that during this period no one shall die in infancy, nor will anyone die of old age, since the span of life will be greatly increased, and medicine will be available for any illness (Rev. 22:2).

One who shall die at the age of 100 at that time will be considered to have died as a child. But this age (100 years) apparently will be the age of accountability, since "the sinner being a hundred years old shall be accursed." This confirms the fact that then death will not be from what we now call "natural causes," but will be the result of the judgment of God. Psalm 101:8 has been rendered, "Morning by morning I will destroy all the wicked of the land, that I may cut off all wicked doers from the city of the Lord." This has been taken to mean that every morning there will be a summary judgment of all wickedness since, under conditions which shall exist then, there will be no incentive to sin. It seems that one who commits a transgression will have until the following morning to repent and make the matter right.[6]

CHARACTERIZED BY SOARING POPULATION

Because of the fact that those who enter the millennium will be in their natural bodies, and the fact that the only deaths during this period will be those who rebel against Christ's righteous rule, the population of the earth will increase rapidly.

And out of them shall proceed thanksgiving and the voice of them that make merry: and I will multiply them and they shall not be few; I will also glorify them, and they shall not be small (Jer 30:19).

There shall yet old men and old women dwell in the streets of Jerusalem, and every man with his staff in his hand for very age. And the streets of the city shall be full of boys and girls playing in the streets thereof (Zec 8:4, 5).

And it shall come to pass, that ye shall divide it by lot for an inheritance unto you, and to the strangers that sojourn among you, which shall beget children among you: and they shall be unto you as born in the country among the children of Israel; they shall have inheritance with you among the tribes of Israel (Eze 47:22).

CHARACTERIZED BY WORSHIP

The whole world will unite in the worship of God and His Son, Jesus Christ.

> And it shall come to pass, that from one new moon to another, and from one sabbath to another, shall all flesh come to worship before me, saith the LORD (Is 66:23).
>
> For then will I turn to the people a pure language, that they may all call upon the name of the LORD, to serve him with one consent (Zep 3:9).
>
> Hearken unto me, ye that know righteousness, the people in whose heart is my law; fear ye not the reproach of men, neither be ye afraid of their revilings. For the moth shall eat them up like a garment, and the worm shall eat them like wool: but my righteousness shall be for ever, and my salvation from generation to generation (Is 51:7, 8).
>
> And it shall come to pass, that every one that is left of all the nations which came against Jerusalem shall even go up from year to year to worship the King, the LORD of hosts, and to keep the feast of tabernacles. And it shall be, that whoso will not come up of all the families of the earth unto Jerusalem to worship the King, the Lord of hosts, even upon them shall be no rain (Zec 14:16, 17).

CHARACTERIZED BY THE FULNESS OF THE HOLY SPIRIT

When this period begins, Joel's prophecy will be fulfilled: "And it shall come to pass afterward, that I will pour out my spirit upon all flesh; and your sons and your daughters shall prophesy, your old men shall dream dreams, your young men shall see visions: And also upon the servants and upon the handmaids in those days will I pour out my spirit" (Joel 2:28, 29).

Isaiah predicts: "So shall they fear the name of the LORD from the west, and his glory from the rising of the sun. When the enemy shall come in like a flood, the Spirit of the LORD shall lift up a standard against him. And the Redeemer shall come to Zion, and unto them that turn from transgression in Jacob, saith the LORD. As for me, this is my covenant with them, saith the LORD; My spirit that is upon thee, and my words which I have put in thy mouth, shall not depart out of thy mouth, nor out of the mouth of thy seed . . . saith the LORD, from henceforth and for ever" (Is 59:19-21).

George N. H. Peters, in his book, *The Theocratic Kingdom*, wrote:

> The remarkable, astounding outpouring of the Holy Spirit as presented in the Millennial descriptions . . . so powerful in its transforming, glorifying, and imparting miraculous gifts to the saints; so pervading in and over the Jewish nation that all shall be righteous from the least to the greatest; so wide-reaching over the Gentiles that they shall rejoice in the light bestowed; and so extended in its operation that the whole earth shall ultimately be covered with glory—this, with the magnificent portrayals of the Millennial and succeeding ages, is so sublime with the indwelling, abiding, communicated Divine, that no one can contemplate it, without being profoundly moved at the display of spirituality.[7]

CHARACTERIZED BY FULL KNOWLEDGE

During the millennium ". . . the earth shall be full of the knowledge of the LORD, as the waters cover the sea" (Is 11:9, *see also* Hab 2:14).

"And all thy children shall be taught of the LORD; and great shall be the peace of thy children" (Is 54:13).

"But this shall be the covenant that I will make with the house of Israel; After those days, saith the LORD, I will put my law in their inward parts, and write it in their hearts; and will be their God, and they shall be my people. And they shall teach no more every man his neighbour, and every man his brother, saying, Know the LORD: for they shall all know me, from the least of them unto the greatest of them" (Jer 31:33, 34).

Not many people really know the Lord now, but all will know Him in the millennium.

CHARACTERIZED BY THE UNIVERSAL RULE OF CHRIST

God intended man to rule over the earth, but man sinned against God and forfeited his right to rule. God's purpose will be fulfilled in Christ when He shall rule over all the earth. God said to His Son: "Ask of me, and I shall give thee the heathen for thine inheritance, and the uttermost parts of the earth for thy possession" (Ps 2:8).

In one of the Messianic Psalms, David says of God's Son: "He shall have dominion also from sea to sea, and from the river unto the ends of the earth. They that dwell in the wilderness shall bow before him; and his enemies shall lick the dust. . . . all kings shall fall down before him: all nations shall serve him. . . . all nations shall call him blessed" (Ps 72:8, 9, 11, 17).

Speaking of Christ as the smiting stone in Daniel 2:35, God says, "The stone that smote the image became a great mountain, and filled the whole earth."

> And in the days of these kings shall the God of heaven set up a kingdom, which shall never be destroyed: and the kingdom shall not be left to other people, but it shall break in pieces and consume all these kingdoms, and it shall stand for ever (Dan 2:44). And there was given him dominion, and glory, and a kingdom, that all people, nations, and languages, should serve him: his dominion is an everlasting dominion, which shall not pass away, and his kingdom that which shall not be destroyed (Dan 7:14).

> But in the last days it shall come to pass, that the mountain of the house of the LORD shall be established in the top of the mountains, and it shall be exalted above the hills; and people shall flow unto it. And many nations shall come, and say, Come, and let us go up to the mountain of the LORD, and to the house of the God of Jacob; and he will teach us of his ways, and we will walk in his paths: for the law shall go forth of Zion, and the word of the LORD from Jerusalem (Micah 4:1, 2).

> And the LORD shall be king over all the earth: in that day shall there be one LORD, and his name one (Zec 14:9).

It is clear from His title in Revelation 19:16, KING OF KINGS AND LORD OF LORDS, that Christ will be the supreme ruler over all the earth.

A very helpful comment has been made by Ryrie:

> Authority over the 12 tribes of Israel will be vested in the hands of the 12 apostles (Matt. 19:28). Other princes and nobles will likewise share in government duties (Jer. 30:21; Isa. 32:1). It seems, too, that many lesser people will have responsibilities in various departments of the millennial government. The parable of the pounds (Luke 19:11-27) indicates that those who have proved their faithfulness will be given more authority. The Church, too, will share in governing the earth (cf. Rev. 5:10). Many of the normal procedures of the millennial government will be carried out by subordinates, but all will be subject to the King of kings and Lord of lords.[8]

The Conclusion of This Period

At the conclusion of this period, Satan, who will have been bound in the bottomless pit for one thousand years (Rev 20:1-3), will be loosed and go out to deceive the nations of the earth. He will gather a large army to follow him, and they will come against Jerusalem with the intention of killing the followers of Christ and possibly destroying Christ Himself. It is probable that the devil's appeal to his followers will be to establish their own government and to overthrow that of Christ.

It is difficult to understand why they will revolt against Christ, because this age will be a time when the whole world is converted. At the beginning of this period all who enter will be converted, but children will be born to those parents; and though some of these children will be converted, others of them will merely profess to follow and obey Him under His absolute rule. Everyone during this time will be compelled to recognize His power and might, for He will rule strictly (with a "rod of iron") and will immediately judge any open rebellion against Him. Those who do not truly in their hearts submit to Christ will render feigned obedience to Him. Psalm 66:3 is rendered in the Amplified Bible: "Say to God, How awesome and fearfully glorious are Your works! Through the greatness of Your power shall your enemies submit themselves to You—with feigned and reluctant obedience."

During the millennium, the devil will not be here to tempt people; the world system will be changed, lacking the evil that it now has to tempt people; but the sin nature will still exist so that people can and will rebel against Christ. In every age, people have a choice to make as to whether they will obey God or rebel against Him. They will be given this opportunity at the close of the millennium, and many of them ("the number of whom is as the sand of the sea," v. 8), will follow Satan in this last revolt. This will prove that Satan's imprisonment for one thousand years did not change his character in the least, and it will also prove that men's hearts are not changed by a perfect environment such as the millennium afforded.

Dr. René Pache, in his book, *The Return of Jesus Christ*, remarks:

> Now the time comes when eternity is going to seal the final outcome of each one. God, who knows the most secret thoughts, could

very well send into eternal Hell the hearts which have rebelled against His grace. But would there not be temptation for such men to say,

"Lord, what have we done to merit such punishment? Have we not conformed ourselves like the others? And have we not always been obedient?"

In order to take away from them every pretext of speaking thus and to give them the occasion of manifesting the depth of their wicked heart, God will permit them to be tempted. . . . temptation is for the creature the price of liberty. God does not wish to be served by slaves but by beings who have fully chosen to love Him and to obey Him.[9]

When this last revolt occurs, God in a very few words gives us the final outcome: "fire came down from God out of heaven and devoured them" (v. 9). Then we read: "And the devil that deceived them was cast into the lake of fire and brimstone, where the beast and false prophet are, and shall be tormented day and night for ever and ever" (Rev 20:10). God says of the devil that he "deceiveth the whole world" (Rev 12:9). He was self-deceived in his desire to be like God; he began his career by deceiving Eve in the garden; he has deceived people throughout the history of the world; and he is still deceiving them right to the time of his final judgment by God. He has had a downward course since he fell from his high and exalted position as the "anointed cherub" (Eze 28:11-15; Is 14:12-15). During the tribulation he will be cast out of the atmospheric heavens, which he now occupies as the prince of the powers of the air (Eph 2:2), to the earth (Rev 12:7-13). At the close of the tribulation, he will be bound and cast into the bottomless pit for a thousand years (Rev 20:1-3). Then at the close of the millennium he will be finally cast into the lake of fire and brimstone to be tormented for ever and ever. The beast and false prophet had been cast into this lake of fire and brimstone one thousand years before (Rev 19:20) and will still be there. Their presence teaches clearly that death is not annihilation, and the wicked exist forever. Walvoord states: "There would be no way possible in the Greek language to state more emphatically the everlasting punishment of the lost than that used here in mentioning both day and night and the expression 'for ever and ever' (Gr. *eis tous aiōnas ton aiōnōn*), literally 'to the ages of the ages.' The lake of fire prepared for the devil and the wicked angels [Matthew 25:41] is also the destiny of all who follow Satan."[10]

After Satan and his followers are destroyed and cast into the lake of fire we read that the great white throne judgment will take place (Rev 20:11-15), followed by the eternal state (Rev 21, 22).

Six times in Revelation 20:2-7 the term *thousand years* is mentioned. Many scriptures teach that Christ will rule over an endless kingdom (2 Sa 7:16; Ps 72:5; Ps 89:3, 4, 34-37; Is 9:6, 7; Dan 7:13, 14; Lk 1:30-33; Rev 11:15). Some people see a conflict here. According to Paul, the time will come when Christ will have put an end to all powers and rulers which challenge His authority; and He will destroy the last enemy, death (1 Co 15:24-28). Then He will deliver the kingdom to God, "that God may be all in all." Dr. Alva J. McClain, in his book *The Greatness of The Kingdom,* summarizes:

> 1. When the last enemy of God is put down by our Lord, as the Mediatorial King, the purpose of the Mediatorial Kingdom will have been fulfilled (I Corinthians 15:25-26).
>
> 2. At this time Christ will hand over the Mediatorial Kingdom to God, to be merged into the eternal Kingdom, so that the Mediatorial Kingdom is perpetuated forever, but no longer having a separate identity (I Cor. 15:24, 28).
>
> 3. This does not mean the end of our Lord's rule. He only ceases to rule as a Mediatorial King. But as the eternal Son, second person to the one true God, He shares the throne with the Father in the final Kingdom (Rev. 22:3-5; cf. 3:21).[11]

"Today people are praying for peace, marching for peace, wearing peace symbols and signs, even dying for peace, but there is no peace in the world." The time is soon coming when Jesus Christ, the Prince of Peace, will return to this earth and the Scriptures will be fulfilled which say: "In his days shall the righteous flourish; and abundance of peace so long as the moon endureth"; "Of the increase of his government and peace there shall be no end"; "And my people shall dwell in a peaceable habitation"; "and he shall speak peace unto the heathen" (Ps 72:7; Is 9:7; 32:18; Zec 9:10).

Though there will not and cannot be peace in this world until the Prince of Peace returns, yet there can be peace today in the heart of the individual who will put his complete trust in this Christ. Through

His death on the cross He made it possible that we who are enemies of God, and of whom it is said, "And the way of peace have they not known" (Ro 3:17), can have "peace with God" (Ro 5:1), and "the peace of God" (Phil 4:7). Isaiah 53:5 in the Amplified Bible reads: "But He was wounded for our transgressions, He was bruised for our guilt and iniquities; the chastisement needful to obtain peace and well-being for us was upon Him, and with the stripes that wounded Him we are healed and made whole." Paul explains that Christ "made peace through the blood of his cross" (Col 1:20), "for *He is our peace* (Eph 2:14), and "therefore being justified by faith, we have peace with God through our Lord Jesus Christ" (Ro 5:1). When we in our hearts trust in the Lord Jesus Christ and what He did for us on the cross, God says we have peace with God—the enmity with God is gone. We cannot have peace today among the nations, but, praise God, we can have peace in our hearts.

Not only can we have "peace with God" but the Bible speaks of "the peace of God" (Phil 4:7). Every Christian has "peace with God," but only those Christians who trust Him wholly, who stay their minds on the Lord, who yield themselves completely to the Lord, who are not anxious about anything, but prayerful about everything, who will "let the peace of God rule in their hearts" (Col 3:15), know this "peace of God." God's promises are true: "Thou wilt keep him in perfect peace whose mind is stayed on thee: because he trusteth in thee" (Is 26:3).

"Be careful [anxious] for nothing; but in everything by prayer and supplication with thanksgiving let your requests be made known unto God. And the peace of God, which passeth all understanding, shall keep your hearts and minds through Christ Jesus" (Phil 4:6, 7).

"Peace I leave with you, my peace I give unto you: not as the world giveth, give I unto you. Let not your heart be troubled, neither let it be afraid" (Jn 14:27).

Not only may peace be yours, but prosperity also. God's Word says, "Let the Lord be magnified, which hath pleasure in the prosperity of his servant" (Ps 35:27). God tells us specifically how we may prosper:

> If they obey and serve him, they shall spend their days in prosperity, and their years in pleasure (Job 36:11).

Blessed is the man that walketh not in the counsel of the ungodly, nor standeth in the way of sinners, nor sitteth in the seat of the scornful. But his delight is in the law of the Lord; and in his law doth he meditate day and night. And he shall be like a tree planted by the rivers of water, that bringeth forth his fruit in his season; his leaf also shall not wither; and whatsoever he doeth shall prosper (Ps 1:1-3).

Believe his prophets, so *shall ye prosper* (2 Chr 20:20).

This book of the law shall not depart out of thy mouth; but thou shalt meditate therein day and night, that thou mayest observe to do according to all that is written therein: for then thou shalt make thy way prosperous, and then thou shalt have good success (Jos 1:8).

My prayer for every reader is that you may have "peace and prosperity" in this life, then for one thousand years, and then for all eternity.

13

THE GREAT WHITE THRONE JUDGMENT

YES, THERE WILL BE a last judgment where the unsaved will be judged and suffer the penalty decreed. This will take place at the great white throne judgment. "And as it is appointed unto men once to die, but after this the judgment" (Heb 9:27). "But the LORD shall endure for ever: he hath prepared his throne for judgment" (Ps 9:7).

THE JUDGE

John wrote: "And I saw a great white throne, and him that sat on it. . . . And I saw the dead, small and great, stand before God" (Rev 20:11, 12). According to the Word of God, Jesus Christ will be the judge. Jesus said, "For the Father judgeth no man, but hath committed all judgment unto the Son. . . . For as the Father hath life in himself; so hath he given to the Son to have life in himself; and hath given him authority to execute judgment also, because he is the Son of man" (Jn 5:22, 26, 27).

Paul said concerning Jesus Christ: "And he commanded us to preach unto the people, and to testify that it is he which was ordained of God to be the Judge of quick and dead. . . . Because he hath appointed a day, in the which he will judge the world in righteousness by that man whom he hath ordained; whereof he hath given assurance unto all men, in that he hath raised him from the dead. . . . I charge thee therefore before God, and the Lord Jesus Christ, who shall judge the quick and the dead at his appearing and his kingdom" (Ac 10:42; 17:31; 2 Ti 4:1).

Jesus Christ is the judge of "the quick and the dead." The word

199

quick means living. In Matthew 25:31-46, we read of a future day when Christ returns to earth and will judge those who are alive.

In Romans 14:10 and 2 Corinthians 5:10, the Bible speaks of a future day when those who have died in Christ and those who are caught up at the rapture will be judged by Him at the judgment seat of Christ.

In Revelation 20:11-15, God speaks of a future judgment when every unsaved person will come before Jesus Christ to be judged.

THE JUDGED

Those who will be judged are called "the dead, small and great" (v. 12). These are the ones of whom it is said, "the rest of the dead lived not again until the thousand years were finished" (Rev 20:5).

There is no such thing taught in the Word of God as a general judgment, when everyone who has ever lived will be judged at the same time. The Bible speaks of two resurrections. Daniel says: "And many of them that sleep in the dust of the earth shall awake, some to everlasting life, and some to shame and everlasting contempt" (Dan 12:2). Jesus promised: "And thou shalt be blessed; for they cannot recompense thee: for thou shalt be recompensed at the resurrection of the just" (Lk 14:14). He said in John 5:28, 29: "Marvel not at this: for the hour is coming, in the which all that are in the graves shall hear his voice, and shall come forth: they that have done good, unto the resurrection of life; and they that have done evil, unto the resurrection of damnation." Paul said, "And have hope toward God, which they themselves also allow, that there shall be a resurrection of the dead, both of the just and unjust" (Ac 24:15).

The resurrection of life for the just to everlasting life is called the first resurrection (Rev 20:5, 6). Christ was the firstfruits of the first resurrection (1 Co 15:20, 23); then those who are saved in this church age, "they that are Christ's at his coming" (1 Co 15:23), will be resurrected at the rapture (1 Th 4:16, 17). Old Testament saints will be resurrected at the conclusion of the tribulation (Is 26:19; Dan 12:1-3), as will the tribulation martyrs (Rev 20:4).

In his book *Things To Come*, Dr. Pentecost summarizes:

> The order of events in the resurrection program would be: (1) the resurrection of Christ as the beginning of the resurrection program (I Cor. 15:23); (2) the resurrection of the Church age saints

at the rapture (I Thess. 4:16); (3) the resurrection of the tribulation period saints (Rev. 20:3-5), together with (4) the resurrection of Old Testament saints (Dan. 12:2; Isa. 26:19) at the second advent of Christ to the earth, and finally (5) the final resurrection of the unsaved dead (Rev. 20:5, 11-14) at the end of the millennial age. The first four stages would all be included in the first resurrection or resurrection to life, inasmuch as all receive eternal life and the last would be the second resurrection, or the resurrection unto damnation, inasmuch as all receive eternal judgment at that time.[1]

All those taking part in the first resurrection will be raised before the millennium. Those taking part in the second resurrection will be raised after the millennium (Rev 20:7-15). All of the unrighteous of all ages from Cain to those who rebel during and at the close of the millennium will stand at this great white throne to be judged. The "small and great" will be there—the beggar and the banker, the pauper and the prince, the simpleton and the scientist, the big sinners and the little sinners, rulers and subjects, the refined and the vulgar, the civilized and the barbarous—all will appear before the Judge, awaiting their eternal doom. The drunkards, the harlots, the thieves, the adulterers, the rejectors, the neglectors, the infidels, the modernists, the self-righteous will be there. The "fearful, and unbelieving, and the abominable, and murderers, and whoremongers, and sorcerers, and idolators, and all liars" will be there (Rev 21:8). Even though their bodies have been buried or in the depths of the sea for centuries or millennia, they will be reunited with their souls and spirits and stand before the Lord. God says in Romans 14:11: "As I live, saith the Lord, every knee shall bow to me, and every tongue shall confess to God." And in Philippians 2:10, 11, He says: "That at the name of Jesus every knee should bow, of things in heaven, and things under the earth; And that every tongue should confess that Jesus Christ is Lord, to the glory of God the Father." Dr. John R. Rice comments on these verses:

> They will not love Jesus, they will not trust Him for salvation, and it will be too late for them to be saved. But the stiff knee of every rebellious and Christ-rejecting sinner will bow before Jesus in humility, and every blaspheming tongue will at that time confess that Jesus Christ is the Lord and Master that they ought to have served and loved. . . .

The "knee" refers to the physical body. The "tongue" refers to the physical body. Resurrected sinners in bodies fresh from the graves and the sea will stand before God to be judged in the flesh for deeds done in the flesh and then to be cast, both soul and body, into Hell, the lake of fire. . . .

The last grave will be opened in every cemetery. A thousand years before, the saints will have been raised and their graves left empty; now the remaining graves will give up their dead as spirits come out of Hell to possess them and to be judged before God.[2]

A true incident recounted some time ago in *Moody Monthly* emphasizes the unavoidable fact of the resurrection awaiting all men:

More than a hundred years ago an infidel died in Hanover, Germany. Before his death he ordered that above his grave large slabs of granite should be placed, bound together with iron bands, and above it all a huge block weighing almost two tons. It was done. On the stone the inscription was put, "This grave is purchased for eternity; it shall never be opened." Somehow, a little poplar seed was enclosed in the mold within the tomb. God in His power caused it to sprout. A little shoot found a crevice in between the iron-bound slabs. Its hidden power in the course of time broke the iron bands asunder and moved every stone out of its original position. The whole structure is displaced completely and the grave is opened thereby. The tree still lives and waves its branches over the rent sepulcher, which the infidel declared should never be opened. It just needed a tiny seed, one of God's marvels in creation to answer the challenge of the infidel. If a tiny seed can burst open a grave, how much more can an omnipotent Lord with His omnipotent power make good His promise?[3]

THE JUDGMENT

As I have already stated, the Bible does not teach a general judgment, but a number of judgments are mentioned in the Word of God. There are at least seven judgments spoken of in the Scriptures, the first three mentioned dealing with believers only, and the other four dealing with other groups.

THE JUDGMENT OF THE BELIEVER'S SINS

This judgment is past, deals with our justification, and was accomplished for us by Christ when He suffered on the cross for our sins.

At Calvary He bore the penalty of our sins: "Who his own self bare our sins in his own body on the tree" (1 Pe 2:24). Because the believer's sins have been judged, we can joyfully sing:

> Jesus paid it all,
> All to Him I owe;
> Sin had left a crimson stain,
> He washed it white as snow.
>
> ELVINA M. HALL

Jesus promised: "Verily, verily, I say unto you, He that heareth my word, and believeth on him that sent me, hath everlasting life, and shall not come into condemnation [or judgment]; but is passed from death unto life" (Jn 5:24). God gives the Christian blessed assurance in Romans 8:1: "There is therefore now no condemnation to them which are in Christ Jesus." The true believer in Christ is saved and free from present condemnation and also free from fear of any future judgment at the great white throne.

THE JUDGMENT OF THE BELIEVER'S SELF

This judgment is present, deals with our sanctification, and is to be done by the believer himself. This is one of the most reassuring verses in the Bible: "For if we would judge ourselves, we should not be judged" (1 Co 11:31). If Christians would examine themselves, judge the things that are wrong in their lives, and confess them to God, He will not have to judge or chasten. He promises: "If we confess our sins, he is faithful and just to forgive us our sins, and to cleanse us from all unrighteousness" (1 Jn 1:9). If we do not judge ourselves, God will have to judge us and "when we are judged, we are chastened of the Lord, that we should not be condemned with the world" (1 Co 11:32).

THE JUDGMENT OF THE BELIEVER'S WORKS

This judgment is future, deals with our glorification, and will take place immediately after the rapture of the church (Ro 14:10); 1 Co 4:5; 2 Co 5:10; 2 Ti 4:8). This is known as the judgment seat of Christ, where our works as Christians will be brought into review. The faithful Christians will be rewarded; the unfaithful Christians will suffer loss (1 Co 3:9-15). (See chapter 8, "The Judgment Seat of Christ—A Practical Prophetic Truth").

THE JUDGMENT OF THE NATIONS

This judgment is future, and will take place at the return of Jesus Christ at the close of the tribulation. Jesus told His disciples of that day: "When the Son of man shall come in his glory, and all the holy angels with him, then shall he sit upon the throne of his glory: And before him shall be gathered all nations: and he shall separate them one from another, as a shepherd divideth his sheep from the goats" (Mt 25:31, 32). As we read the following verses, 33-46, we see that the teaching of this passage is that there will be three classes of people at this judgment: (1) *sheep,* who are saved Gentiles, those who have been saved on earth during the tribulation period between the rapture and the revelation of Christ; (2) *goats,* who are unsaved Gentiles; and (3) *my brethren,* who are the people of Israel. The scene is on the earth; there is no resurrection at this judgment; no books are opened. The basis of this judgment is how people have treated the Jews, those whom Christ calls "my brethren." The good works mentioned here do not teach that the people who did them were saved by their good works, but the works are the proof of their faith and salvation. There is a twofold outcome of this judgment: the goats, the unsaved Gentiles, will be sent away into everlasting punishment (vv. 41, 46); and the righteous will inherit the millennial kingdom (v. 34) and enter into life eternal (v. 46).

THE JUDGMENT OF THE JEWS

This judgment is future, and speaks of the time when the Jews will be dealt with by God. Ezekiel 20:33-38 records God's statements about this judgment. God will purge out the rebels from among the Jews during the latter part of the tribulation. This is known as "the time of Jacob's trouble" (Jer 30:7), and two-thirds of the Jews will be purged out; the remaining one-third will be saved and enter the millennial kingdom (Zec 13:8, 9; Ro 11:26).

THE JUDGMENT OF THE ANGELS

This judgment is future, and will take place perhaps at the time Satan is judged, which will be after the millennium and preceding the great white throne judgment (Rev 20:10). Jude says, "And the angels which kept not their first estate, but left their habitation, he hath reserved in everlasting chains under darkness unto the judgment of the great day" (v. 6). These are fallen angels who followed Satan in his rebellion against God. Revelation 12:4, speaking of Satan, says: "And his tail drew the third part of the stars of heaven." A note at this verse in the Pilgrim Bible reads: "*Stars*. These are the *Angels* who followed Satan in his rebellion against God. . . ." Peter speaks of these angels: "For if God spared not the angels that sinned, but cast them down to hell, and delivered them into chains of darkness, to be reserved unto judgment" (2 Pe 2:4). These angels have been chained in pits of darkness ("hell" in the Greek is *tartaros*) waiting for the judgment of "the great day." There are other fallen angels at large, still under the direction of Satan, making up that kingdom of evil spirits arrayed against God and Christ (Mt 12:24-27; Eph 2:2; 6:11, 12). Satan, who led them astray, along with them will be "cast into the lake of fire and brimstone, where the beast and false prophet are [they had been there one thousand years and were not burnt up], and shall be tormented day and night for ever and ever" (Rev 20:10).

THE JUDGMENT OF THE GREAT WHITE THRONE

This is in the future and is the last judgment of mankind. We read about it in Revelation 20:11-15. God will wind up all the affairs of heaven and earth before establishing a new heaven and a new earth. This is not a throne to determine the guilt or innocence of those who appear there. There will be no questions asked—all the evidence and facts are in. This judgment is to determine the sentence of those who have already been declared guilty. Jesus says of the unsaved, "He that believeth on him is not condemned: but he that believeth not is condemned already, because he hath not believed in the name of the only begotten Son of God" (Jn 3:18).

God brings forth His books: "the books were opened: and another book was opened, which is the book of life" (v. 12). It required several books to register the wicked, but a single book was all that was needed to register the righteous. Jesus said, "Wide is the gate, and broad is the way, that leadeth to destruction, and many there be which go in thereat: because strait is the gate, and narrow is the way, which leadeth unto life, and few there be that find it" (Mt. 7:13, 14). Daniel 7:10 says, "The judgment was set, and the books were opened."

The book of life will be there only to prove to the unbelievers that their names are not there. Many people take for granted that because their names are on a church roll, they are also listed in the book of life. Jesus said to His disciples, "Many will say to me in that day, Lord, Lord, have we not prophesied in thy name? and in thy name have cast out devils? and in thy name done many wonderful works? And then will I profess unto them, I never knew you: depart from me, ye that work iniquity" (Mt 7:22, 23). Some names are written in the book of life (Lk 10:20; Phil 4:3), and some are not (Rev 13:8; 17:8; 20:15). Only those whose names are in this Book go to heaven (Rev 21:27). My friend, ask yourself this question:

> Is my name written there,
> On the page white and fair?
> In the book of Thy kingdom,
> Is my name written there?

If you are not sure, Peter tells us, "give diligence to make your calling and election sure. . . ." (2 Pe 1:10). "Believe on the Lord Jesus Christ and thou shalt be saved" (Ac 16:31). When you repent of your sins and receive Jesus Christ as your personal Saviour and Lord, you can be sure, and then you can "rejoice, because your names are written in heaven" (Lk 10:20), and sing:

> Yes, my name's written there,
> On the page white and fair,
> In the book of Thy kingdom,
> Yes, my name's written there.
>
> M. A. K.

Certain other books will also be opened. These contain an exact record of all that has happened in each sinner's life. Everyone will be judged "according to their works" (Rev 20:12, 13). God is fair and just in His judgments. God is a very accurate bookkeeper, and He has stated: "be sure your sin will find you out" (Num 32:23). These books will reveal the unrighteous thoughts and deeds, the neglected opportunities, and the degree of sinfulness and guilt of every unsaved person.

There are degrees of punishment taught in the Word of God. Jesus said to some cities which had rejected Him, "It shall be more tolerable for Tyre and Sidon at the day of judgment, than for you. . . . it shall be more tolerable for the land of Sodom in the judgment, than for thee" (Mt 11:22, 24). He also said, "And that servant, which knew his lord's will, and prepared not himself, neither did according to his will, shall be beaten with many stripes. But he that knew not, and did commit things worthy of stripes, shall be beaten with few stripes. For unto whomsoever much is given, of him shall much be required: and to whom men have committed much, of him they will ask the more" (Lk 12:47, 48). Christ spoke of the scribes and said of them, "the same shall receive greater damnation" (Lk 20:47). The difference in degrees will not be in the length of punishment, but in the severity of punishment.

Words Will Be Judged. Jesus said, "But I say unto you, that every idle word that men shall speak, they shall give account thereof in the day of judgment. For by thy words thou shalt be justified, and by thy words thou shalt be condemned (Mt 12:36, 37). "And Enoch also, the seventh from Adam, prophesied of these, saying, Behold, the Lord cometh with ten thousands of his saints, to execute judgment upon all, and to convince all that are ungodly among them of all their ungodly deeds which they have ungodly committed, and of all their hard speeches which ungodly sinners have spoken against him" (Jude 14, 15).

Actions Will Be Judged. The Bible says, "for the LORD is a God of knowledge, and by him *actions are weighed*" (1 Sa 2:3). King Belshazzar was told by God, "Thou art weighed in the balances, and art found wanting" (Dan 5:27). Every one at this judgment will be "found wanting."

Works Will Be Judged. Twice in this passage (Rev 20:12, 13) God says people will be judged "according to their works." The thought of God judging every person according to his works is found as many as forty-two times in the Bible (See Ps 62:12; Pr 24:12; Is 3:11; Jer 17:10; 32:19; Eze 7:3, 27; Ro 2:6; Gal 6:7; 2 Ti 4:14; Rev 2:23; 18:6). At this judgment, every lost sinner will experience the truth of these words: "Be not deceived; God is not mocked: for whatsoever a man soweth, that shall he also reap" (Gal 6:7).

Secret Things Will Be Judged. Ecclesiastes 12:14 says: "For God shall bring every work into judgment, with every secret thing, whether it be good, or whether it be evil." Paul said, "In the day when God shall judge the secrets of men by Jesus Christ according to my gospel" (Ro 2:16). Jesus said, "For there is nothing covered, that shall not be revealed; neither hid, that shall not be known" (Lk 12:2). Think of the sins hidden in the hearts of millions of people. People think they are hidden, but at this judgment everything will be exposed, every skeleton will come out of the closet.

Every Work Will Be Judged. The verse quoted above says, "For God shall bring every work into judgment." The writer of Hebrews says, "Neither is there any creature that is not manifest in his sight: but all things are naked and opened unto the eyes of him with whom we have to do" (Heb 4:13). Yes, the sinner's words, actions, works, secrets—all will be open to the eyes of Jesus Christ.

William R. Newell, in his great book, *Romans Verse By Verse*, as he was commenting on Chapter 2 of Romans, gave seven principles of God's judgment:

1. God's judgment is according to truth (verse 2).
2. According to accumulated guilt (verse 5).
3. According to works (verse 6).
4. Without respect of persons (verse 11).
5. According to performance, not knowledge (verse 13).
6. God's judgment reaches the secrets of the heart (verse 16).
7. According to reality, not religious profession (verses 17-29).[4]

The sentence that is given at this judgment is revealed in Revelation 20:14, 15: "And death and hell were cast into the lake of fire. This is the second death. And whosoever was not found written in the book of life was cast into the lake of fire." "Death" here has reference to the grave which received the body; "hell" here is a translation of the Greek word *hades*. Man is body, soul, and spirit (1 Th 5:23). Only the body goes to the grave, never the soul and spirit. The soul and spirit of an unsaved person go immediately to *hades* at the time of death (*See* Lk 16:22, 23—"hell" there in the Greek is *hades*).

There has been much confusion about hell in people's minds because three different Greek words have been translated by the same English word in the King James Version of the Bible. The three

Greek words are *tartaros, hades,* and *geenna,* which have all been translated by the one word *hell.*

The word *tartaros* occurs only once in the New Testament: "God spared not the angels that sinned, but cast them down to hell [*tartaros*], and delivered them into chains of darkness, to be reserved unto judgment" (2 Pe 2:4). *Tartaros* is the place of confinement for the angels that sinned until judgment day.

The word *hades* occurs eleven times in the New Testament, ten times translated hell (Mt 11:23; 16:18; Lk 10:15; 16:23; Ac 2:27, 31; Rev 1:18; 6:8; 20:13, 14), and one time translated grave (1 Co 15:55). Thayer defines *hades* as "the infernal regions, the common receptacle of disembodied spirits." There is torment in *hades,* but it is not the final abode of the unsaved. *Hades* will one day deliver up the dead; they will be judged; and then they will be cast into the lake of fire.

Gerald L. Stover gave a very helpful explanation of *hades:*

1. The Hebrew word is *Sheol,* appearing 65 times in the Old Testament. Its New Testament equivalent is the Greek, *Hades,* which appears 11 times. That they are to be identified as referring to the same place is proven by comparing Psalm 16:10 with Acts 2:31.

2. That these words are place names, referring to a locality, is an absolute certainty. They refer to the unseen world of disembodied spirits.

3. In the Old Testament and up to the time of the atoning work of Jesus Christ in terms of death and resurrection it would seem that the spirits of the lost and the saved went to Sheol or Hades, the two classes being separated by a vast gulf in the unseen world (Luke 16:19-31). That the portion of Hades occupied by the saints in the intermediate state is referred to as *Abraham's bosom* (Luke 16:22) and *paradise* (Luke 23:43).

4. Throughout the Old and New Testaments Sheol and Hades receives the spirits of the lost. After the death of our Lord Jesus Christ and His resurrection, we do not read of a single believer going to Hades. The teaching of the New Testament dispensation is summed up in such words as: "We are confident, I say, and willing rather to be absent from the body, and to be present with the Lord" (II Corinthians 5:8). "For I am in a strait betwixt two, having a desire to depart, and to be with Christ; which is far better" (Philippians 1:23).

If we compare Psalm 68:18 with Ephesians 4:7-11 it is interesting that when Christ ascended into Heaven, He is first of all described as descending into the lower parts of the earth and leading captive to Himself a multitude of persons described in terms of captivity—these He led into Heaven itself. Evidently the saints confined for the while to the blessed part of Sheol or Hades, were delivered by the triumphant Christ and led safely to Heaven at His ascension. Thus no Christian of this dispensation goes to Hades at death. The body goes into the grave and the spirit is released into the presence of the Lord.

Our passage in Revelation 20:12, 13, described then, the resurrection of the wicked dead. They live again in the body, the graves and Hades surrendering their victims and thus body, soul and spirit are united for judgment.[5]

The word *geenna* occurs twelve times in the New Testament (Matthew 5:22, 29, 30; 10:28; 18:9; 23:15, 33; Mark 9:43, 45, 47; Luke 12:5; James 3:6). Eleven of the twelve references are the words of Jesus Christ Himself. Harold J. Berry wrote concerning this word:

> Southeast of Jerusalem there was a valley known as the "valley of the son of Hinnom" (Joshua 15:8). It was also referred to as "Gehenna" from the Hebrew word *ge-hinnom*, which means "valley of Hinnom." During Old Testament times there were children offered to Moloch in this valley (II Chron. 33:1-6; Jer. 7:31). Later, after such heathen practices were stopped, the Jews used the valley to dispose of their rubbish, as well as the bodies of dead animals and unburied criminals. To consume all of this, a fire known as the "Gehenna of fire" burned continuously. To be in the "gehenna of fire" would be the most excruciating torment that the human mind could imagine; thus, Christ used this known place with its gnawing worms and burning fires to teach truths about the unknown place—the final abode of those who reject Him as Saviour.[6]

There are those who do not believe in a literal hell. God's Word definitely teaches "the wicked shall be turned into hell and all the nations that forget God" (Ps 9:17). Twice in these two verses in Revelation 20, verses 14 and 15, God says that the wicked were "cast into the lake of fire." People ask how a human body can live in a lake of fire without being burnt up in a few minutes. God will give the unsaved a body in the second resurrection which will be of such a composition that it will be able to endure the fire without being consumed. God kept the three Hebrew children from burning up in the fire, and He will keep the bodies of the unsaved from burning up for all eternity. What a terrifying thought! Charles H. Spurgeon believed in an eternal hell and spoke to his hearers:

> But, in Hell there is no hope. They have not even the hope of dying—the hope of being annihilated. They are forever—forever— forever—lost! On every chain in Hell, there is written "forever." In the fires there blazes out the word "forever." Up above their heads, they read "forever." Their eyes are galled, and their hearts are pained with the thought that it is "forever." Oh! if I could tell you tonight that Hell would one day be burned out, and that those who were lost might be saved, there would be a jubilee in Hell at the very thought of it. But it cannot be—it is "forever" they are "cast into utter darkness."[7]

May these words, written by J. A. Brown, be used to convict every unsaved man and woman, boy and girl:

When I Stand Before the Judgment Bar

In a day that is not far,
At the blazing judgment bar,
   Even now the awful summons I can hear;
I must meet the mighty God,
I must face His holy Word,
   I must stand before the judgment bar.

I must meet each broken vow,
That I hold so lightly now,
   Every heartache I have caused, each sigh, each tear;
Things that time cannot erase,
I must meet them face to face,
   When I stand before the judgment bar.

Every secret lust and thought
There shall be to judgment brought,
   When the Lord in all His glory shall appear;
All the deeds of darkest night
Shall come out to greet the light
   When I stand before the judgment bar.

I must meet my cankered gold,
For whose greed my life was sold,
    It shall mock me in the judgment's lurid glare,
Saying ye have sold for naught,
All the Saviour's blood had bought,
    And you stand before the judgment bar.

Oh, my record will be there,
Be its pages dark or fair,
    When I stand before the judgment bar;
When the books shall open lie,
In that morning bye and bye,
    Oh, my record! Oh, my record will be there!

Let me turn and seek the Lord,
Let me trust His holy Word,
    Let us bow and call upon Him while He's near;
Then when I my record face,
He will answer in my place
    When I stand before the judgment bar.

Hell stands waiting for every person outside of Christ, yet Christ also stands waiting for every person outside of hell. Jesus Christ made this wonderful promise: "Verily, verily, I say unto you, He that heareth my word, and believeth on him that sent me, hath everlasting life, and shall not come into condemnation; but is passed from death unto life" (Jn 5:24). He says if you hear His Word, believe on Him, receive Him as your personal Saviour and Lord, you "shall not come into condemnation." God also promises in Romans 8:1, "There is therefore now no condemnation [judgment] to them which are in Christ Jesus." The person who is saved, who is in Christ Jesus, will never have to stand at the great white throne judgment. If you are not saved, if you are not in Christ, trust Him now before it is too late.

Daniel Curry, a mighty man of God in the Middle West, dreamed he ascended to heaven and knocked on the gate. He was asked for his name, and then was told that it could not be found, but that if he wished he could appear before the judgment throne and answer for himself. He was carried rapidly away until he came into the presence of a brilliant, shining light. It was a million times brighter then anything he had ever seen on earth and its brightness seemed to blind him. He could see only the light, but soon he heard a voice out of the midst of it, saying, "Daniel Curry, have you always been good?" He had to answer, "No." "Have you always been pure?" Again his answer was, "No." "Have you always been charitable in your opinion of others?" "I cannot say that I have been." "Have you always been fair and precisely just in your dealings with your fellow men?" "No, I haven't been." And as he stood there thinking that the end would come any second, he heard a voice sweeter than the voice of any mother. As he turned he saw One standing by his side with a face sweeter than any face he had ever seen on earth, and that voice of unspeakable sweetness said, "Father, all this man's sin, all his mistakes, every evil action, word and thought; all of his short-comings, put them all down against Me; Daniel Curry stood for me down on the earth; I'll stand for him up here."[8]

"Whosoever therefore shall confess me before men, him will I confess also before my Father which is in heaven. But whosoever shall deny me before men, him will I also deny before my Father which is in heaven" (Mt 10:32, 33).

Those who stand *for* Christ down here will not have to stand *before* Him at the great white throne judgment.

14

ETERNITY AHEAD

CHARLES F. KETTERING said, "My interest is in the future because I am going to spend the rest of my life there."[1] My interest too is in the future, not only my future in this life, but in the eternity ahead, because I shall be in eternity forever and ever.

For every one of us there is an eternity ahead. It is impossible for our finite minds to comprehend how long eternity is. Someone has illustrated it this way: Try to imagine that this earth is nothing but sand. Now try to imagine that a bird could fly from a faraway planet to this earth and carry back with him one tiny grain of sand, and the round trip would take a thousand years. Then try to imagine how long it would take for that bird to carry away the entire earth, a grain of sand every thousand years. The time required for this would be but a moment in comparison to eternity.

ETERNITY AHEAD FOR THE HEAVEN AND THE EARTH

God tells us that after the millennium, the revolt at its close, the doom of the revolters and of Satan, and the great white throne judgment, "And I saw a new heaven and a new earth: for the first heaven and the first earth were passed away; and there was no more sea" (Rev 21:1).

When God says "the first heaven and the first earth were passed away," He is referring to the renovation of the heaven and the earth as spoken of in 2 Peter 3:10: "But the day of the Lord will come as a thief in the night; in the which the heavens shall pass away with a great noise, and the elements shall melt with fervent heat, the earth also and the works that are therein shall be burned up."

The Bible teaches that there are three heavens: 1) the atmospheric heaven immediately surrounding our earth; 2) the planetary heaven where the sun, moon, and stars are; and 3) the third heaven (2 Co 12:2), God's abiding place. The heaven which shall pass away is the atmospheric heaven that has been defiled by the devil and his demons (Eph 2:2; 6:12). Of course, God's heaven has not been defiled, because nothing unclean can enter there.

God's Word speaks of "the first earth . . . passed away" (Rev 21:1) and "the earth also and the works that are therein shall be burned up" (2 Peter 3:10). There is a difference of opinion among Bible scholars as to how this will take place. Some say that the present heaven and earth will be annihilated and God will create a new heaven and earth. Others say that instead of annihilation of the heaven and earth, there will be renovation.

The future change in the heaven and the earth will be made by fire, as Peter records, "the heavens being on fire shall be dissolved, and the elements shall melt with fervent heat" (2 Peter 3:12). In the past, God renovated the earth by water. Peter spoke of that in 2 Peter 3:6: "Whereby the world that then was, being overflowed with water, perished." When he said that the earth "perished," he did not mean that it was annihilated. Likewise, when God renovates the heaven and earth, the earth will not be annihilated but the fire will purge away all sin and everything which has been contaminated by sin, both in this earth and in the atmospheric heaven.

After quoting 2 Peter 3:7-13, Clarence Larkin, in his book *The Book of Revelation,* expounded:

> A surface reading of the above passage would lead one to believe that the earth as a planet, and the sidereal heavens, are to be destroyed by fire and pass away. But a careful study of the Scriptures will show us that this is not so, that what is to happen is, that this present earth, and the atmosphere surrounding it, is to be Renovated by Fire, so that its exterior surface shall be completely changed, and all that sin has brought into existence, such as thorns and thistles, disease germs, insect pests, etc., shall be destroyed, and the atmosphere purified and forever freed from evil spirits and destructive agencies.
> That this is the correct view of the passage is clear from Peter's words in verses 5 and 6.

"By the word of God the heavens were of old, and the earth standing out of the water and in the water; whereby the world that then was, being overflowed with water, PERISHED."

As we have seen the Apostle Peter was referring here not to the Flood, but to the Primeval Earth, which was made "formless and void" by a "Baptism of Water" that completely submerged it and destroyed all animal life.

Now as the Framework of the "Primeval Earth" was not destroyed by its "Watery Bath," so the Framework of the "Present Earth" is not to be destroyed by its "Baptism of Fire."

This is confirmed by the Apostle's use of the Greek word "Cosmos," which means the "land surface," the inhabitableness of the earth and not the earth as a planet. It is the exterior surface of the earth then that is to "Melt With Fervent Heat" and the "Works Therein Burnt Up." The intense heat will cause the gases in the atmosphere to explode, which the Apostle describes as the "heavens (the atmosphere) passing away with a great noise." The result will be the destruction of all animal and vegetable life, and the alteration of the earth's surface.

The Greek word "Parerchomai," translated "pass away," does not mean "termination of existence" or "annihilation," but means to pass from "one condition of existence to another." The Apostle Paul in his letter to Titus (Titus 3:5), speaking of the "Regeneration" of men, uses the same word that Jesus used when, in Matt. 19:28, He promised His Disciples that in the "Regeneration," that is in the "New Earth," they should sit on "Twelve Thrones" judging the "Twelve Tribes" of Israel. Now no one supposes that the "Regeneration of a man is his Annihilation." It is simply a Renewing Process by which he is brought back to the condition of man spiritually as before the Fall. The word "Restitution" in Acts 3:21, means the same thing. The "Dissolving" of which Peter speaks (2 Peter 3:11), is the same word Jesus used when He said of the colt—"Loose him and let him go." The teaching of the Scriptures is, that "Creation" is at present in a "State of Captivity," waiting to be Loosed from the Bondage that sin has caused. Rom. 8:19-23.

As to the "Departing as a Scroll" of the heavens, and the "Flying Away" of the earth and heavens, of which John speaks, (Rev. 6:14; 20:11), a total disappearance of all the material worlds is not at all the idea, for he tells us that afterwards he saw—"the New Jerusalem coming down out of Heaven, and nations living and walking in the

Light of it on the earth, and the Kings of the Earth bringing their Glory and Honor Into It." Rev. 21:2, 24.

The Holy Spirit by Solomon said,

"One generation passeth away, and another generation cometh, but the Earth Abideth Forever." Ecc. 1:4.

It is specifically promised that "the Meek shall Inherit the Earth," (Matt. 5:5), and that the Children of Israel shall dwell in it forever, (Isa. 60:21; 66:22), and if God's people are to inhabit it forever, it must EXIST FOREVER. It is clear then that this earth as a planet is not to be annihilated, but that it is to be Cleansed and Purified by Fire and made fit for the home of those peoples and nations that are to occupy it after its renovation.[2]

God promises in Isaiah 65:17: "For, behold, I create new heavens and a new earth: and the former shall not be remembered, nor come into mind." Then He uses the eternal stability of these new creations to emphasize a promise to the nation of Israel: "For as the new heavens and the new earth, which I will make, shall remain before me, saith the LORD, so shall your seed and your name remain" (Is 66:22). After Peter spoke of the time when "the heavens shall pass away with a great noise, and the elements shall melt with fervent heat, the earth also and the works that are therein shall be burned up" (2 Pe 3:10), he continued in verse 13: "Nevertheless we, according to his promise, look for new heavens and a new earth, wherein dwelleth righteousness." John said in Revelation 21:1: "And I saw a new heaven and a new earth." Peter says, "But in accord with His promise we are looking for new heavens and a new earth in which righteousness is at home" (2 Pe 3:13, Berkeley Version).

Revelation 21:1 closes with these words: "and there shall be no more sea." Today about three-fourths of the surface of the earth is water, and more than half of the land surface is uninhabitable. There will be geological changes in the earth so that on the new earth there will be more than eight times as much space for habitation as on the present earth. The curse will be completely lifted (Rev 22:3) when this new earth comes into being.

ETERNITY AHEAD FOR THE SAVED

Not only will there be a new heaven and a new earth in the future, but there also will be a new city called "the holy city, new Jerusalem"

(Rev 21:2). According to this verse John saw this city "coming down from God out of heaven." It is not heaven, for it comes down from God out of heaven. It takes up its abode on the new earth and will be the dwelling place for all eternity for God's saints. It is said of Abraham, "For he looked for a city which hath foundations, whose builder and maker is God" (Heb 11:10). It is also said of Abraham and his descendants:

> These all died in faith, not having received the promises, but having seen them afar off, and were persuaded of them, and confessed that they were strangers and pilgrims on the earth. For they that say such things declare plainly that they seek a country. And truly, if they had been mindful of that country from whence they came out, they might have had opportunity to have returned. But now they desire a better country, that is, an heavenly: wherefore God is not ashamed to be called their God: for he hath prepared for them a city (Heb 11:13-16).

Jesus promised: "Let not your heart be troubled: ye believe in God, believe also in me. In my Father's house are many mansions: if it were not so, I would have told you. I go to prepare a place for you. And if I go and prepare a place for you, I will come again, and receive you unto myself; that where I am, there ye may be also" (Jn 14:1-3).

Horatius Bonar, in his book on Revelation, writes glowingly of the holy city:

> Blessed City! City of peace, and love, and song! Fit accompaniment of the new heavens! Fit metropolis of the new earth, wherein dwelleth righteousness! How eagerly should we look for it! How worthy of it should we live! It has not yet arrived. Eye hath not seen it. But God points to it above, and assures us that it shall come. The right of citizenship is to be had now; and they who are to dwell in it are not angels, but men; not the unfallen, but the fallen. It is as such that we apply for the "freedom of the city." He who is its Builder and Maker gives it freely. He who is its Prince, whose blood has bought and opened it, gives it freely. He waits to receive applications; nay, He entreats men to apply. He announces that whosoever will only take Him at His word, and trust Him for entrance into it, shall have it. He specially proclaims to us His own sacrifice, His infinite propitiation, His divine bloodshedding on the

cross, and gives us to know that whosoever will receive the testimony to this great work of atonement shall enter in through the gates into the city. It is the blood that brings us to the mercy seat; it is the blood that brings us into the city. It will be a joy to enter that joyous city. By this joy we beseech you now to make sure of your citizenship, by making sure of your connection with the King. He who has the King has the city.[3]

The writer of Hebrews names the inhabitants of that new city: "But ye are come unto mount Sion, and unto the city of the living God, the heavenly Jerusalem, and to an innumerable company of angels, to the general assembly and church of the firstborn, which are written in heaven, and to God the Judge of all, and to the spirits of just men made perfect, and to Jesus the mediator of the new covenant, and to the blood of sprinkling, that speaketh better things than that of Abel" (Heb 12:22-24). This passage teaches that saints of all ages will be in this city. Notice those who are listed: an innumerable company of angels, the church, God, spirits of just men made perfect (which refer to all Old Testament saints), and Jesus.

After John saw the holy city come down from God out of heaven, he heard a great voice saying, "Behold, the tabernacle of God is with men, and he will dwell with them, and they shall be his people, and God himself shall be with them, and be their God" (Rev 21:3). God walked in the Garden of Eden with Adam and Eve; He appeared to the patriarchs of Israel; He dwelt in the innermost part of the tabernacle in the Old Testament time; He was in Christ when Christ was in the flesh on this earth; He dwells in the church by His Holy Spirit; but His actual dwelling with His people on this earth awaits the eternal state.

William R. Newell wrote of God's dwelling with men:

His "*delight* was with the sons of men" (Proverbs 8:31). Man was made in God's "image" and "likeness." Doubtless we will never know all that these terms mean! God was manifest in the flesh in Christ, the Son of man. Jesus, though crowned with glory and honor, remains man forever.

What the "delight" of God will be in this new earth "with men," and what their capacity for knowing God, and progressing in that blessed and only real knowledge, can be measured only by eternity, and the infinity of God Himself; which is to say, it is utterly without limits![4]

The description of the holy city, new Jerusalem, the home of the saints, is given in Revelation 21:10-22:6. This city will be 1500 miles long, 1500 miles wide, and 1500 miles high (Rev 21:16; a furlong is one-eighth of a mile). The base of it would stretch from farthest Maine to farthest Florida, and from the Atlantic Ocean to the state of Colorado. It would cover all of Ireland, Britain, France, Spain, Italy, Germany, Austria, Prussia, most of Turkey, and half of European Russia. Someone has calculated that if fifteen feet were allowed to each story in this city, there would be 528,000 stories. Every one of the stories would contain 2,250,000 square miles. All the stories combined would total 1,188,000,000,000 square miles (one trillion, one hundred and eighty-eight billion). It is utterly impossible to conceive the immensity of the city! The Department of Eugenics of the Carnegie Institute has estimated that the total population of the world since man first appeared on the earth is thirty billion.[5] On this estimate of population and the figures given above of the square miles in the city, there would be thirty-nine and three-fifths square miles for every man, woman, and child from Adam to the present time. (Of course, I am not saying that the city will be divided into the stories as given above).

F. W. Boreham, a very brilliant and interesting writer and minister, told the story of an Australian engineer by the name of Tammas, who was one of his parishioners, and with whom Boreham was talking:

> "Did you ever think about the size of the city?" he asked. And without waiting for a reply he proceeded to reveal the significance of his statistics. "Man, it's amazing; it's astounding; it beats everything I ever heard of! John says that each of the walls of the city measures twelve thousand furlongs. Now, if you work that out"—he bent closely over his notebook—"it will give you an area of 2,250,000 square miles! Did you ever hear the like of that? The only city foursquare that I ever saw was Adelaide in South Australia. The ship that brought me out from the old country called in there for a couple of days, and I thought it a fine city. But, as you know, very well, the city of Adelaide covers only one square mile. Each of the four sides is a mile long. London covers an area of 140

square miles. But this city—the City Foursquare! It is 2,250,000 times as big as Adelaide. It is 15,000 times as big as London! It is twenty times as big as all New Zealand! It is ten times as big as Germany, and ten times as big as France! It is forty times as big as all England! It is ever so much bigger than India! Why, it's an enormous continent in itself. I had no idea of it until I went into the figures with my blue pencil here." He would allow no comment at this stage. "Wait a minute," he pleaded, as Gavin turned to ask a question, "wait a minute. I've been going into the matter of population, and it's even more wonderful still. Look at this! Working it out on the basis of the number of people to the square mile in the city of London, the population of the City Foursquare comes out at a hundred thousand millions—seventy times the present population of the globe!"[6]

In the description of the eternal home of God's people there are a number of things which shall not be there. Leon Tucker used to say that the book of Romans is the book of the "much mores" (Ro 5:9, 10, 15, 17, 20; 11:12, 24) and that the book of Revelation is the book of the "no mores." In chapter 21 there are ten "no mores": no more sea, no more death, no more sorrow, no more crying, no more pain, no more temple, no more sun, no more moon, no more night, and no more sin. And in the next chapter, it is said there will be no more curse (22:3).

As we think of eternity ahead for the saved, a number of things come to mind as to what they shall do throughout eternity. The saved will include those who have been glorified either through death and resurrection, or through transformation. The church will have experienced glorification by resurrection and transformation; the Old Testament saints and the martyred tribulation saints will have experienced glorification by resurrection. Others included among the saved will be those who were saved during the tribulation and entered the millennium in natural bodies, as well as the children born during the millennium who did not follow Satan in his rebellion at the close of the millennium. It is not clear whether they will be translated as Dr. John F. Walvoord suggests: "It is assumed, though the Scriptures do not state it, that the millennial saints at the end of the millennium will be translated prior to their entrance into the eternal state and thus will qualify for entrance into the heavenly

Jerusalem"[7]; or will continue "living in the natural state that God originally intended for Adam and his race,"[8] as Dr. Herman A. Hoyt states. God says of them, "And the nations of them which are saved shall walk in the light of it [the city]: and the kings of the earth do bring their glory and honour into it" (Rev 21:24).

They shall worship him

> And when he had taken the book, the four beasts and four and twenty elders fell down before the Lamb, having every one of them harps, and golden vials full of odours, which are the prayers of saints. And they sung a new song, saying, Thou art worthy to take the book, and to open the seals thereof: for thou wast slain, and hast redeemed us to God by thy blood out of every kindred, and tongue, and people, and nation; and hast made us unto our God kings and priests: and we shall reign on the earth. And I beheld, and I heard the voice of many angels round about the throne and the beasts and the elders: and the number of them was ten thousand times ten thousand, and thousands of thousands; saying with a loud voice, Worthy is the Lamb that was slain to receive power, and riches, and wisdom, and strength, and honour, and glory, and blessing. And every creature which is in heaven, and on the earth and under the earth, and such as are in the sea, and all that are in them, heard I saying, Blessing, and honour, and glory, and power, be unto him that sitteth upon the throne, and unto the Lamb for ever and ever. And the four beasts said, Amen. And the four and twenty elders fell down and worshipped him that liveth for ever and ever. . . . And I heard as it were the voice of a great multitude, and as the voice of many waters, and as the voice of mighty thunderings, saying, Alleluia: for the Lord God omnipotent reigneth" (Rev 5:8-14; 19:6).

Robert Ervin Hough, in his book *The Christian After Death* wrote: "Here the heart lags, the mind is dull, memory weak, and the distractions of the earthly lot obtrude unasked upon the holiest moments. Jarring notes spoil the praise, and coldness of spirit chill the thanksgiving. It is only His matchless grace that encourages the believer to know that his poor worship is accepted. But in Heaven how different it will be! What glorious unison of full-hearted, pure, untainted, and unceasing worship the redeemed shall be able to render, as they sing the song of Moses and the Lamb!"[9]

THEY SHALL SERVE HIM

"And his servants shall serve him" (Rev 22:3). Forever God's people will serve Him. There will be constant labor for the Lord, yet there will be no weariness or failure in our work. Walter Scott wrote: "Ours will be a service without cessation, without weariness, without flagging energy. In joy and freedom our service then will be one of pure love; without a flaw, and without one legal thought. How varied the character of service! How gladly the whole being enters upon an eternal life of service to *Him!*"[10]

THEY SHALL SEE HIS FACE

"And they shall see his face" (Rev 22:4). God told Moses, "Thou canst not see my face: for there shall no man see me, and live. And I will take away mine hand, and thou shalt see my back parts: but my face shall not be seen" (Ex 33:20, 23). Jesus promised: "Blessed are the pure in heart: for they shall see God" (Mt 5:8). The psalmist prayed: "As for me, I will behold thy face in righteousness: I shall be satisfied, when I awake, with thy likeness" (Ps 17:15). "And I shall see Him face to face, and tell the story—Saved by grace."

Dr. W. A. Criswell, writing concerning seeing His face, said:

> This is what it is to be in heaven, to look upon the face of God, our Lord, and to be with one another and live. That is heaven. Incidentally, gates of pearl; incidentally, streets of gold; incidentally, walls of jasper. But mostly and foremost, our Lord and one another. I can hear the Lord as He will say to you, "On what street would you like to live in glory and what mansion would you like to call your home?" And I can hear a true saint reply, "Dear Lord, any street, any mansion, just so the windows open on the palace of the great King that I may see Him come and go."[11]

THEY SHALL HAVE HIS NAME ON THEIR FOREHEADS

"And his name shall be in their foreheads" (Rev 22:4). They shall openly and publicly hear His name, signifying that they belong to Him. They are branded forever as His very own.

J. A. Seiss writes of His name on their foreheads:

> The Jewish high priest, when fully arrayed as the officer and agent of Jehovah, in addition to his mitre, had a plate of burnished gold upon his brow, on which was engraved the great Name of that almighty

Being for whom he served. These dwellers in the New Jerusalem are all priests then, as well as kings, and so they have the tokens of their sublime office and consecration on their foreheads. The name of their King and God is there, to tell of their dignity, their office, and the transcendent authority and glory of him for whom they officiate. In the courts of kings, the most honoured servants and favourites wear badges and marks in token of the king's confidence, favour, and affection. The noble knights have their ribbons; and those whom the king delighteth to honour have their chains of gold about their necks, their rosettes, their indications of standing with their sovereign. So these all have the Name of the All-Ruling Lamb upon their foreheads, showing exaltation, honour, and blessedness of the very highest degree. They are the enthroned princes of the eternal realm, the servants of the Supreme God, the very organs and expressions of the everlasting Throne.[12]

THEY SHALL BE WITH HIM

Paul, in speaking of the coming of Christ for His own, says that they shall "meet the Lord in the air: and so shall we ever be with the Lord" (1 Th 4:17). John says, "Behold, the tabernacle of God is with men, and he will dwell with them, and they shall be his people, and God himself shall be with them, and be their God" (Rev 21:3). Jesus promised, "I will come again, and receive you unto myself; that where I am, there ye may be also" (Jn 14:3), and He prayed, "Father, I will that they also, whom thou hast given me, be with me where I am" (Jn 17:24). God's people will forever be with Him and His Son to enjoy intimate fellowship for all eternity. God's agelong purpose to dwell with His people will be finally and fully realized.

THEY SHALL BE LIKE HIM

God's people are promised: "Beloved, now are we the sons of God, and it doth not yet appear what we shall be: but we know that, when he shall appear, we shall be like him; for we shall see him as he is" (1 Jn 3:2). Also there is a promise in Philippians 3:20, 21: "For our conversation is in heaven; from whence also we look for the Saviour, the Lord Jesus Christ: who shall change our vile body, that it may be fashioned like unto his glorious body, according to the working whereby he is able even to subdue all things unto himself."

Paul declares in Romans 8:29: "For whom he did foreknow, he also did predestinate to be conformed to the image of his Son."

Dr. Kenneth S. Wuest says concerning our likeness to Christ in I John 3:2:

> This likeness in this context has to do with a physical likeness, not a spiritual one. Saints are spiritually like the Lord Jesus now in a relative sense, and through the sanctifying work of the Holy Spirit, are being conformed more and more to His spiritual likeness. John is speaking here of the Rapture. . . . The Rapture has to do with the glorification of the physical body of the believer. . . . We shall be like our Lord as to His physical, glorified body.[13]
>
> The enswathement of glory will return. Our minds will again function perfectly. Our bodies will be immortal, perfect, free from all the effects of sin that have accumulated in 6,000 years of human history.[14]

C. H. Spurgeon wrote to Andrew Bonar for his picture and autograph to be placed in the book *Studies in Leviticus,* which Bonar had kindly sent him. Bonar repiled, "I will do as you request, but I am sorry you could not wait a while, for I could have sent you a better picture, for I shall be like Him!"[15]

THEY SHALL REIGN WITH HIM ETERNALLY

"And they shall reign for ever and ever" (Rev 22:5). After reigning with Christ through the millennium, they shall continue this reign throughout eternity. They shall never cease to reign with Him. It is said of Christ: "The kingdoms of this world are become the kingdoms of our Lord, and of his Christ; and he shall reign for ever and ever" (Rev 11:15); and now it is said of His people: ". . . and they shall reign for ever and ever."

D. L. Moody had this written in the fly leaf of his Bible:

> The light of Heaven is the face of Jesus.
> The joy of Heaven is the presence of Jesus.
> The melody of Heaven is the name of Jesus.
> The harmony of Heaven is the praise of Jesus.
> The theme of Heaven is the work of Jesus.
> The employment of Heaven is the service of Jesus.
> The duration of Heaven is the eternity of Jesus.
> The fullness of Heaven is Jesus Himself.

Henry Durbanville wrote:

> Heaven is the center of the Christian's universe and he is bound to it by eight golden links:
>
> Our Father is there—Matthew 6:9.
> Our Saviour is there—Hebrews 9:24.
> Our home is there—John 14:2.
> Our name is there—Luke 10:20.
> Our life is there—Colossians 3:1-3.
> Our heart is there—Matthew 6:19-21.
> Our inheritance is there—I Peter 1:3-5.
> Our citizenship is there—Philippians 3:20.[16]

Dr. R. G. Lee said in one of his sermons:

> In Heaven beauty has reached perfection. Dr. Biederwolf tells us of a little girl who was blind from birth and only knew the beauties of earth from her mother's lips. A noted surgeon worked on her eyes and at last his operations were successful, and as the last bandage dropped away she flew into her mother's arms and then to the window and the open door, and as the glories of earth rolled into her vision, she ran screaming back to her mother and said, "Oh, Mama, why didn't you tell me it was so beautiful?" And the mother wiped her tears of joy away and said, "My precious child, I tried to tell you but I couldn't do it." And one day when we go sweeping through those gates of pearl and catch our first vision of the enrapturing beauty all around us, I think we will hunt up John and say, "John, why didn't you tell us it was so beautiful?" And John will say, "I tried to tell you when I wrote the twenty-first and twenty-second chapters of the last book in the Bible after I got my vision, but I couldn't do it."
>
> Heaven—the land where they never have any heartaches, where no graves are ever dug.
>
> Heaven—where there is no hand-to-hand fight for bread.
>
> Heaven—where no hearse rolls its dark way to the tomb.
>
> Heaven—where David is triumphant, though once he bemoaned Absalom.
>
> Heaven—where Abraham is enthroned who once wept for Sarah.
>
> Heaven—where Paul is exultant, though once he sat with his feet in the stocks.
>
> Heaven—where John the Baptist is radiant with joy though his head was chopped off in the dungeon.

Heaven—where Savonarola wears a crown, though once he burned at the stake.

Heaven—where Latimer sings praises though once he simmered in the fire.

Heaven—where many martyrs sit in the presence of Jesus though their blood once reddened the mouths of lions.

Heaven—where many saints rest in peace who once were torn on torture racks.

Let Heaven come into your mind—where there are no tears, no partings, no strife, no agonizing misunderstanding, no wounds of heart, no storm to ruffle the crystal sea, no alarm to strike from the cathedral towers, no dirge throbbing from seraphic harps, no tremor in the everlasting song.[17]

I pray that the reader will be in eternity, worshiping Him, serving Him, seeing His face, having His name on the forehead, being with Him, being like Him, and reigning with Him. The way to heaven is given by Jesus: "I am the way, the truth, and the life: no man cometh unto the Father, but by me" (Jn 14:6). A poor woman once told the preacher Rowland Hill that the way to heaven was short, easy, and simple, comprising only three steps: out of self, into Christ, and into glory.

Mr. Spurgeon told the story of one who dreamed a dream, when in great distress of mind, about religion. He thought he stood in the outer court of Heaven, and he saw a glorious host marching up, singing sweet hymns, and bearing the banners of victory; and they passed by him through the gate, and when they vanished he heard in the distance sweet strains of music.

"Who are they?" he asked.

"They are the goodly fellowship of the prophets, who have gone to be with God."

And he heaved a deep sigh as he said, "Alas! I am not one of them, and never shall be, and I cannot enter there."

By and by there came another band, equally lovely in appearance, and equally triumphant, and robed in white. They passed within the portals, and again were shouts of welcome heard within.

"Who are they?"

"They are the goodly fellowship of the apostles."

"Alas!" he cried, "I belong not to that fellowship, and I cannot enter there."

He still waited and lingered, in the hope that he might yet go in, but the next multitude did not encourage him, for they were the noble army of martyrs. He could not go with them nor wave their palm branches. He waited still, and saw that the next was a company of godly ministers and officers of Christian churches; but he could not go with them. At last, as he walked, he saw a larger host than all the rest put together, marching and singing most melodiously; and in front walked the woman that was a sinner, and the thief that died upon the cross, close by the Saviour; and he looked long, and saw there such as Manasseh and the like; and when they entered he could see who they were, and he thought—

"There will be no shouting about them."

But to his astonishment, it seemed as if all Heaven was rent with sevenfold shouts as they passed in. And the angels said to him, "These are they that are mighty sinners, saved by mighty grace."

And then he said, "Blessed be God! I can go in with them."

And so he awoke.

Blessed be God! you and I, too, can go in with that company. I cannot hope to go in anywhere but with that company. Such is my own sense of how I expect to enter Heaven, and we will go together, brother sinner, or sister sinner, trusting in the precious blood and washed in the blood of the Lamb.[18]

Thank God, I can say with Spurgeon: Blessed be God, I will be in that company, because I am trusting in the precious blood of Jesus Christ, who is "the Way to Go," "the Truth to Know," and "the Life to Live." This is how a person gets to heaven.

ETERNITY AHEAD FOR THE LOST

There are many questions asked in the Bible. Two are asked in 1 Peter 4:17, 18: "what shall the end be of them that obey not the gospel of God? And if the righteous scarcely be saved, where shall the ungodly and the sinner appear?" The "end" means the destination, the condition, the estate. In the last part of this chapter, I want to see how the Word of God answers these questions.

I realize that many people in this country and in the world do not accept the teaching of the Bible about the future estate of the lost, but facts are facts—you can argue against them, but you can't change them.

R. A. Torrey, in a message entitled, "The Bible Hell," said,

I would rather believe and proclaim unpleasant truth than to believe and proclaim pleasant error, and as awful as the thought is, I have been driven to the conclusion that there is a Hell. . . . The New Testament does not hold out one single ray of hope for men and women who die without Christ. Any one who dares to do so dares to do what God has not done. He takes a fearful responsibility upon himself. "Forever and ever" is the never ceasing wail of that restless sea of fire. As appalling as it is, let us face the facts and act accordingly.[19]

Here are the facts about eternity ahead for the lost. These facts ought to be faced and acted upon.

THEY SHALL BE CAST INTO THE LAKE OF FIRE

Five times in the book of Revelation the lake of fire is mentioned (Rev 19:20; 20:10, 14, 15; 21:8). After the white throne judgment, the sentence for the lost is given: "And whosoever was not found written in the book of life was cast into the lake of fire." Hell fire is mentioned a number of times in the Bible (Mt 5:22; 18:9; Mk 9:47; Ja 3:6). Fire is referred to often in relation to Hell (Mt 13:40, 42, 50; 18:8, 9; 25:41; Mk 9:43-48; Jude 7; Rev 14:10).

THEY SHALL BE TORMENTED FOREVER

The rich man in Luke 16 was in torment (vv. 23, 24, 25, 28). Those who die unsaved "shall be tormented with fire and brimstone in the presence of the holy angels, and in the presence of the Lamb: And the smoke of their torment ascendeth up forever and ever" (Rev 14:10, 11). They will never be able to get one drop of water (Lk 16:24).

A young man named David, who had often heard this story, was impressed by verse 24 where in agony the rich man pleads that one might be sent to dip the tip of his finger in water and cool his parched tongue. Although under conviction, David did not immediately receive Christ. Every night, however, as he came in from his evening of pleasure he took a glass of water befor retiring. Later he confessed, "I don't believe I ever lifted that cup to my lips without the story of Luke 16 coming before my mind's eye. I found myself wondering if this would be the last drink of water I would ever take! I feared I would wake up in torment, begging for just a drop to cool my dry tongue." Finally, David was led to put his trust in the Saviour when he heard a message on John 6:35, "He that believeth on me shall never thirst!"

THEY SHALL HAVE NO REST DAY NOR NIGHT

God says of the unsaved in this life: "But the wicked are like the troubled sea, when it cannot rest, whose waters cast up mire and dirt. There is no peace, saith my God, to the wicked" (Is 57:20, 21). Jesus invites people, "Come unto me, all ye that labour and are heavy laden, and I will give you rest" (Mt 11:28). If people do not come to Christ to be saved and get His rest, they will be restless in this life, and for all eternity it will be true of them "they have no rest day nor night" (Rev 14:11).

THEY SHALL WEEP AND WAIL AND GNASH THEIR TEETH

Jesus said of the lost: "The Son of man shall send forth his angels, and they shall gather out of his kingdom all things that offend, and them which do iniquity; and shall cast them into a furnace of fire: there shall be wailing and gnashing of teeth. . . . So shall it be at the end of the world: the angels shall come forth, and sever the wicked from among the just, and shall cast them into the furnace of fire: there shall be wailing and gnashing of teeth" (Mt 13:41, 42, 49, 50 *see also* Lk 13:28).

Dr. Franklin Logsdon wrote of this dungeon of ceaseless grief:

> Tears will never be hotter, nor grief more bitter. Nor shall there be any relief. Memory will aggravate the sorrowful condition as recollection after recollection will remind the lost of the opportunities which were theirs to enter into eternal life, to be delivered from the power of darkness—the sermons heard, the gospel tracts offered, the testimonies borne to them, the pressing invitations urged upon them, all of which went unheeded. Many will remember their saying, "Not tonight; I'll get saved by and by."
>
> Self-disdain. The gnashing or gritting of the teeth is almost beyond comprehension. Nor can anyone be sure of its full meaning. A minister of the Gospel, who had been saved out of a horrible life of crime, was reflecting on his past one day. He had spent fourteen years as a prisoner in a state penitentiary. He said, "How good of the Lord, not only to save a sinner like me, but to erase so much of

the past from my mind. But one matter which comes back to me so frequently to put chills in my being is the outbursts of prisoners during the long night hours. Unable to rest, they would condemn themselves in fearfully vile language for their stupidity in getting caught, gritting their teeth as the verbal putrification emanated from their lips." This illustration may fall far short of usefulness in this connection, but one in a lost eternity with all its torment and grief will have no one to blame but himself. One can only imagine with what self-disdain such will flay themselves for being there.[20]

THEY SHALL BE IN THE BLACKNESS OF DARKNESS FOREVER

Jude wrote of the lost, "to whom is reserved the blackness of darkness forever" (Jude 13). What a reservation! The lost are described as children of darkness in 1 Thessalonians 5:5, and Jesus said of them that they "loved darkness rather than light because their deeds were evil" (Jn 3:19). Jesus said, "I am the light of the world: he that followeth me shall not walk in darkness, but shall have the light of life" (Jn 8:12), but if people do not follow Jesus, they shall have "the blackness of darkness forever."

THEY SHALL BE SEPARATED FROM GOD FOREVER

People who are lost are separated from God in this life. They are spoken of as "dead in trespasses and sins . . . without Christ . . . without God . . . far off" (Eph 2:1, 12, 13). When the lost person dies, there is a great gulf that separates the lost from the saved (Lk 16:26). This gulf is fixed; no one can help him. The unsaved person will be separated for all eternity from God and His people.

Senator Tombs of Georgia, and George Pierce, his very good friend, were having a conversation. As they were talking, George said, "Do you know, Senator, one of these days you are going to be terribly hurt. An awful thing is going to happen to you. You are going to be eternally separated from that dear wife you love so much." Senator Tombs said, "Why, man, have you lost your mind? You know that I love my wife more than I love my own life. You know there isn't anything I wouldn't do for her. What in the world are you talking about?" George replied, "Senator, your wife is a wonderful Christian. One day she is going to be with the Lord; but you are not a Christian, so you will die and go to hell and be eternally separated from your wife." The senator said, "Tell me, how can I be saved? I don't want to be separated from my wife. I love her dearly." They went down on their knees and prayed, and the senator was saved.

Jesus will say to many at the judgment, "Depart from me, ye that work iniquity" (Mt 7:23).

THEY SHALL BE UNJUST AND FILTHY FOREVER

Jesus said of the lost: "He that is unjust, let him be unjust still: and he which is filthy, let him be filthy still" (Rev 22:11). A note in the *Pilgrim Edition* of the Bible at this verse says: "This means that when the things written in this book have taken place, there will be no more opportunity for men to be saved and changed into the likeness of the Lord Jesus Christ. Whatever they are at the end of this time, they will be to all eternity."

Evangelist Robert L. Sumner, in his book, *Hell Is No Joke*, spoke of this:

> Suffice it to say that Hell is a land where passions run wild but are never gratified. The appetites you feed now will cry unsuccessfully for appeasement throughout all eternity. All appetites will bring the same reaction in Hell whether they be for dope, tobacco, liquor, lust or some lesser sin in the eyes of the finite. As another has already suggested, Hell is a place where the Belshazzars will not have their wine, where the Ahabs will not have their Naboth's vineyards, where the Felixes will not have their Drusillas, where the Herods will not have their sensuous dances, and where the Judases will not have their cankered gold.[21]

The Bible makes it clear that Hell is eternal, or everlasting.

The two Greek words *aion* and *aionios* which speak of the being of God, the glory of God, the Son of God, His reign, His glory, His throne, His priesthood, His postresurrection life, mean eternal or everlasting. Jesus Christ said in Matthew 25:46: "And these shall go away into everlasting [*aionios*] punishment: but the righteous into life eternal [*aionis*]." The same Greek word *aionios* describes the duration of the life of the righteous and the duration of the punishment of the unsaved. Therefore, everlasting punishment will last just as long as everlasting life. The unsaved will be in hell as long as God lives; and that will be forever, because God will never die.

Dr. Kenneth S. Wuest, Greek scholar who made a thorough study of the duration of future punishment, after quoting a number of

Greek scholars such as Moulton and Milligan, Cremer, Thayer, Liddell and Scott to prove his point, concluded with these words: "Thus, God's Word clearly teaches that the sufferings of the lost will be unending."[22]

What a contrast between eternity ahead for the saved and the lost! Salem Kirban, in his book *Your Last Goodbye*, shows some of this contrast:

HELL	HEAVEN
Eternal Torment in the Lake of Fire for your sin	Eternal bliss in Heaven for your acceptance of Christ
No hope ever for escape	Heaven is yours forever
A place of conscious torment constantly	A place of conscious joy forever
Anguishing torment by fire that is never quenched and never consumes you	No sickness, no sorrow, no death but eternal abundance of life that never ends
Eternal darkness that brings weeping and grinding of teeth	Eternal light for there is no night there . . . singing praises to God
Eternal separation from loved ones who are believers in Christ. No hope of communication between you and those living on earth to warn them of the reality of Hell	Eternal reunion with loved ones who are believers in Christ
The torment of a memory that will add to your constant suffering, realizing that a decision of repentance and faith on your part, while living on earth, could have changed your destination	Eternal happiness in a New Heaven and a New Earth with all the former things passed away and remembered no more
Eternal torment of unsatisfied lustful cravings	Complete fulfillment of all of God's Promises[23]

If you who are not saved will repent and receive Christ as personal Saviour and Lord (Lk 13:3; Jn 1:12), in the eternity ahead you will be with the Lord and His people. I say to you, as an old teacher said to his students, "Gentlemen, many will be wishing you a happy New Year. Your old teacher wishes you a happy eternity!"

15

"WHAT MANNER OF PERSONS OUGHT YE TO BE?"

PETER SAYS: "But the day of the Lord will come as a thief in the night; in the which the heavens shall pass away with a great noise, and the elements shall melt with fervent heat, the earth also and the works therein shall be burned up. Seeing then that all these things shall be dissolved, what manner of persons ought ye to be in all holy conversation and godliness?" (2 Pe 3:10, 11). Then he tells us the kind of a person we ought to be in the light of the fact that Jesus is coming and judgment will follow (vv. 11, 12, 14, 17, 18).

As I have written the preceding chapters concerning the any-moment return of Christ, the judgment seat of Christ which follows for the Christians, the awful tribulation and judgments following for the unsaved, my desire in this chapter is to help you to see, and to be, the kind of person God wants you to be.

Jesus said, "If ye know these things, happy are ye if ye do them" (Jn 13:17), and the writer of Hebrews says, "Therefore we ought to give the more earnest heed to the things which we have heard, lest at any time we should let them slip [or slip away from them]" (Heb 2:1).

The old-time expositor, Albert Barnes, made a helpful comment concerning this:

> The fact of the imminent return of Christ ought to be allowed to exert a deep and abiding influence on us, to induce us to lead holy lives. We should feel that there is nothing permanent on the earth; that this is not our abiding home, and that our great interests are

in another world. We should be serious, humble and prayerful, and should make it our great object to be prepared for the solemn scenes through which we are soon to pass. A habitual contemplation of the truth that all we see is soon to pass away would produce a most salutary effect on the mind. It would make us serious. It would lead us not to desire to accumulate what must so soon be destroyed. It would prompt us to lay up our treasures in Heaven. It would cause us to ask with deep earnestness whether we are prepared for these amazing scenes should they suddenly burst upon us.[1]

In 2 Peter 3:11, 12, 14, 17, 18, we are told ten things we ought to be in times like these.

WE OUGHT TO BE PERSONS WHO ARE HOLY

In verse 11, Peter uses the phrase *holy conversation,* which means a holy manner of life. The Greek word for holy, *hagios,* means basically, set apart for the service of God. As Peter speaks of the coming of the Lord in 1 Peter 1:13-16, he says, "But as he which hath called you is holy, so be ye holy in all manner of conversation; because it is written, Be ye holy; for I am holy." The only way Christians can be holy is to "present your bodies a living sacrifice, holy, acceptable unto God" (Ro 12:1) and be "filled with the Holy Ghost" (Ac 4:31).

WE OUGHT TO BE PERSONS WHO ARE GODLY

Also in verse 11, Peter speaks of *godliness.* This is the Greek word *eusebeia,* which, according to W. E. Vine "characterized by a God-ward attitude, does that which is well-pleasing to Him."[2] We are told to "exercise thyself rather unto godliness" and Paul says "godliness is profitable unto all things, having promise of the life that now is, and of that which is to come" (1 Ti 4:7, 8). Paul says, "But godliness with contentment is great gain," and exhorts us to "follow after . . . godliness" (1 Ti 6:6, 11). He says in Titus 2:12: "Teaching us that, denying ungodliness and worldly lusts, we should live soberly, righteously, and godly, in this present world."

WE OUGHT TO BE PERSONS WHO ARE LOOKING FOR HIS COMING

Verse 12 exhorts us to be *looking for,* which means "to expect, or wait for." Paul said in Philippians 3:20, "For our conversation [citizenship, A.S.V.] is in heaven: from whence also we look for the Saviour, the Lord Jesus Christ" and in Titus 2:13: "Looking for that blessed hope, and the glorious appearing of the great God and our Saviour Jesus Christ." God promises in Hebrews 9:28: "unto them that look for him shall he appear the second time without sin unto salvation."

WE OUGHT TO BE PERSONS WHO ARE EARNESTLY DESIRING HIS COMING

In the American Standard Version, *hasting* is rendered "earnestly desiring." Paul, just before he was martyred, wrote: "Henceforth there is laid up for me a crown of righteousness, which the Lord, the righteous judge, shall give me at that day: and not to me only, but unto all them that love his appearing" (2 Ti 4:8). Dr. N. A. Woychuk stated:

> The original phrasing is more emphatic, "Not to me only, but also to all those who have *set their love* on His appearing." The word, used as a *perfect* participle, signifies earnest desire, looking with great expectation. Here are believers, like the Apostle Paul, who have *set their love* upon His appearing, because they have found in Jesus "all their salvation and all their desire" (2 Sam. 23:5). Their "soul waiteth for the Lord more than they that watch for the morning" (Psa. 130.6), and they scan the eastern horizon longingly and pray, "Even so, come, Lord Jesus" (Rev. 22:20).
>
> A dear servant of God once suggested that there are four attitudes of heart and mind respecting the "appearing" of Christ: The worst of these is *indifference.* "Where is the promise of his coming?" they say, "For since the fathers fell asleep, all things continue as they were from the beginning of the creation" (2 Pet. 3:4). How all such need to be reminded that the "Lord is not slack concerning his promise" (2 Pet 3:9).
>
> The next state is *fear.* This is good because it requires faith to "fear." "Praise our God, all ye his servants, and ye that fear him, both small and great" (Rev. 19:5).
>
> Better still than fear is *hope.* "Hope" is expectation with desire. God has endowed such a person with knowledge enough to be able to wish it. Paul calls it the *blessed* hope: "Looking for that blessed hope, and the glorious appearing of the great God and our Saviour Jesus Christ" (Titus 2:13).

But the Spirit of God takes the devoted ones yet one step higher—
love. "Love" is as much above "hope" as "hope" is above fear. *Hope*
may selfishly desire merely what the person gives, but *love* is set on
the Person Himself. They "have *set their love* on His appearing."[3]

Then Dr. Woychuk gave seven reasons why we should love His
appearing, or earnestly desire His coming:

1) Because Satan's powerful and unceasing attacks upon the believers will abruptly come to an end. . . .

2) Because all of creation which groans and travails, as a result of
the curse, "shall be delivered from the bondage of corruption into
the glorious liberty of the children of God" (Rom. 8:21).

3) Because at that moment "we shall all be changed" (I Cor.
15:51) and "we know that when he shall appear, we shall be like
him; for we shall see him as he is" (I John 3:2).

4) Because death shall then be indeed "swallowed up in victory"
(I Cor. 15:54). . . .

5) Because it shall be a supreme honor to our blessed Lord when
the believers—His mystical body—clothed in His unveiled perfec-
tions, shall be exhibited before the whole universe. That will be the
day when He "shall be glorified in his saints" and be "admired in all
them that believe" (II Thessalonians 1:10).

6) Because at that moment all the saints in their united strength
and beauty, as the Bride of Christ, shall proceed to the "marriage
supper of the Lamb" (Rev. 19:9) where the purposes of Divine love
shall be at last fully consummated, and the Lord shall "rest in His
love," and rejoice over her "with singing" (Zeph. 3:17).

7) Why *love* Christ's appearing? Because we *love Him,* our
blessed Lord and Saviour, Jesus Christ—the One "who first loved
us," the One who "died the just for the unjust that He might bring
us to God."[4]

WE OUGHT TO BE PERSONS WHO ARE DILIGENT

Peter exhorts us to *be diligent,* which means "do your best, make
haste, take care, hurry on." Peter uses the thought of diligence three
times in his second epistle: "And beside this, giving all diligence, add
to your faith virtue; and to virtue knowledge; and to knowledge
temperance; and to temperance patience; and to patience godliness;
and to godliness brotherly kindness; and to brotherly kindness
charity" (1:5-7). "Wherefore the rather, brethren, give diligence to

make your calling and election sure: for if ye do these things, ye shall never fall" (1:10). "Be *diligent* that ye may be found of him in peace, without spot, and blameless" (3:14).

Jesus told His servants, "Occupy till I come" (Lk 19:13), which means to buy up the opportunities, to be busy. He gave each of His servants a pound to trade with, and they were to use it diligently. When He returns, some will have been diligent and will receive rewards, while others will have been lazy and will be judged as wicked servants (Lk 19:11-27).

WE OUGHT TO BE PERSONS WHO ARE PEACEFUL

Peter tells us to "be diligent that ye may be found of him in peace." Dr. Kenneth S. Wuest comments: "The idea is, 'Do your best to be found with respect to Him, in relation to Him,' thus, with respect to His coming and at that time by Him. 'In peace' refers to the saints living at peace with one another."[5] Paul writes in 2 Corinthians 13:11 "live in peace" and in 1 Thessalonians 5:13, "And be at peace among yourselves." He also wrote, "If it be possible, as much as lieth in you, live peaceably with all men" (Ro 12:18). The writer of Hebrews exhorts, "*Follow peace* with all men" (Heb 12:14). When Jesus Christ the Prince of peace returns, He does not want to find Christians fighting and squabbling with one another. In view of the Saviour's return at any moment, Christians should neither provoke nor prolong strife, but make every effort to live peacefully with others.

WE OUGHT TO BE PERSONS WHO ARE WITHOUT SPOT

Peter says in verse 14 that we should be "without spot" which means being free from censure, irreproachable, free from all defilement in the sight of God. James wrote, "Pure religion and undefiled before God and the Father is this, To visit the fatherless and widows in their affliction, and to keep himself unspotted from the world" (Ja 1:27). We have been redeemed "with the precious blood of Christ, as of a lamb without blemish and without spot" (1 Pe 1:19) "who through the eternal Spirit offered himself without spot to God" (Heb 9:14). He "loved the church, and gave himself for it, that he might sanctify and cleanse it with the washing of water by the word, that he might present it to himself a glorious church, not having spot, or wrinkle, or any such thing; but that it should be holy and without blemish" (Eph 5:25-27).

WE OUGHT TO BE PERSONS WHO ARE BLAMELESS

The last word in verse 14, *blameless*, speaks of what cannot be blamed or found fault with. Paul wrote to the Corinthians: "So that ye come behind in no gift; waiting for the coming of our Lord Jesus Christ: who shall also confirm you unto the end, that ye may be blameless in the day of our Lord Jesus Christ" (I Co 1:7, 8), and in Philippians 2:14-16 he says: "Do all things without murmurings and disputings: That ye may be blameless and harmless, the sons of God, without rebuke, in the midst of a crooked and perverse nation, among whom ye shine as lights in the world." In his prayer for Christians he said, "I pray God your whole spirit and soul and body be preserved blameless unto the coming of our Lord Jesus Christ" (1 Th 5:23). Rev. Francis W. Dixon, writing on 2 Pe 3:10-18, says:

> Study verses 11 and 14 carefully, and ask yourself this question: What would my immediate reaction be if I were suddenly told that the Lord was coming in two hours' time? Is it not true that many Christians, on receiving such a message, would need every bit of two hours to prepare for His coming? Apologies would have to be made—look up Matthew 5:23-24; debts would have to be paid— look up Romans 13:8; books would have to be burnt—look up Acts 19:19; loved ones would have to be warned—look up Genesis 19:14; checks would have to be written—look up Malachi 3:8; confessions would have to be made—look up Matthew 18:15-16; etc., etc.! Well, the fact is, He is coming—and *He may come tonight*—and the practical effect of this truth should be an incentive to holy living. If we are expecting Him to come we shall desire to be found of Him "without spot" and "blameless" (verse 14)—look up Colossians 3:2-5 and I John 2:28.[6]

WE OUGHT TO BE PERSONS WHO ARE ON GUARD

Peter says in verse 17: "Ye therefore, beloved, seeing ye know these things before, beware lest ye also, being led away with the error of the wicked, fall from your own stedfastness." *Beware* is *phulasso* in the Greek, which is a military term meaning to guard or be on your guard. In this verse we are commanded to be on guard against two things: 1) getting drawn away from the faith by the error of the unbelievers, and 2) as a consequence, losing our own steadfastness.

The world today is full of wicked people who will lead Christians astray if we are not on our guard. The word *error* here means a wandering, a straying about, and if we are not careful, the wicked all about us will lead us astray from the right way, so that we will be wandering and straying about, going hither and thither in the things of sin.

We need to be on guard also concerning the danger of falling from our steadfastness. The word *steadfast* means firmly fixed in faith or duty, constant, unchanging, steady. Surely lack of backbone, stamina, consistency, and faithfulness has characterized many of God's people down through the years. In Psalm 78:8 God says of people in that day that they were "a generation that set not their heart aright, and whose spirit was not steadfast with God"; and in verse 37 of this same Psalm the psalmist lamented, "For their heart was not right with him, neither were they stedfast in his covenant." Paul exhorted, "Therefore, brethren, stand fast, and hold the traditions which ye have been taught, whether by word, or our epistle" (2 Th 2:15). James exhorted, "Be ye also patient; stablish your hearts: for the coming of the Lord draweth nigh" (Ja 5:8). In Revelation we are urged: "But that which ye have already hold fast till I come"; "Remember . . . hold fast"; "Behold, I come quickly: hold that fast which thou hast, that no man take thy crown" (Rev 2:25, 3:3, 11). These are great incentives to stand fast, hold fast, and be steadfast. Paul encourages us: "Therefore, my beloved brethren, *be ye stedfast,* unmoveable, always abounding in the work of the Lord, forasmuch as ye know that your labour is not vain in the Lord" (1 Co 15:58). May it be said of us, as it was said of the Christians in the church at Jerusalem: "And they continued stedfastly in the apostles' doctrine and fellowship, and in breaking of bread, and in prayers" (Ac 2:42). The result of steadfastness will be to hear the returning Saviour saying: "Well done, thou good and faithful servant: thou hast been faithful over a few things, I will make thee ruler over many things: enter thou into the joy of thy lord" (Mt 25:21).

WE OUGHT TO BE PERSONS WHO ARE GROWING

This is the last of Peter's exhortations to us in this chapter: "But grow in grace, and in the knowledge of our Lord and Saviour Jesus Christ" (v. 18). Alford comments: "Not only do not fall from your own steadfastness but be so firmly rooted as to throw out branches and yield increase."[7] This spiritual growth has two aspects: 1) growth in grace and 2) growth in the knowledge of our Lord and Saviour Jesus Christ.

Growing in grace means growing in the Christian life. We are to grow in our love for the Lord Jesus Christ and to "grow up into him in all things, which is the head, even Christ . . . Till we all come in the unity of the faith, and of the knowledge of the Son of God, unto a perfect man, unto the measure of the stature of the fulness of Christ" (Eph 4:15, 13). Paul said, "Christ in you [is] the hope of glory: Whom we preach, warning every man, and teaching every man in all wisdom; that we may present every man perfect [full-grown, mature, fully developed] in Christ Jesus" (Col. 1:28).

Growing "in the knowledge of our Lord and Saviour Jesus Christ" means getting to really know and understand Him completely. Paul's prayer was "That I may know him, and the power of his resurrection, and the fellowship of his sufferings, being made comformable unto his death" (Phil 3:10).

N. Vincent, in *The Biblical Illustrator*, spoke of growing in the knowledge of Christ:

> (1) Growing in the knowledge of Christ implies a fuller apprehension of His Godhead. (2) A clearer sight of His humanity. (3) A more plain discerning and full persuasion that He was foreordained to be a Redeemer. (4) A greater insight into His sufferings. (5) A more fruitful eyeing of His resurrection and going to His Father. (6) Greater satisfaction about His imputed righteousness. (7) A more constant and fiducial eyeing of His intercession, and the pity and compassions of Him that intercedes. (8) Being better acquainted with His great power, and continual presence with His Church which is so nearly related to Him. (9) A better understanding of Him as "Mediator of the New Covenant." (10) A more earnest looking for His appearing.[8]

John Jardine wrote of the evidences that Christians are growing in the knowledge of Christ:

"1. He will be rising higher and higher in the estimation of your souls. 2. You will be growing in a filial dependence on Him. 3.

The more you grow in the knowledge of Christ the more you will be assimilated to His glorious image. 4. The more you grow in the knowledge of Christ you will the more cheerfully worship, honour, and obey Him."[9]

Rev. Francis W. Dixon, pastor of the Lansdowne Baptist Church, of Bournemouth, England, in one of his studies on this third chapter of II Peter, gives some very helpful suggestions on how to grow in grace:

(1) *To grow in grace we must be truly born again, i.e., we must have LIFE.* There must be life before there can be growth—look up and compare John 3:3-6; Ephesians 2:1; and I John 5:11-13. We cannot grow into grace—we are born into grace, then we are to grow. It is no good trying to live the Christian life before we have received that life, for dead things do not grow. Growth is the evidence of life and the result of life.

(2) *To grow in grace we must have the care of others and the comfort of HOME.* A baby is entirely dependent upon its mother. We need care, the care of spiritual foster-parents, and the comfort and help of a Christian Church. Spiritual tramps and religious gypsies do not grow. Link on to a live fellowship of God's people—you need their help—look up and compare Acts 2:42 and Hebrews 10:23-25.

(3) *To grow in grace we must have plenty of sleep or REST.* Sleep is not a luxury; it is a necessity. We spend one-third of our lives sleeping. Before we can become strong, fully-grown, robust Christians we need to know how to rest upon the promises of God—look up 2 Peter 1:4-12, and compare Isaiah 26:3; Matthew 11:28-29; Philippians 4:6 and I Peter 5:7.

(4) *To grow in grace we must have plenty of fresh AIR.* Prayer is "the Christian's native air . . . and vital breath"—look up Isaiah 40:31; Daniel 6:10; Matthew 6:6; Luke 18:1 and James 5:16. A prayerless Christian will always be a stunted Christian—look up the Psalmist's prescription for growth in Psalm 55:17!

(5) *To grow in grace we must have plenty of good FOOD.* We grow by what we eat—look up Deuteronomy 8:3; Matthew 4:4; John 6:51; I Corinthians 3:2; Hebrews 5:12-14 and I Peter 2:2. "The Word of God is the food of the mighty." If we are to grow we must not only have plenty of food, but plenty of the *right* food. Regular devotional Bible reading is the secret of growth in grace.

(6) *To grow in grace we must have plenty of EXERCISE.* There

must be the exercise of open confession of Christ (Matthew 5:16; Mark 5:19 and Romans 10:9-10); soul-winning activity (John 1:41); and generous giving (Luke 6:38 and 2 Corinthians 9:7). Spiritual exercise in these three ways will soon result in spiritual growth.

(7) *We must GO ON GROWING in grace until we see Him face to face.* We should never stop growing in this life—look up Philippians 1:6, and compare Revelation 22:4.[10]

Besides Peter's exhortations to us as to what manner of persons we ought to be in view of the second coming of Christ, God's Word in other verses exhort us as to our manner of living as we wait for Christ to return. I will briefly mention a few.

WE OUGHT TO BE PERSONS WHO ARE PURE

"Beloved, now are we the sons of God, and it doth not yet appear what we shall be: but we know that, when he shall appear, we shall be like him; for we shall see him as he is. And every man that hath this hope in him purifieth himself, even as he is pure" (1 Jn 3:2, 3).

WE OUGHT TO BE PERSONS WHO ARE PATIENT

"Be patient therefore, brethren, unto the coming of the Lord. Behold, the husbandman waiteth for the precious fruit of the earth, and hath long patience for it, until he receive the early and latter rain. Be ye also patient; stablish your hearts: for the coming of the Lord draweth nigh" (Ja 5:7, 8).

WE OUGHT TO BE PERSONS WHO ARE SOBER

"But of the times and the seasons, brethren ye have no need that I write unto you. For yourselves know perfectly that the day of the Lord so cometh as a thief in the night. For when they shall say, Peace and safety; then sudden destruction cometh upon them, as travail upon a woman with child; and they shall not escape. But ye, brethren, are not in darkness, that that day should overtake you as a thief. Ye are all the children of light, and the children of the day: we are not of the night, nor of darkness. Therefore let us not sleep, as do others; but let us watch and be sober" (1 Th 5:1-6).

WE OUGHT TO BE PERSONS WHO ARE PRAYERFUL

"But the end of all things is at hand: be ye therefore sober, and watch unto prayer" (1 Pe 4:7).

WE OUGHT TO BE PERSONS WHO ARE FAITHFUL

"For the kingdom of heaven is as a man traveling into a far country, who called his own servants, and delivered unto them his goods . . . After a long time the lord of those servants cometh, and reckoneth with them. And so he that had received five talents came and brought other five talents, saying, Lord, thou deliveredst unto me five talents: behold, I have gained beside them five talents more. His lord said unto him, Well done, thou good and faithful servant: thou hast been faithful over a few things, I will make thee ruler over many things: enter thou into the joy of thy lord" (Mt 25:14, 19-21).

WE OUGHT TO BE PERSONS WHO ARE OBEDIENT

"I give thee charge in the sight of God, who quickeneth all things, and before Christ Jesus, who before Pontius Pilate witnessed a good confession; That thou keep this commandment without spot, unrebukeable, until the appearing of our Lord Jesus Christ" (1 Ti 6:13, 14).

WE OUGHT TO BE PERSONS WHO ARE SINCERE AND WITHOUT OFFENSE

"That ye may approve things that are excellent; that ye may be sincere and without offense till the day of Christ" (Phil 1:10).

WE OUGHT TO BE PERSONS WHO ARE LOVING

"And the Lord make you to increase and abound in love one toward another, and toward all men, even as we do toward you: To the end he may stablish your hearts, unblameable in holiness before God, even our Father, at the coming of our Lord Jesus Christ with all his saints" (1 Th 3:12, 13).

WE OUGHT TO BE PERSONS WHO ARE MODERATE OR GENTLE

"Let your moderation be known unto all men. The Lord is at hand" (Phil 4:5).

WE OUGHT TO BE PERSONS WHO ARE ABIDING IN CHRIST

"And now, little children, abide in him; that, when he shall appear, we may have confidence, and not be ashamed before him at his coming" (1 Jn 2:28).

We Ought to Be Persons Who Are Good Examples

"The elders which are among you I exhort, who am also an elder, and a witness of the sufferings of Christ, and also a partaker of the glory that shall be revealed: Feed the flock of God which is among you, taking the oversight thereof, not by constraint, but **willingly**; not for filthy lucre, but of a ready mind; Neither as being lords over God's heritage, but being examples to the flock. And when the chief Shepherd shall appear, ye shall receive a crown of glory that fadeth not away" (1 Pe 5:1-4).

We Ought to Be Persons Who Are True Disciples

"Then said Jesus unto his disciples, If any man will come after me, let him deny himself, and take up his cross, and follow me. For whosoever will save his life shall lose it: and whosoever will lose his life for my sake shall find it. For what is a man profited, if he shall gain the whole world, and lose his own soul? or what shall a man give in exchange for his soul? For the Son of man shall come in the glory of his Father with his angels; and then he shall reward every man according to his works" (Mt 16:24-27).

We Ought to Be Persons Who Are Seeking Those Things Which Are Above

"If ye then be risen with Christ, seek those things which are above, where Christ sitteth on the right hand of God. Set your affection on things above, not on things on the earth. For ye are dead, and your life is hid with Christ in God. When Christ, who is our life, shall appear, then shall ye also appear with him in glory" (Col 3:1-4).

We Ought to Be Persons Who Are Assembling Ourselves Together

"Not forsaking the assembling of ourselves together, as the manner of some is; but exhorting one another: and so much the more, as ye see the day approaching" (Heb 10:25).

Those ought's mentioned above refer to those who are saved, and I pray that the daily anticipation of Christ's return will inspire each one of us who is a Christian to live lives that will bring glory to God and souls to Jesus Christ.

Now I want to say just one more thing and this will be to those who are not saved.

WE OUGHT TO BE PERSONS WHO ARE READY

Jesus warned people who are not ready: "Therefore be ye also ready: for in such an hour as ye think not the Son of man cometh" (Mt 24:44). It is true that at any moment Jesus may return and gather His own to take away. Those who are not ready will be left to go through the awful tribulation period and then into hell forever. Two Thessalonians 2:10-12 makes it clear that all those who have heard the truth and have not believed it will be sent strong delusion by God and they all will" be damned who believed not the truth, but had pleasure in unrighteousness." If you will repent of your sin and receive Christ right now, God will save you and you will be ready when He comes. May God help you to do it this moment, for the next moment may be too late.

"I WANT TO BE READY WHEN THE LORD COMES"

Recently I read a tract about the second coming of Jesus. It told the story of young John who was servant to a rich doctor in London. John's master loved the Lord Jesus Christ and often had church meetings in the large living room of his home. At one of these meetings the doctor talked about the coming again of the Lord Jesus to take to heaven all those who believe in Him. Everyone else would be left behind.

After the meeting was over, the doctor said, "Well, John, I just want to tell you that if Jesus comes before I die, I shall no longer want the things I now have. He will take me away with Him, and then you may have my house and all my money."

Such an offer took John by surprise. He could only stammer out his thanks. That night he lay awake wondering why his master had offered him all that wealth. Suddenly he thought, "Why should I want a house and furniture, a car, horses, and money after the Lord comes? How terrible it would be to be left behind, even if all my master's belongings were mine!"

Soon he could bear the thought no longer. He slipped out of bed, ran quickly down the hall to the room where his master slept, and knocked on the door.

"Why, John," asked the doctor, "what's the matter? What do you want?" "Please sir," answered John, "I don't want your house after the Lord comes, or your car, or horses, or money."

"Well, John, what do you want?"

"Oh sir, I want to be ready when the Lord comes, to go with Him to heaven."

Right there in the doctor's bedroom, John put his trust in the Lord Jesus Christ and was saved and knew that he was ready for the Lord's coming.[11]

NOTES

PREFACE

1. Wilbur M. Smith, *World Crises and the Prophetic Scriptures*, p. 14.
2. M. R. DeHaan, *Coming Events in Prophecy*, p. 9. Used by permission.

CHAPTER 1

1. James M. Gray, *Mountain Peaks: A Textbook of Prophecy*, 2:138.
2. William Culbertson, *Christ the Hope of the World!*, p. 9.
3. Rufus W. Clark, quoted by Gray, p. 144.
4. R. A. Torrey, quoted by Culbertson, p. 11.
5. Torrey, "He Is Coming," *Gospel Herald*, Sept. 1, 1962, p. 17.
6. Gray, quoted by Culbertson, p. 11.
7. A. P. Stirrett, "I Never Had a Call," *Sudan Witness* 39, no. 2 (April-June, 1963): 4.
8. Gray, *Mountain Peaks*, p. 143.
9. Ibid.

CHAPTER 2

1. Charles C. Ryrie, *Dispensationalism Today*, p. 29.
2. *Scofield Reference Bible*, p. 5.
3. *Pilgrim Bible*, p. 1689.
4. Clifton L. Fowler, *Building the Dispensations*, p. 20.
5. W. Graham Scroggie, *Ruling Lines of Progressive Revelation* (London: Marshall, Morgan, & Scott, 1918), pp. 62-63.
6. H. A. Ironside, *In the Heavenlies* (New York: Loizeaux, n.d.), p. 67.
7. C. E. Mason, Jr., "Eschatology" (mimeographed notes for course at Philadelphia College of Bible, rev. 1962), pp. 5-6.
8. Lewis Sperry Chafer, *Major Bible Themes*, pp. 96-97.
9. Louis T. Talbot, *God's Plan of the Ages*, pp. 29-30. Used by permission.
10. A. C. Gaebelein, *Pilgrim Bible*, p. 8, footnote 1.
11. Frederick A. Tatford, *God's Program of the Ages*, p. 28.
12. *Scofield Reference Bible*, p. 1115.
13. William W. Orr, *God's Plan of the Ages*, p. 29.

CHAPTER 3

1. Charles C. Ryrie, *The Bible and Tomorrow's News*, p. 45. Used by permission of Victor Books.
2. "Seven Minutes to Midnight?" *Christianity Today*, Feb. 2, 1968, p. 31.
3. Pitirim A. Sorokin, quoted by Wilbur M. Smith, *World Crises and the Prophetic Scriptures*, pp. 16-17.
4. Smith, p. 16.
5. A. R. Pazhwak, *Saturday Review*, Dec. 9, 1967, cover.

6. W. H. Pickering, quoted by Hal Lindsey, "The Pieces Fall Together," *Moody Monthly,* Oct., 1967, p. 26.
7. *Pilgrim Bible,* p. 1570.
8. Hoyt, *The End Times,* p. 10.
9. John F. Walvoord, quoted by Paul Bauman, *The Prophetic Word in Crisis Days,* pp. 124-25.
10. J. Dwight Pentecost, *Prophecy for Today,* pp. 189-90.
11. Ord L. Morrow, *Behold He Cometh,* p. 50.
12. John F. Walvoord, *The Return of the Lord,* p. 17. Used by permission.

CHAPTER 4

1. John F. Walvoord, *The Nations in Prophecy,* p. 172.
2. E. Schuyler English, "Is the U.S. in Bible Prophecy?", *The Pilgrim,* p. 93.
3. Homer Duncan, "Sound the Trumpet," *Missionary Crusader,* July, 1968, p. 6.
4. Alexis de Tocqueville, quoted by John A. Stormer, *The Death of a Nation,* pp. 20-21. All quotes from this book by permission of the author.
5. Stormer, p. 21.
6. Vance Havner, quoted by Rawlings, "What's Wrong with America?", *Christian Youth Today,* April, 1970, p. 15.
7. Rawlings, p. 14.
8. "Decline and Fall of U.S.—View of Top Newsmen," *U.S. News and World Report,* Sept. 30, 1968, p. 8.
9. Rawlings, p. 14.
10. May Craig, quoted by Stormer, p. 19.
11. Duncan, pp. 5-7.
12. "Has America Passed Her Peak?", *Christianity Today,* March 1, 1968, pp. 28-29. Copyright 1968 by *Christianity Today;* reprinted by permission.
13. *Calgary Farm and Ranch Review,* quoted by *The Prairie Overcomer,* July, 1959, p. 245.
14. Walvoord, pp. 174-75.
15. H. Rap Brown, quoted by Stormer, p. 35.
16. Lenin, quoted by Stormer, p. 35.
17. Phillip Abbot Luce, *Road to Revolution,* p. 9.
18. J. Edgar Hoover, quoted by Brubaker, "Persecution Ahead?", *Radar News,* July, 1969, p. 2.
19. "Black Manifesto," full text, may be ordered from The American Council of Christian Churches of California, 450 Ave. 64, Pasadena, Calif. 91105.
20. Rev. I. H. Jackson, quoted by Ray Brubaker, "Persecution Ahead?", *Radar News,* July, 1969, p. 1.
21. Stormer, p. 34.
22. Dr. Thorsten Sellen, quoted by Ray Brubaker, *The United States in Prophecy,* p. 20.
23. J. Edgar Hoover, quoted by William H. Walker, pp. 40-41.
24. Hugh Ross Williamson, quoted by Brubaker, "Sins of Sodom," *Radar News,* Feb., 1968, p. 7.
25. Leonard Ravenhill, quoted by Brubaker, p. 7.
26. Dr. Graham Blaine, Jr., quoted by Jack Wyrtzen, *Sex Is Not Sinful?,* p. 10.
27. Stormer, p. 74.
28. Hoover, quoted by Stormer, p. 75.
29. Dr. Goodrich Schauffler, quoted by Brubaker, *Repent America,* p. 20.
30. Hermann Sasse, quoted by Brubaker, p. 20.
31. Dr. Mary Steichen Calderone, quoted by Wyrtzen, p. 7.
32. Vance Packard, *The Sexual Wilderness,* p. 188.
33. Brubaker, "America at the Crossroads," *Radar News,* Jan., 1969, p. 1.
34. *The Courier Mail,* quoted by Brubaker, *Repent America,* p. 21.
35. *Pageant,* quoted by Brubaker, p. 22.
36. Stormer, p. 70.
37. *Redbook,* quoted by Stormer, p. 82.
38. Stormer, p. 67.
39. "Anything Goes: Taboos in Twilight," *Newsweek,* Nov. 13, 1967, pp. 74-76. Copyright Newsweek, Inc., 1967; used by permission.

40. Rev. Harry Williams, quoted by Stormer, p. 80.
41. Howard Moody, quoted by Stormer, p. 80.
42. Rev. Allan Pyatt, quoted by Wyrtzen, p. 10.
43. Gordon Clanton, quoted by Wyrtzen, p. 10.
44. Rev. Ernest Harrison, quoted by Wyrtzen, p. 10.
45. Truman Douglas, quoted by Wyrtzen, p. 11.
46. Pitirim Sorokin, quoted by Carl G. Johnson, *Scriptural Sermon Outlines*, Grand Rapids: Baker Book House, 1965.
47. Bruce Dunn, "Watching a Nation Die," *Moody Monthly*, July-Aug., 1964, p. 19.
48. Frederick C. Grant, quoted by Stormer, p. 117.
49. Quoted by Stormer, p. 118.
50. Ibid.
51. Harold Lindsell, "The Crisis of the Church," *Christianity Today*, Sept. 11, 1970, pp. 5-6. Copyright 1970 by *Christianity Today; reprinted by permission.*
52. William K. Harrison, quoted by Brubaker, "News Interview with General William Harrison," *Radar News*, Feb., 1967, p. 3.
53. William H. Walker, *Will Russia Conquer the World?*, p. 42.
54. William H. Wilbur, quoted by Phyllis Schlafly and Chester Ward, *Strike from Space*, p. 2. All quotes from this book used by permission.
55. Nikita Krushchev, quoted by Schlafly and Ward, p. 58.
56. Ibid., p. 59.
57. Stefan T. Possony, quoted by Schlafly and Ward, p. 18.
58. Schlafly and Ward, p. 52.
59. John C. Hubbell, "The Threat of Russia's Rising Strategic Power," *Reader's Digest*, Feb., 1968, p. 55. Used by permission of The Reader's Digest.
60. Ibid., p. 58.
61. Ibid., pp. 60-61.
62. Dr. George S. Benson; "The Cuban Missile Crisis"; Beckley, West Virginia, *Post-Herald;* Aug. 11, 1967. Used by permission.
63. Oleg Penkovskiy, as quoted by Schlafly and Ward, pp. 214-15.
64. Schlafly and Ward, p. 225.
65. Ibid., p. 214.
66. U.S. Bomb Casualty Commission, "The A-Bombed Cities—Twenty-five Years Later," *U.S. News & World Report*, Aug. 10, 1970, p. 55.
67. Gerrit Verkuyl, ed., *The Holy Bible: The New Berkeley Version in Modern English* (Grand Rapids: Zondervan, 1969), p. 763, note o.

CHAPTER 5

1. J. Dwight Pentecost, *Prophecy for Today*, p. 183. Used by permission of the publisher.
2. Lord Balfour, quoted by L. Sale-Harrison, *The Remarkable Jew*, p. 62.
3. Paul Goodman, quoted by F. A. Tatford, *Five Minutes to Midnight* (London: Victory Press, 1970), p. 82.
4. Wilbur M. Smith, *Israeli-Arab Conflict and the Bible*, p. 152.
5. Moshe Dayan, quoted by Palmer Gordon Brown, "Miracles of the 1967 War," *Prophetic Witness*, Jan., 1970, p. 17.
6. Yitzhak Rabin, quoted by Brown, p. 17.
7. de Gramont, quoted by Brown, p. 17.
8. Brown, p. 17.
9. Israel Eldad, quoted in "Should the Temple Be Rebuilt?", *Time*, June 30, 1967, p. 56.
10. Ibid.
11. John F. Walvoord, *The Church in Prophecy*, p. 174.
12. Jacob Gartenhaus, "This Is the Time," *The Highland Park Evangelist*, July 31, 1968, p. 4.
13. Hal Lindsey, *The Late Great Planet Earth*, p. 57. Quotes from this book used by permission of the publisher.
14. Walvoord, p. 174.
15. F. A. Tatford, *The Jew and Prophecy* (Eastbourne, Sussex, Eng.: Bible and Advent Testimony, 1968), p. 16. Used by permission of the author.
16. M. R. DeHaan, *Signs of the Times*, p. 74.

17. American Security Council, "Operation Alert," Washington, D. C.
18. Walvoord, p. 175.
19. Lehman Strauss, *The End of This Present World,* p. 80. Used by permission of the publisher.
20. John F. Walvoord, *We Believe in the Blessed Hope,* (Dallas: Dallas Theological Seminary), p. 6.
21. Douglas Horton, quoted by F. A. Tatford, *A One World Church and Prophecy* (Eastbourne, Sussex: Bible and Advent Testimony Movement), p. 5.
22. *Pilgrim Bible,* p. 1664, note 6.
23. Charles C. Ryrie, *The Bible and Tomorrow's News,* pp. 119-20.
24. Walvoord, p. 9.
25. Dean Acheson, quoted by Hal Lindsey, "The Pieces Fall Together," *Moody Monthly,* Oct., 1967, p. 28.
26. Jean Monnet, as quoted in "What Chance for a United States of Europe?", *Reader's Digest,* Oct., 1970, pp. 158-59, 162. Used by permission of The Reader's Digest.
27. De Murville, quoted by Lindsey, p. 28.
28. *Pilgrim Bible,* p. 1121.
29. Premier of Belgium, quoted by Lindsey, p. 28.
30. Tatford, *The Common Market,* p. 16. Used by permission of the author.
31. William W. Orr, *Jesus Is Coming . . . This Year?,* p. 10.
32. Sir Isaac Newton, Voltaire, as quoted by Theodore H. Epp, "Will This Generation See the Return of the Lord?", part 2, *Good News Broadcaster,* Sept., 1965, p. 7. Used by permission.
33. John Wesley White, *Re-Entry,* p. 24.
34. Ibid., pp. 32-33.
35. Gavin Hamilton, "Signs of the Times," *Christian Victory,* June 1970, p. 30.
36. M. R. DeHaan, *The Days of Noah,* pp. 36-37. Used by permission of the publisher.
37. A. T. Robertson, *Word Pictures in the New Testament* (Nashville: Broadman, 1930), 1:189.
38. W. E. Vine, *Expository Dictionary of New Testament Words,* 4:53.
39. Arthur I. Brown, *Into the Clouds,* p. 24.
40. *Encyclopedia Americana,* quoted by Theodore Epp, "Startling Signs," *Good News Broadcaster,* Nov., 1965, p. 9.
41. Louis S. Bauman, *Light from Bible Prophecy,* pp. 90-91.
42. *Science News,* quoted by *Radar News,* Jan., 1968, p. 1.
43. As quoted in *Radar News,* p. 1.
44. Dr. Raymond Ewell, quoted by *Radar News,* p. 7.
45. The London *Times,* quoted by Bauman, p. 91.
46. Norman White, quoted by Bauman, p. 91.
47. Dale Yocum, quoted by *The Evangel,* Feb., 1965, p. 12.
48. *Changing Times,* quoted by *The Evangel,* Dec., 1968, p. 23.
49. R. W. Neighbor, quoted by *Radar News,* Aug., 1968, p. 6.
50. Robert Little, quoted by *Moody Monthly,* July-Aug., 1967, p. 24.
51. *Scofield Reference Bible,* p. 1034.
52. McCrossan, as quoted by Arthur I. Brown, *I Will Come Again,* p. 44.
53. Milton B. Lindberg, quoted by Brown, pp. 46-47.
54. J. Dwight Pentecost, *Things to Come,* p. 281.
55. Robert Little, *Here's Your Answer* (Chicago: Moody, 1967), p. 114.
56. Theodore H. Epp, *Back to the Bible Broadcaster,* Nov., 1965, p. 9. Used by permission of Back to the Bible Broadcast.
57. Ibid., Oct., 1965, p. 8.
58. Ibid., Sept., 1965, p. 6.
59. Ibid., July-Aug., 1965.
60. Lindsey, p. 28.
61. John H. Linton, *The Bible Herald,* no. 2, p. 2.
62. Ibid., pp. 6-8.
63. Stephen Olford, "The Coming of Christ" in *Prophetic Truth Unfolding Today,* pp. 138-39.

CHAPTER 6

1. M. R. DeHaan, *Signs of the Times,* p. 181.
2. S. Franklin Logsdon, *Profiles of Prophecy,* p. 17. Used by permission.
3. Charles C. Ryrie, *The Bible and Tomorrow's News,* p. 138.
4. M. R. DeHaan, "What Is Delaying Christ's Coming?" in *Founder's Week Messages—1963,* p. 47.

CHAPTER 7

1. John F. Walvoord, *The Return of the Lord,* p. 119.
2. W. Myrddin Lewis, *Hidden Mysteries,* p. 87. Used by permission of the author.
3. Isaac M. Haldeman, "The Judgment Seat of Christ," in *Great Gospel Sermons,* 1:93-94.
4. Lewis, p. 87.
5. J. Dwight Pentecost, *Things to Come,* pp. 222-23. Used by permission.
6. E. Schuyler English, "The Church and the Tribulation" in *Prophetic Truth Unfolding Today,* p. 31.
7. Pentecost, pp. 225-26.
8. F. E. Marsh, *Fully Furnished,* p. 382.
9. Ibid., p. 390.
10. Lehman Strauss, *God's Plan for the Future,* p. 115. Used by permission.
11. Keith L. Brooks, *Prophecy Answered,* pp. 60-62. Used by permission of Good News Publishers, Westchester, Illinois 60153.
12. M. R. DeHaan, *The Judgment Seat of Christ,* p. 21.
13. Theodore Epp, *Present Labor and Future Rewards* (Lincoln, Neb.: Back to the Bible, 1960), p. 75. Used by permission.
14. Lehman Strauss, *We Live Forever* (Neptune, N.Y.: Loizeaux, 1947), pp. 81-82.
15. Emery H. Bancroft, *Christian Theology* (Grand Rapids: Zondervan, 1949), p. 361. Used by permission of publisher.
16. Haldeman, pp. 85-87.
17. Donald G. Barnhouse, *Expositions of Bible Doctrines,* vol. 9, *God's Discipline,* pp. 195, 198.
18. W. H. Griffith Thomas, quoted by Robert T. Ketcham, *Why Christ Was a Carpenter,* p. 147. Used by permission of Regular Baptist Press.
19. Lewis, pp. 86, 88-89.
20. John H. Linton, *Tears in Heaven and Other Sermons,* pp. 13-16.
21. Ibid., pp. 23-24.
22. H. H. Savage, in *Founder's Week Messages—1962,* pp. 55, 49.
23. L. Sale-Harrison, *The Judgment Seat of Christ,* p. 42, 51-52, 53, 55.
24. John R. Rice, *Tears in Heaven,* pp. 8-9. Used by permission of the publishers.
25. S. Franklin Logsdon, *Profiles of Prophecy,* pp. 26, 28-29.
26. Marsh, p. 367.
27. Robert T. Ketcham, *Why Was Christ a Carpenter?,* pp. 127-28.
28. Ibid., pp. 144-147.
29. Herbert Lockyer, "The Advent and Youth," *Prophetic Witness,* March, 1969, pp. 55-56.
30. Ibid.
31. Kenneth F. Dodson, *The Prize of the Upcalling,* pp. 86-88. Used by permission.
32. Linton, p. 35.

CHAPTER 8

1. William R. Newell, *The Book of the Revelation,* p. 221.
2. Herman A. Hoyt, *The End Times,* p. 148.
3. Newell, p. 118.
4. Charles E. Fuller, *The Tribulation,* The Prophetic Bible Lessons Series, no. 3 (Los Angeles: Gospel Broadcasting Assoc., n.d.).

CHAPTER 9

1. Vance Havner, "Lessons from Baruch," in *Founder's Week Messages—1964,* p. 69.

2. John F. Walvoord, *The Rapture Question,* pp. 191-99.
3. Henry C. Thiessen, quoted by Gerald B. Stanton, *Kept from the Hour,* p. 49.
4. Gerald B. Stanton, *Kept from the Hour,* pp. 49-50. Quotes from the book used by permission of the publisher.
5. Alexander Reese, *The Approaching Advent of Christ* (London: Marshall, Morgan & Scott, n.d.), p. 283.
6. Thiessen, as quoted by Stanton, p. 127.
7. Stanton, p. 126.
8. William R. Newell, *The Book of Revelation,* pp. 400-401.
9. John Linton, *Will the Church Escape the Great Tribulation?,* p. 95.
10. Stanton, pp. 128-29.
11. Homer Duncan, *An Outline of Things to Come,* p. 35.
12. Stanton, p. 259.
13. Ibid., p. 264.
14. Ibid., pp. 93-99.
15. Hoyt, *The End Times,* p. 95.
16. Henry C. Thiessen, *Will the Church Pass Through the Tribulation?,* p. 33.
17. Stanton, pp. 106-7.
18. Stanton, p. 135.
19. Thiessen, pp. 52, 53.

CHAPTER 10

1. Moshe Dayan, quoted by Hal Lindsey, *The Late Great Planet Earth,* p. 59.
2. Jack Van Impe, *The Coming War with Russia,* n. 4.
3. Richard W. DeHaan, *Israel and the Nations in Prophecy,* p. 119.
4. Lowth, quoted by Lindsey, p. 65.
5. Gesenius, quoted by Lindsey, pp. 64-65.
6. Wilbur M. Smith, *World Crises and the Prophetic Scriptures,* p. 252.
7. DeHaan, p. 121.
8. DeHaan, p. 122.
9. Edward Gibbon, *The History of the Decline and Fall of the Roman Empire,* 1:204.
10. O. E. Phillips, *Russia and the World Crisis* (Philadelphia: Hebrew Christian Fellowship, n.d.), p. 3.
11. Louis Goldberg, "What Will Happen in the Middle East?", *Moody Monthly,* 1970, p. 20.
12. Walter Chamberlain, quoted by Lindsey, pp. 62-63.
13. *The Evangel,* July, 1968, pp. 11-12.
14. George T. B. Davis, quoted by William H. Walker, *Will Russia Conquer the World?,* p. 13.
15. Clifton Brannon, *Will Russia Rule the World?,* p. 14.
16. Ibid., p. 14.
17. Joseph Alsop, "Russia's Menacing New Challenge in the Middle East," *Reader's Digest,* August, 1970, pp. 50-51. Used by permission of The Reader's Digest.
18. Arthur W. Kac, *The Rebirth of the State of Israel,* p. 150.
19. Theodore H. Epp, *Russia's Doom Prophesied,* p. 8.
20. Charles C. Ryrie, *The Bible and Tomorrow's News,* p. 154.
21. Walker, pp. 11-12.
22. John F. Walvoord, quoted by Bauman, *The Prophetic Word in Crisis Days,* p. 120.
23. J. Dwight Pentecost, *Prophecy for Today,* p. 112.
24. DeHaan, pp. 130, 135.
25. M. R. DeHaan, *Signs of the Times,* p. 37.
26. David L. Cooper, *When Gog's Armies Meet the Almighty,* p. 17. Used by permission of The Biblical Research Society.
27. Epp, pp. 40-42.
28. H. D. M. Spence and Joseph Excell, eds., *Pulpit Commentary,* vol. 28, *Ezekiel,* 2:287.
29. Matthew Henry, *Matthew Henry's Commentary,* 4:974.
30. *The International Standard Bible Encyclopaedia,* 1:522.
31. Spence and Excell, p. 298.

32. William W. Orr, *What Will God Do with Russia?*, p. 29.
33. Walvoord, p. 117.
34. Spence and Excell, p. 302.
35. "Fuel for History's Greatest Fire," *Christian Victory*, June, 1970, p. 10.
36. Cooper, p. 106.
37. Henry, p. 974.
38. Jack Van Impe, *The Coming War with Russia*, pp. 14-16, 32.

CHAPTER 11

1. J. McKee Adams, quoted by Wilbur M. Smith, *World Crises and the Prophetic Scriptures*, pp. 144-45.
2. Frederick L. Brooks, quoted by Lehman Strauss, *The End of This Present World*, p. 90.
3. A. Sims, quoted by Pentecost, *Things to Come*, pp. 341-42.
4. Pentecost, p. 340.
5. John F. Walvoord, *Daniel*, pp. 277-78.
6. F. A. Tatford, *Prophecy's Last Word*, p. 167.
7. William R. Newell, *The Book of the Revelation*, p. 312.
8. Louis T. Talbot, *The Revelation of Jesus Christ*, pp. 225-26. Used by permission.
9. Walter Scott, *Exposition of the Revelation of Jesus Christ*, pp. 393-94.
10. Ford C. Ottman, *The Unfolding of the Ages*, pp. 423-24.

CHAPTER 12

1. Pitirim Sorokin and Nicholas Golovin, quoted by Lehman Strauss, *God's Plan for the Future*, pp. 167-68.
2. Harry Hager, quoted by Strauss, p. 170.
3. J. Dwight Pentecost, *Things to Come*, p. 476.
4. M. R. DeHaan, *The Great Society*, pp. 7-8.
5. J. Vernon McGee, *Reveling Through Revelation*, 2:74.
6. Robert J. Little, *Here's Your Answer* (Chicago: Moody Press, 1967), pp. 113-14.
7. George N. H. Peters, quoted by Pentecost, p. 487.
8. Charles C. Ryrie, *The Bible and Tomorrow's News*, pp. 182-83.
9. René Pache, *The Return of Jesus Christ*, p. 431.
10. John F. Walvoord, *The Revelation of Jesus Christ*, pp. 304-5.
11. Alva J. McClain, quoted by Pentecost, p. 494.

CHAPTER 13

1. J. Dwight Pentecost, *Things to Come*, p. 411. Used by permission of the publisher.
2. John R. Rice, *The Last Judgment of the Unsaved Dead*, pp. 10, 12. Used by permission of the publisher.
3. *Moody Monthly*, quoted by A. H. Yetter, "The Resurrection of the Unbelieving Dead," *Christian Victory*, November, 1970, pp. 38-39.
4. William R. Newell, *Romans Verse by Verse* (Chicago: Moody, 1938), p. 54.
5. Gerald L. Stover, *Truth for Tomorrow*, pp. 85-86. Used by permission of the publisher.
6. Harold J. Berry, quoted by Theodore H. Epp, *Practical Studies in Revelation*, p. 450.
7. Charles H. Spurgeon, quoted by Carl G. Johnson, *Ready for Anything*, p. 80.
8. Johnson, p. 45.

CHAPTER 14

1. Charles F. Kettering, quoted by Salem Kirban, *Your Last Goodbye*, p. 289. Used by permisison.
2. Clarence Larkin, *The Book of Revelation*, pp. 199-201. Used by permission of the author, Rev. Clarence Larkin.
3. Horatius Bonar, quoted by Wilbur M. Smith, *The Biblical Doctrine of Heaven*, pp. 256-57.
4. William R. Newell, *The Book of the Revelation*, p. 346.

5. Department of Eugenics, quoted by Robert Ervin Hough, *The Christian After Death*, p. 112.
6. F. W. Boreham, quoted by Smith, pp. 246-47.
7. John F. Walvoord, *The Millennial Kingdom*, p. 328.
8. Herman A. Hoyt, *The End Times*, p. 230.
9. Robert Ervin Hough, *The Christian After Death*, p. 115.
10. Walter Scott, *Exposition of the Revelation of Jesus Christ*, p. 441.
11. W. A. Criswell, *Expository Sermons on Revelation*, 5:132-33. Used by permission of publisher.
12. J. A. Seiss, *The Apocalypse*, p. 510.
13. Kenneth S. Wuest, *In These Last Days*, pp. 144-45.
14. Kenneth S. Wuest, *Philippians in the New Testament*, p. 104.
15. Carl G. Johnson, *Ready for Anything*, p. 75.
16. Henry Durbanville, quoted by A. Naismith, *1200 Notes, Quotes and Anecdotes* (Chicago: Moody Press, 1962), p. 94.
17. R. G. Lee, *Bread from Bellevue Oven*, pp. 70-71.
18. Johnson, pp. 35-36.
19. R. A. Torrey, *The Biblical Evangelist*, May, 1969, pp. 1, 8.
20. S. Franklin Logsdon, *Profiles of Prophecy*, pp. 135-36.
21. Robert L. Sumner, *Hell Is No Joke*, p. 26.
22. Kenneth S. Wuest, *Treasures from the Greek New Testament* (Grand Rapids: Eerdmans, 1966), p. 43.
23. Kirban, pp. 343-44. Used by permission.

CHAPTER 15

1. Albert Barnes, quoted by Francis W. Dickson, "The Kind of People We Ought to Be," (Notes of Bible Studies conducted at Lansdowne Baptist Church, Bournemouth, Eng., Spring, 1967), Study 10.
2. W. E. Vine, *Expository Dictionary of New Testament Words*, 2:162.
3. N. A. Woychuk, *To Them Who Love His Appearing*, pp. 17-18.
4. Ibid., pp. 18-20.
5. Kenneth S. Wuest, *In These Last Days*, pp. 74-75.
6. Dixon, Study 10.
7. Alford, quoted by Wuest, *In These Last Days*, p. 76.
8. N. Vincent, quoted by J. S. Exell, ed., *The Biblical Illustrator*, vol. 26, *1 and 2 Peter*, p. 215.
9. John Jardine, quoted by Exell, p. 219.
10. Frances W. Dixon, "The Birth and Growth of a Child of God" (Notes of Bible Studies conducted at Lansdowne Baptist Church, Bournemouth, Eng., Spring, 1967), Study 12.
11. *I Don't Want Your Money*, (Oradell, N.J.: American Tract Society).

BIBLIOGRAPHY

Alderman, Paul R. *The Unfolding of the Ages*. Neptune, New Jersey: Loizeaux, 1965.

Allis, Oswald T. *Prophecy and the Church*. Philadelphia: Presb. & Ref., 1969.

Appelman, Hyman. *Ye Must Be Born Again*. Grand Rapids: Zondervan, 1939.

Barndollar, W. W. *The Validity of Dispensationalism*. Des Plaines, Ill.: Reg. Bapt., 1964.

Barnhouse, Donald G. *Exposition of Bible Doctrines*. Philadelphia: The Evangelical Found., 1964.

Bauman, Louis S. *Light from Bible Prophecy*. New York: Revell, 1940.

———. *Russian Events in the Light of Bible Prophecy*. New York: Revell, 1942.

Bauman, Paul. *The Prophetic Word in Crisis Days*. Findlay, Ohio: Dunham, 1961.

Beckwith, George D. *God's Prophetic Plan*. Grand Rapids: Zondervan, 1962.

Blackstone, W. E. *Jesus Is Coming*. New York: Revell, 1908.

Bradbury, John W. *Hastening the Day of God*. Wheaton, Ill.: Van Kampen, 1953.

———. *Light for the World's Darkness*. New York: Loizeaux, 1944.

———. *The Sure Word of Prophecy*. New York: Revell, 1943.

Brannon, Clifton. *Will Russia Rule the World?* Grand Rapids: Zondervan, 1957.

Brooks, Keith L. *Prophecy Answered*. Westchester, Ill.: Good News, 1960.

Brown, Arthur I. *Into the Clouds*. Findlay, Ohio: Fundamental Truth, 1938.

———. *I Will Come Again*. Findlay, Ohio: Fundamental Truth, 1947.

Brubaker, Ray M. *Jerusalem in Prophecy*. St. Petersburg: God's News Behind the News, n.d.

————. *Repent America.* St. Petersburg: God's . . . News, n.d.

————. *The United States in Prophecy.* St. Petersburg: God's . . . News, n.d.

————. *Will Communism Triumph?* St. Petersburg: God's . . . News, n.d.

Buswell, J. Oliver, Jr. *Unfulfilled Prophecies.* Grand Rapids: Zondervan, 1937.

Cardey, Elmer L. *The Countdown of History.* Grand Rapids: Baker, 1962.

Chafer, Lewis Sperry. *The Kingdom in History and Prophecy.* Grand Rapids: Dunham, 1915.

————. *Major Bible Themes.* Chicago: Moody, 1942.

Cohen, Gary G. *Understanding Revelation.* Collingswood, N.J.: Christian Beacon, 1968.

Cooper, David L. *When Gog's Armies Meet the Almighty.* Los Angeles: Biblical Research Soc., 1940.

Criswell, W. A. *Expository Sermons on Revelation.* Grand Rapids: Zondervan, 1962.

Crowley, Dale. *The Soon Coming of Our Lord.* New York: Loizeaux, 1958.

Culbertson, William. *Christ the Hope of the World!* Chicago: Moody Bible Inst., n.d.

DeHaan, M. R. *Coming Events in Prophecy.* Grand Rapids: Zondervan, 1962.

————. *The Days of Noah.* Grand Rapids: Zondervan, 1963.

————. *The Great Society.* Grand Rapids: Radio Bible Class, 1965.

————. *The Jew and Palestine in Prophecy.* Grand Rapids: Zondervan, 1950.

————. *The Judgment Seat of Christ.* Grand Rapids: Radio Bible Class, n.d.

————. *The Millennium.* Grand Rapids: Radio Bible Class, n.d.

————. *The Second Coming of Christ.* Grand Rapids: Zondervan, 1944.

————. *Signs of the Times.* Grand Rapids: Zondervan, 1951.

————. *Revelation.* Grand Rapids: Zondervan, 1946.

DeHaan, Richard. *Israel and the Nations in Prophecy.* Grand Rapids: Zondervan, 1968.

Dodson, Kenneth F. *The Prize of the Up-Calling.* Grand Rapids: Baker, 1969.

Duncan, Homer. *An Outline of Things to come.* Lubbock, Tex.: Missionary Crusader, n.d.

————. *The Budding of the Fig Tree.* Lubbock, Tex.: Missionary Crusader, n.d.

———. *Prepare Now for the Second Coming of Christ*. Lubbock, Tex.: Missionary Crusader, n.d.

Eade, Alfred Thompson. *The Expanded Panorama Bible Study Course*. Westwood, N.J.: Revell, 1961.

English, E. Schuyler. *Re-Thinking the Rapture*. Traveler's Rest, S. C.: Southern Bible, 1954.

———, ed. *Pilgrim Bible*. 2d ed. N.Y.: Oxford, 1952.

Epp, Theodore H. *Brief Outlines of Things to Come*. Chicago: Moody, 1952.

———. *Practical Studies in Revelation*. 2 vols. Lincoln, Nebr.: Good News Broadcasting, 1969.

———. *Rightly Dividing the Word*. Lincoln, Nebr.: Good News Broadcasting, 1954.

———. *Russia's Doom Prophesied*. Lincoln, Nebr.: Back to the Bible, 1959.

Exell, Joseph S., ed. *The Biblical Illustrator*. Grand Rapids: Baker, 1954.

Feinberg, Charles L. *Focus on Prophecy*. Westwood, N.J.: Revell, 1964.

———, ed. *Prophetic Truth Unfolding Today*. Westwood, N.J.: Revell, 1968.

Ford, W. Herschel. *Seven Simple Sermons on the Second Coming*. Grand Rapids: Zondervan, 1945.

———. *Simple Sermons on Prophetic Themes*. Grand Rapids: Zondervan, 1968.

Founder's Week Messages—1962. Chicago: Moody, 1962.

——— 1963. Chicago: Moody, 1963.

——— 1964. Chicago: Moody, 1964.

Fowler, Clifton L. *Building the Dispensations*. Denver: Maranatha, 1940.

Fraser, Neil M. *The Gladness of His Return*. Neptune, N.J.: Loizeaux, 1967.

Freligh, H. M. *Studies in Revelation*. Harrisburg, Pa.: Christian Pubns., 1969.

Gaebelein, Arno C. *The Harmony of the Prophetic Word*. New York: "Our Hope," n.d.

———. *The Return of the Lord*. New York: "Our Hope," 1925.

Gartenhaus, Jacob. *"Unto His Own."* Atlanta: Intl. Brd. Jewish Missions, 1965.

Graham, Billy. *World Aflame*. New York: Doubleday, 1965.

Gray, James M. *Mountain Peaks—A Textbook of Prophecy*. 2 vols. New York: Revell, 1918.

Great Gospel Sermons. Vol. 1. New York: Revell, 1949.

Gromacki, Robert Glenn. *Are These The Last Days?* Westwood, N.J.: Revell, 1970.

Harrison, Norman B. *His Sure Return*. Chicago: BICA, 1926.

Harrison, William K. *Hope Triumphant*. Chicago: Moody, 1966.

Haddon, Jeffrey K. *The Gathering Storm in the Churches*. New York: Doubleday, Anchor Books, 1969.

Havner, Vance. *It Is Time*. New York: Revell, 1943.

———. *Living in Kingdom Come*. Westwood, N.J.: Revell, 1967.

Henry, Matthew. *Matthew Henry's Commentary*. 5 vols. Westwood, N.J.: Revell, n.d.

Hitchcock, Floyd. *Lectures on the Revelation*. Springfield, Mo.: Johnson Print Shop, n.d.

Hoover, J. Edgar. *Masters of Deceit*. New York: Henry Holt, 1958.

Hough, Robert Ervin. *The Christian After Death*. Chicago: Moody, 1947.

Hoyt, Herman A. *The End Times*. Chicago: Moody, 1969.

Ironside, H. A. *The Lamp of Prophecy*. Grand Rapids: Zondervan, 1940.

Jamieson, Robert; Fausset, A. R.; and Brown, David. *A Commentary Critical, Experimental and Practical on the Old and New Testaments*. Vols. 1-2. Grand Rapids: Eerdmans, 1948.

Johnson, Carl G. *Ready for Anything*. Minneapolis: Bethany Fellowship, 1968.

Kac, Arthur W. *The Rebirth of the State of Israel*. London: Marshall, Morgan, & Scott, 1958.

Ketcham, Robert T. *Why Was Christ a Carpenter? and Other Sermons*. Des Plaines, Ill.: Reg. Bap., 1966.

Kirban, Salem. *Guide to Survival*. Huntingdon Valley, Pa.: Salem Kirban, 1968.

———. *Your Last Goodbye*. Huntingdon Valley, Pa.: Salem Kirban, 1969.

Kirby, Gilbert W. *Remember I Am Coming Soon*. London: Victory Press, 1964.

Koch, Kurt. *Day X*. Western Germany: Evangelization Publ., 1967.

Kurtz, Edward Cuyler. *"And Behold, the Camels Were Coming."* Grand Rapids: Zondervan, 1941.

Larkin, Clarence. *The Book of Revelation*. Philadelphia: Clarence Larkin, Est., 1919.

Lee, Robert G. *Bread from Bellevue Oven*. Murfreesboro, Tenn.: Sword of the Lord, 1947.

Lewis, W. Myrddin. *Hidden Mysteries*. W. Myrddin Lewis, 1965.

Lindsey, Hal. *The Late Great Planet Earth*. Grand Rapids: Zondervan, 1970.

Linton, John. *Tears in Heaven and Other Sermons*. Philadelphia: Westbrook, 1942.

———. *Will the Church Escape the Great Tribulation?* Ontario, Canada: John Linton, n.d.

Logsdon, S. Franklin. *Profiles of Prophecy.* Grand Rapids: Zondervan, 1964.

Lockyer, Herbert. *All the Doctrines of the Bible.* Grand Rapids: Zondervan, 1964.

Luce, Phillip Abbott. *Road To Revolution.* San Diego: Viewpoint, 1967.

Ludwigson, R. *Bible Prophecy Notes.* R. Ludwigson, 1951.

Marsh, F. E. *Fully Furnished.* London: Pickering & Inglis, 1924.

McClain, Alva J. *Daniel's Prophecy of the Seventy Weeks.* 3rd Ed. Grand Rapids: Zondervan, 1940.

———. *The Greatness of the Kingdom,* Grand Rapids: Zondervan, 1959.

McGee, J. Vernon. *Revealing Through Revelation, Part 1.* Los Angeles: Church of the Open Door, 1962.

———. *Reveling Through Revelation, Part 2.* Los Angeles: Church of the Open Door, 1962.

Miles, F. J. *Prophecy: Past, Present, and Prospective.* Grand Rapids: Zondervan, 1943.

Moody, D. L. *Heaven and How to Get There.* Chicago: Moody, n.d.

Morrow, Ord L. *Behold He Cometh.* Lincoln, Nebr.: Back to the Bible, 1963.

Munhall, L. W. *The Lord's Return and Kindred Truth.* Philadelphia: L. W. Munhall, 1888.

Munsey, William Elbert. *Eternal Retribution.* Murfreesboro, Tenn.: Sword of the Lord, 1951.

Murch, James DeForest. *The Protestant Revolt.* Arlington, Va.: Crestwood, 1967.

Newell, William R. *The Book of the Revelation.* Chicago: Scripture Press, 1935.

Orr, James, ed. *The International Standard Bible Encyclopaedia.* Grand Rapids: Eerdmans, 1949.

Orr, William W. *Antichrist, Armageddon and the End of the World.* Temple City, Calif.: Grace Gospel Fellowship, n.d.

———. *God's Plan of the Ages.* Findlay, Ohio: Dunham, n.d.

———. *Jesus Is Coming . . . This Year?* Findlay, Ohio: Dunham, n.d.

———. *What Will God Do with Russia?* Temple City, Calif.: Grace Gospel Fellowship, n.d.

Ottman, Ford C. *The Unfolding of the Ages.* Fincastle, Va.: Scripture Truth, 1905.

Pache, René. *The Future Life.* Trans. by Helen I. Needham. Chicago: Moody, 1962.

———. *The Return of Jesus Christ.* Trans. William Sanford LaSor. Chicago: Moody, 1955.

Packard, Vance. *The Sexual Wilderness.* New York: David McKay, 1968.

Penkovskiy, Oleg. *The Penkovskiy Papers.* New York: Doubleday, 1965.

Pentecost, J. Dwight. *Prophecy for Today.* Grand Rapids: Zondervan, 1961.

———. *Things to Come.* Grand Rapids: Dunham, 1958.

Pettingill, William L. *God's Prophecies for Plain People.* Findlay, Ohio: Fundamental Truth, 1923.

Pfeiffer, Charles F., and Harrison, Everett F., eds. *Wycliffe Bible Commentary.* Chicago: Moody, 1962.

Pink, A. W. *The Redeemer's Return.* Swengel, Pa.: Bible Truth Depot, 1918.

Pont, Charles E. *The World's Collision.* Boston, Mass.: W. A. Wilde, 1956.

Rice, John R. *Hell! What the Bible Says About It.* Murfreesboro, Tenn.: Sword of the Lord, 1942.

———. *Tears in Heaven.* Murfreesboro, Tenn.: Sword of the Lord, 1941.

———. *The Last Judgment of the Unsaved Dead.* Murfreesboro, Tenn.: Sword of the Lord, 1943.

Roberson, Lee. *Some Golden Daybreak.* Orlando, Fla.: Christ for the World, 1957.

Rogers, E. W. *Concerning the Future.* Chicago: Moody, 1962.

Ryrie, Charles Caldwell. *The Bible and Tomorrow's News.* Wheaton, Ill.: Scripture Press, 1969.

———. *Dispensationalism Today.* Chicago: Moody, 1965.

———. *Revelation.* Chicago: Moody, 1968.

Sale-Harrison, L. *The Judgment Seat of Christ.* New York: Sale-Harrison Pubns., 1938.

———. *The Remarkable Jew.* New York: Sale-Harrison Pubns., 1928 & 1934.

Sauer, Erich. *From Eternity to Eternity.* Grand Rapids: Eerdmans, 1954.

———. *The Triumph of the Crucified.* Grand Rapids: Eerdmans, 1951.

Schlafly, Phyllis, and Ward, Chester. *Strike from Space.* New York: Devin-Adair, 1966.

Scofield, C. I. *Prophecy Made Plain.* London: Pickering & Inglis, n.d.

———, ed. *Scofield Reference Bible.* N.Y.: Oxford, 1945.

Scott, Walter. *Exposition of the Revelation of Jesus Christ.* London: Pickering & Inglis, n.d.

Scroggie, W. Graham. *The Lord's Return.* London: Pickering & Inglis, n.d.

Seiss, J. A. *The Apocalypse*. Grand Rapids: Zondervan, n.d.

Smith, J. B. *A Revelation of Jesus Christ*. Scottdale, Pa.: Mennonite Pub. House, 1961.

Smith, Oswald J. *What Will Happen Next?* Oswald J. Smith, 1934.

Smith, Wilbur M. *The Biblical Doctrine of Heaven*. Chicago: Moody, 1968.

———. *Egypt in Bible Prophecy*. Boston: W. A. Wilde, 1957.

———. *Israeli-Arab Conflict and the Bible*. Glendale, Calif.: Gospel Light, 1967.

———. *World Crises and the Prophetic Scriptures*. Chicago: Moody, 1952.

Spence , H. D. M., and Excell, Joseph, eds. *The Pulpit Commentary*. Vol. 28. London & N.Y.: Funk & Wagnalls, 1880-93.

Stanton, Gerald B. *Kept from the Hour*. Grand Rapids: Zondervan, 1956.

Stormer, John A. *The Death of a Nation*. Florissant, Mo.: Liberty Bell, 1968.

Stover, Gerald A. *Truth for Tomorrow*. Denver: Baptist Pubns., 1966.

Strauss, Lehman. *The End of This Present World*. Grand Rapids: Zondervan, 1967.

———. *God's Plan for the Future*. Grand Rapids: Zondervan, 1965.

———. *Life After Death*. Westchester, Ill.: Good News, 1961.

Stroh, Grant. *The Next World-Crisis in the Light of Former World-Crises*. Chicago: BICA, 1914.

Strombeck, J. F. *First the Rapture*. Moline, Ill.: Strombeck, 1950.

Sumner, Robert L. *Hell Is No Joke*. Grand Rapids: Zondervan, 1959.

Talbot, Louis T. *The Revelation of Jesus Christ*. Grand Rapids: Eerdmans, 1937.

———. *God's Plan of the Ages*. Grand Rapids: Eerdmans, 1936.

Tatford, Frederick A. *The Common Market*. Lowestoft, England: Green & Co., n.d.

———. *Five Minutes to Midnight*. London: Victory Press, 1970.

———. *God's Program of the Ages*. Grand Rapids: Kregel, 1967.

———. *The Jew*. Sowestoft, England: Green & Co., n.d.

———. *Prophecy's Last Word*. London: Pickering & Inglis, 1947.

Trotter, William. *Plain Papers on Prophetic and Other Subjects*. Kansas City: Walterick, n.d.

Thiessen, Henry C. *Will the Church Pass Through the Tribulation?* Grand Rapids: Zondervan, 1940.

Trumbull, Charles G. *Prophecy's Light on Today*. New York: Revell, 1937.

Van Impe, Jack. *The Coming War with Russia*. Old Time Gospel Hour Press, n.d.

Vine, W. E. *Expository Dictionary of New Testament Words.* Westwood, N.J.: Revell, 1940.

Walker, William H. *Will Russia Conquer the World?* Neptune, N.J.: Loizeaux, 1962.

Walvoord, John F., *The Church in Prophecy.* Grand Rapids: Zondervan, 1964.

———. *Daniel.* Chicago: Moody Press, 1971.

———. *Israel in Prophecy.* Grand Rapids: Zondervan, 1962.

———. *The Millennial Kingdom.* Grand Rapids: Dunham, 1959.

———. *The Nations in Prophecy.* Grand Rapids: Zondervan, 1967.

———. *The Rapture Question.* Grand Rapids: Dunham, 1957.

———. *The Return of the Lord.* Grand Rapids: Dunham, 1955.

———. *The Revelation of Jesus Christ.* Chicago: Moody, 1966.

———. *We Believe in the Blessed Hope.* Dallas, Tex.: Dallas Theological Seminary, n.d.

West, Nathaniel. *The Thousand Years in Both Testaments.* Chicago: Revell, 1880.

Westwood, Tom. *Golden Daybreak.* Glendale, Calif.: Tom Westwood, n.d.

White, John Wesley. *Re-entry.* Grand Rapids: Zondervan, 1956.

Witty, Robert G. *Signs of the Second Coming.* Nashville, Tenn.: Broadman, 1969.

Wolff, Richard. *Israel Act III.* Wheaton, Ill.: Tyndale, 1967.

Wood, Leon J. *Is the Rapture Next?* Grand Rapids: Zondervan, 1956.

Woychuk, N. A. *For All Eternity.* New York: Books, Inc., 1955.

———. *To Them Who Love His Appearing.* St. Louis: Bible Memory Assn., 1968.

Wuest, Kenneth S. *In These Last Days.* Grand Rapids: Eerdmans, 1966.

———. *Philippians in the New Testament.* Grand Rapids: Eerdmans, 1966.

Wyrtzen, Jack. *Sex Is Not Sinful?* Grand Rapids: Zondervan, 1970.

Zoller, John. *Heaven.* John Zoller, 1968.

SUBJECT INDEX

SCRIPTURE INDEX

268